The COMPLETE GUIDE to the UK NATIONAL PARKS

CONWAY
Bloomsbury Publishing Plc
50 Bedford Square, London, WC1B 3DP, UK
Bloomsbury Publishing Ireland Limited,
29 Earlsfort Terrace, Dublin 2, D02 AY28, Ireland

BLOOMSBURY, CONWAY and the Conway logo are trademarks of Bloomsbury Publishing Plc

First published in Great Britain 2026

Copyright © Mike Appleton, 2026
Logo © National Parks UK, 2026
Maps © David Broadbent, 2026

Mike Appleton has asserted his right under the Copyright, Designs and Patents Act, 1988, to be identified as Author of this work

For legal purposes the Acknowledgements on page 284 constitute an extension of this copyright page

This book is a guide for when you spend time outdoors. Undertaking any activity outdoors carries with it some risks that cannot be entirely eliminated. For example, you might get lost on a route or caught in bad weather. Before you spend time outdoors, we therefore advise that you always take the necessary precautions, such as checking weather forecasts and ensuring that you have all the equipment you need. Any walking routes that are described in this book should not be relied upon as a sole means of navigation, so we recommend that you refer to an Ordnance Survey map or authoritative equivalent.

This book may also reference businesses and venues. Whilst every effort is made by the author and the publisher to ensure the accuracy of the business and venue information contained in our books before they go to print, changes to such information can occur during the production and lifetime of a publication. Therefore, we also advise that you check with businesses or venues for the latest information before setting out.

All internet addresses given in this book were correct at the time of going to press. Bloomsbury Publishing Plc does not have any control over, or responsibility for, any third-party websites referred to or in this book. The author and the publisher regret any inconvenience caused if some facts have changed or sites have ceased to exist, but can accept no responsibility for any such changes.

All rights reserved. No part of this publication may be: i) reproduced or transmitted in any form, electronic or mechanical, including photocopying, recording or by means of any information storage or retrieval system without prior permission in writing from the publishers; or ii) used or reproduced in any way for the training, development or operation of artificial intelligence (AI) technologies, including generative AI technologies. The rights holders expressly reserve this publication from the text and data mining exception as per Article 4(3) of the Digital Single Market Directive (EU) 2019/790

A catalogue record for this book is available from the British Library

Library of Congress Cataloguing-in-Publication data has been applied for

ISBN: 978-1-84486-738-7; ePDF: 978-1-84486-741-7; ePub: 978-1-84486-739-4

2 4 6 8 10 9 7 5 3 1

Typeset in Tisa Pro by Austin Taylor
Printed and bound in China by RR Donnelley Asia Printing Solutions Ltd

To find out more about our authors and books visit www.bloomsbury.com and sign up for our newsletters
For product safety related questions contact productsafety@bloomsbury.com

Mike Appleton

The COMPLETE GUIDE to the UK NATIONAL PARKS

National Parks UK

C✦NWAY
LONDON · OXFORD · NEW YORK · NEW DELHI · SYDNEY

CONTENTS

Foreword
6

Introduction
8

ENGLAND

Northumberland
10

Lake District
28

Yorkshire Dales
46

North York Moors
64

Peak District
82

The Broads
100

Exmoor
120

Dartmoor
138

New Forest
156

South Downs
174

WALES

Eryri
192

Pembrokeshire Coast
210

Bannau Brycheiniog
230

SCOTLAND

Cairngorms
248

Loch Lomond & The Trossachs
266

Acknowledgements
284

Picture credits
285

Index
286

FOREWORD

The United Kingdom's National Parks are different from protected landscapes in many other countries, because they are so closely intertwined with the people who live there – people who have shaped the land for centuries.

My relationship with National Parks, therefore, spans not only my own life, but also the wide range of roles these precious places serve.

As a child, the Yorkshire Dales National Park was my playground, my school, and even the site of my first proper employment – serving ice creams to grateful walkers from a little roadside van in the beautiful limestone country near my home.

As a young man, increasingly fixated on adventure and wild places, the National Parks became my proving ground – my training ground – and the setting for many of my happiest, wildest, most adventurous memories. I remember yomping over the peaks of Bannau Brycheiniog, the Cairngorms, Eryri and the Lake District in particular. Those were good times of sore feet, soggy sandwiches and the earned respite of log fires in cosy pubs.

Like many people, I moved to a big city to seek my fortune. And as that never quite materialised, I often found myself yearning for open spaces. The relative accessibility of the South Downs became an important cycling escape from the city streets.

National Parks play many roles for many people. They protect our most iconic landscapes. They offer space to run and walk, to sit and swim, to watch wildlife, to breathe, and to play with children. They are also vital places that help us fall in love with nature – to forge a strong connection with it and become motivated to care for it.

Our National Parks are not fossilised snapshots of some distant paradise long past. They are living landscapes, shaped by centuries of farming, industry and settlement – places where culture and nature still meet. And one of the greatest challenges our human world now faces is learning how culture, industry, and settlement can live harmoniously alongside nature.

National Parks are proving grounds for this essential redressing of our society's relationship with the natural world. They are crucial for our future: helping to tackle climate change by storing carbon and slowing floods, sheltering rare species and restoring vital habitats.

Even more importantly, they show the rest of the country – and the world – how food, nature, and people *can* and *must* thrive together. These living landscapes are test cases demonstrating that regenerative farming can unite food production with conservation.

We must not take our National Parks for granted. They need our care. They are under great pressure from climate change, land-use demands, and extremely severe funding cuts.

↑ View from Foel Eryr in the Preseli, Pembrokeshire Coast.

Our National Parks are essential for our country's health, hope, and connection. Let's cherish and protect our shared breathing spaces – and make sure we enjoy them and look after them for generations to come.

Alastair Humphreys
Author and Adventurer

INTRODUCTION

I've always had a deep fascination for National Parks. When I was growing up, I spent a lot of time in the Yorkshire Dales, playing in the rivers and caves and getting to know the locals. Fast forward a few decades, and I'm now lucky enough to work in the same National Park I idolised as a child.

'Explore more. Discover incredible landscapes, wildlife, lifestyles and adventures. Find your self' is the mantra for each of the UK's 15 National Parks, but I always felt I glossed over what they were really about, or simply turned a blind eye. Long walks typically led to pubs and overnight stays, but I never really got under the surface of why they are special. My relationship was more transactional, and I never took the time to ask myself why these breathing spaces are so vital.

By writing this book, I wanted to answer that question while spreading my wings a little further than the Dales. I wanted to explore more, to visit, interact and uncover all 15 of our amazing national heritages, and understand what makes our connection to these landscapes so significant. In doing so, I hoped my love of the Yorkshire Dales would be replicated throughout.

We're facing several concurrent crises: climate change and biodiversity loss, a general disconnect with nature and reduced health outcomes. National Parks help to provide the solution to each of those challenges, and several more, but they need to be cherished, loved and protected. I wanted to demonstrate it's not just about nice tea rooms, jagged hills and a post-wander beer. I'm asking the reader to look at the whole, and to ask how they can get the most out of a visit – and their

↓ Yorkshire Dales National Park.

→ Steep Hill, Robin Hood's Bay.

hard-earned pennies – while respecting what is so important.

I was lucky enough to visit each National Park over the course of six months. I'm not going to say it was a total bind, far from it, but I did set myself an onerous task. I allowed just a few days in each Park to see and experience as much as I could, talk and be with the people who care for and protect them, and then try to give a comprehensive flavour of everything visitors can do there.

Landscape, as it should, features strongly, but I wanted 'people' to be a key focus, and I set about interviewing a number of 'Champions' of each of the 15 Parks. Each Champion – and they are champions, leaders and standard bearers in more ways than one – was selected for their love of their area. Ten-minute chats turned into hours-long online calls, texts and emails as we travelled beyond their story and what makes each Park special, to reflecting on the National Park movement, its successes, challenges and the future. Seeing the likes of Loch Lomond, Eryri and the other 13 spaces through their eyes helped remove any bias I might have had in my work. I've also made friends for life.

I have also provided two guided walks, and three additional suggestions, for each of the National Parks in the book. I selected them based on suggestions from the amazing people who work in our National Parks, and my own wanderings through these landscapes. They range from the easy and accessible Miles Without Stiles routes (no stiles, steps or gradients) to those that are more challenging. There are mere pootles and epics, chances to do more if you have the energy, and a few that will simply get the legs and lungs working. While these are great for starters, you should not confine yourself to the five I've named for each National Park, but get out there and explore more.

Our National Parks are facing challenges that, without public support, will be difficult, if not impossible, to overcome. They are at the forefront of restoring nature and wildlife, while ensuring they can sustain vibrant local economies. When you think about it, it's a lot to ask of them, their people and their communities. Yet, we do so because they are public spaces, a respite from our busy lives. They don't always succeed in getting the balance right, but when they do, it is pure magic. I hope this book allows you to understand why they are precious, bolsters your confidence to step off the beaten track, and helps you to support these wonderful local businesses and people.

Above all, I want you to love, care for and protect your National Parks as much as I do. At times, I found my true self in these vast spaces, and I hope you do too.

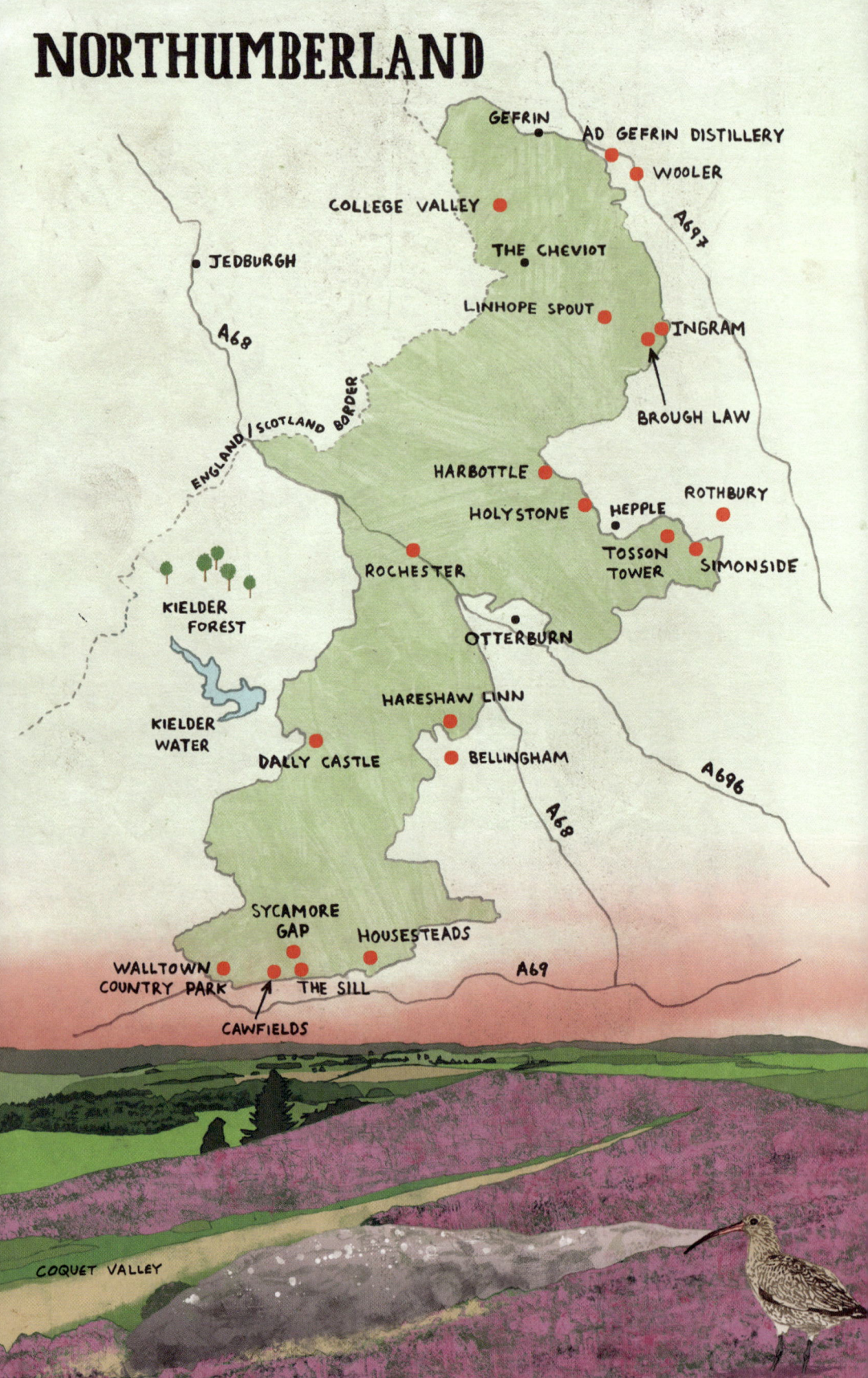

NORTHUMBERLAND

DESIGNATED: **6 April 1956**
SIZE: **1,049 sq km (405 sq miles)**, HIGHEST PEAK: **The Cheviot at 815m (2,674ft)**
ANNUAL VISITOR NUMBERS: **1.63 million (2023)**, POPULATION: **2,000**
OFFICIAL WEBSITE: **www.northumberlandnationalpark.org.uk**

If projections are to be believed, more than 75 million people could be living in the UK by 2050. Head into any town or city, and you'll likely be stuck on congested roads and then fighting to find a parking spot. If we're honest, public transport can be a little hit or miss; the trains are packed, or sometimes late, and it can all be too frustrating. Humans are a tribal species; we strive for connection with each other – more than 52,000 will pack into St James' Park to watch Newcastle United, for example, to feel the joy of shared moments. Yet, we do like a little bit of alone time, don't we?

The build-up before the 'drop' may be obvious here, but it's clear that our National Parks provide that breathing space. They are fulfilling their original vision of welcoming people from all walks of life to experience nature for health and well-being, and while some are indeed struggling under the weight of visitors, that's not the case for all. So, when I was told that Northumberland is the last true wilderness in England, I was excited. There are fewer than 2,000 people who live within the boundary

⬇ The walk to Breamish Valley as the sun pokes out.

of this 1,049 sq km (405 sq mile) National Park. Larger towns and villages circumvent its perimeter, while hamlets and tiny communities are the lifeblood of the National Park itself. There's no real town or typical base here, and that means by venturing into the National Park's wilder centre and north, you will find many places that are still pure and unspoilt.

Sparse it may be, but Northumberland was, and is still, shaped by people. This is a land of Romans, tribes, conflicts, battles, hillforts, burial cairns and other settlements. Humans have lived here for thousands of years, and the signs of their habitation and occupation remain. The present-day population is protecting and guarding this landscape not only for the past but also for the future. Wildlife is allowed to flourish here too, with red squirrels, deer and birds able to live alongside communities.

Then there's the sky; such a trivial thing as we go about our day-to-day business, yet so full of life and bountiful light when dark. We take it for granted; the sky is always above us, but we often don't get to see the real wonders owing to light pollution. But Northumberland has England's most pristine dark skies and is an International Dark Sky Park. Looking at the night sky here, you can almost

⬆ Crag Lough.

➡ Managed deer at Ingram Valley Farm.

forget you're on a busy island just off the west coast of Europe.

It's no surprise that such beauty has seen Northumberland named as the country's best National Park. It scored 90 per cent in a *Which?* survey (2024) of customers, beating out the Pembrokeshire Coast and Lake District. Understandably, it also received a 90 per cent satisfaction rate among visitors and was hailed for its 'peace and quiet'. Let's be honest; the lack of people is a clear reason why it's a favourite, but visitors remain important to Northumberland and its communities. It needs a transient, seasonal population to bolster the economy and ensure those smaller hamlets remain connected. The National Park also doesn't shy away from visitors, and they encourage people to visit the hotspots, albeit responsibly.

The felling of the famous tree at Sycamore Gap brought furious reactions from people around the country, while others were more sanguine. Humans have always had an impact on the land – a rather famous wall was built across the southern wilderness of this National Park in AD 122, after all. Over centuries, visitors made a pilgrimage to this special tree at Hadrian's Wall, and now more will come to see the loss of a national icon. Therefore, park officials could be forgiven for wanting people to stay away as they decided what to do next with this memorable spot. The loss was, however, eventually embraced; people are encouraged to visit, and now the saplings from the sycamore will be sent across the country as a sign of growth, togetherness and the fact that life, and nature in particular, does indeed carry on.

Northumberland blew me away. The wildness, the love within communities for their special place and the wholesome togetherness to celebrate everything it has to offer. It is a true National Park – a place for everyone.

➜ The loss of the sycamore at Sycamore Gap was felt worldwide.

THE CHAMPIONS

Rebecca & Ross Wilson
○○○

Rebecca Wilson and her husband, Ross, run Ingram Valley Farm in the Breamish Valley, some of the remotest land in the National Park.

In England, farmers are experiencing the biggest change in land management since the Second World War. Subsidies are being phased out, and those looking after this beautiful landscape will be paid 'public money for public goods'. It's a change that has long been expected but is still very much in transition as the finer details are ironed out. That said, farmers have always sought alternative income away from government support, and innovation is key to thriving.

> 'We couldn't survive here without diversification,' Rebecca says. 'We run a mixed farm of cattle, sheep and deer, and making the economics work based on that alone, in this climate, is difficult, but it always has been. We knew that subsidies were going to dry up eventually. A few years ago, we were talking to the Rural Development Programme for England about how we could diversify, and I suggested we could bring people to this farm to experience the landscape. It was a microcosm of an idea, but it blossomed from there.

Our Star Barn and the Safari are designed to showcase the landscape but to address so many factors, such as accessibility. When we did our market research, we learned that there are a lot of people who can't necessarily climb a hill that's 300m (1,000ft) high. We thought if we could help them do that, then they could see the hillforts they've never seen before, and touch the stone that dates back 480 million years, because that's when the valley was formed by volcanic activity. There is 12,000 years of recent history showcased here. We can connect people to cultivation terraces that are more than 4,000 years old, usher them into the entrance of a hillfort that dates back to the Iron Age, or just let them feel the cotton grass. Those visitors can also help feed the animals, and we can talk about the landscape and how we manage it.'

Rebecca grew up on a farm in Yorkshire but at seven-years-old she was sent to boarding school because she was allergic to pretty much everything there and was severely asthmatic. She was advised not to marry a farmer as a result, but when she was 16, she read Thomas Hardy's *Far from the Madding Crowd* (1874) and was drawn back to the countryside. Newcastle University followed, and then she joined a friend on a trip to Northumberland, where she would eventually meet her own Gabriel Oak.

'I just fell in love with this beautiful landscape, met my Gabriel (husband Ross), and settled here,' she continues. 'I always knew the pressures farming had, but if there's one thing we can't change, it's change itself. Farming is under a lot of political and economic pressure, more so than ever, and we both knew Ingram Valley Farm had to evolve and diversify.'

Rebecca believes that National Parks and the work at Ingram are part of the natural health service. Being outdoors is fantastic for people both mentally and physically, but only if they have access.

'Stargazing is such a big thing for us at Ingram and in Northumberland,' she continues. 'During lockdown, there was less light pollution, and many people saw the stars in urban areas for the first time. The stars are the perfect antidote to the stresses of modern-day life, alongside our landscape. We've seen how a connection with this place helps people come back from trauma and other setbacks. We've worked with Northumberland Communities Together, the Child Poverty Trust and the United Nations, and can see how powerful communing with nature is for physical and mental well-being. This landscape brings people closer together, and we need this at the moment.'

Ingram Valley Safaris takes people on a journey through time and landscape, as well as the realities of a working farm.

'We're really honest, too,' she continues. 'Farming isn't glamorous, and we've had people witness a new lamb being killed by crows. Nature can be brutal; we need to show that. We also have 526ha (1,300 acres) scheduled as an Ancient Monument – one of the largest pieces of scheduled land in England – and that brings pressure. People will spend a lot of time with us, and we will give them vouchers for the café in Ingram. It's important to support that enterprise, as they do a lot for the area. There's a shop in the café too, a little micro-economy that helps support remote rural areas like this. It sustains a whole rural way of life.'

Keeping the farm sustainable as part of a rural community is at the centre of this couple's ethos. Ingram Valley hosts yoga retreats and artist workshops, all utilising employment from the local area. One of their Safari guides is a shepherd, like his father and grandfather before him, and it's this lived experience that not only helps the farm but also enhances the fabric of the Safari.

'I feel like I'm a farmer of paperwork at times, and that is fairly typical with a diverse business and tenancy. I spend most of my time paying bills and filling out forms, and my husband is out there in the elements. I think my biggest joy is creating employment – farming employment opportunities, if you like – and that is my role.

I know we're lucky at Ingram, but I also know that we and farming could do a lot more on every level. I know we need to be more representative of society, and that means being more inclusive. That's hard to think about at a time when political conflicts and authoritarianism are creeping in across the world. But I think if we can treat the world as one National Park, then it's clear there is only one planet and one planet Earth. If humans can pull together and protect our precious resource that is Earth, then hopefully, it will still be here for another 5 billion years. National Parks can lead the way in terms of showcasing to the world how we look after our environment and how the environment looks after us.'

You can follow Ingram Valley Farm at www.ingramvalley.co.uk and @ingramvalleysafaris on Instagram.

Rebecca's favourite thing to do in Northumberland National Park:
'I would walk to Brough Law, lie in the middle of the hillfort, feel Mother Earth, and look up at the stars. If you lie down up there, it is like sleeping on an electric blanket. The earth is warm, and you can feel a special connection to this landscape.'

Facts and fiction

Northumberland is a **historical treasure trove**. Officials at the National Park look after 425 Scheduled Ancient Monuments and 229 listed buildings. As a county, it has more than 70 castle sites, more than any other in England.

Just outside the National Park, in Chillingham is **a breed of cattle** 'rarer than a Siberian tiger or a giant panda' ... apparently. This wild, isolated place has limited their genetics. You can see them at Chillingham Park in the shadows of the Cheviot Hills.

The 1991 action-adventure *Robin Hood: Prince of Thieves* was filmed at Sycamore Gap – the location used to depict the outlaw's journey to Nottingham and Sherwood Forest. Elsewhere, Alnwick Castle was used as a location in the first two **Harry Potter** films, while Danny Boyle's *28 Years Later* (2025) was filmed in Hexham, Lindisfarne, Rothbury and Kielder Forest, all just on the border of the National Park.

Hadrian's Wall is 117.5km (73 miles) long, but to walk its length, you have to march the extra mile, all 11 of them. The route starts at Wallsend in Tyne and Wear and ends in Bowness-on-Solway in Cumbria. In 2023, the trail celebrated its 20th birthday, and it is estimated that more than 10,000 people attempt the route each year.

Myths and legends

The moorland near Threestoneburn Wood, north of Linhope, is called **Kelpie Strand**. A kelpie is a shape-shifting water creature that appears as a grey or white horse to carry folk off to a watery grave. But its power can be harnessed, too. In '"The Kelpies": Ancient Myth in Modern Art', Ark UK writes: 'If caught using a magic bridle, the kelpie's immense strength can be used to safely carry passengers or to haul vast loads.'

Hen Hole, a chasm to the north-west of The Cheviot, is said to be a haven for fairies. It's a wide and dark place, hardly catching sunlight, so the fairies sing to entice people in. According to *Rambles in Northumberland* by Chatto (1835): 'On the north-west side of Cheviot there is a deep chasm called the Hen Hole, in which there is frequently to be seen a snow egg at midsummer. There is a tradition, that a party of hunters, when chasing a roe upon cheviot, were wiled by the fairies into the Hen Hole, and could never again find their way out.'

Brocolitia, also known as the Temple of Mithras, next to Carrawburgh Roman Fort, was built by soldiers to worship a god from the Eastern Empire. English Heritage says: 'According to legend, Mithras captured and killed a sacred bull in a cave, which Mithraic temples were intended to evoke.' Later, they refer to Mithras as 'the god of a Roman religious cult that emerged in the 1st century AD and spread across the provinces'. The temple was built at the fort in AD 200 and was rebuilt or refurbished four times until AD 350, before it was 'incorporated into a Roman rubbish tip'.

In Bellingham, there's **'the Long Pack'** in the graveyard of St Cuthbert's Church. This is allegedly the grave of a burglar who hid in a beggar's pack to break into a local house. He was discovered when he coughed, and was duly despatched by the owner.

WALK 1

Hadrian's Wall Meander

ooo

The classic view of Hadrian's Wall, with Sycamore Gap and Housesteads Fort.

There is no finer introduction to Northumberland than an undulating walk along the ruins of Hadrian's Wall from The Sill. This route takes in the National Landscape Discovery Centre, Steel Rigg, and crosses Sycamore Gap before arriving at Housesteads Fort. It then returns on the other side of the Wall, through Ridley Common.

Built under the orders of Roman Emperor Hadrian in AD 122, the structure was designed not only as a defence tool but also to keep people in. He included gates that acted as customs posts and a milecastle every mile, the remains of which are visible all along the route.

↑ Such a magnificent place and a feat of engineering.

The Wall took 16 years to complete and was 6m (nearly 20ft) high in some places. It is around 117.5km (73 miles) in length.

Begin by carefully crossing the B6318, then walk up the lane to Steel Rigg before turning right and climbing up the steep path to Hadrian's Wall. The route is straightforward and well-marked, crossing past Milecastle 39 and Sycamore Gap. Pause and reflect on the loss of the iconic tree (but see the new shoots of life), and then climb up and enjoy views on both sides. The route continues through some incredible landscapes, along ridges and crags, before the stunning Housesteads Fort comes into view. It's worth staying here for a bit; it's busy, but the remains are extensive.

START/END: The Sill: National Landscape Discovery Centre, Hexham, NE47 7AN
DISTANCE: 13.36km (8.3 miles)
GRADE: Moderate

Around 1km (0.6 miles) after the Fort, turn left and take the long but pleasurable walk back to Steel Rigg. This is a different view of the Wall and the landscape beyond, but a better chance to take a look at Crag Lough, a freshwater lake. The walk then takes you up to the Steel Rigg car park – stay for the views – before you head back down the lane to The Sill, where you can enjoy local Northumbrian produce in the Once Brewed Coffee and Bakehouse.

An amazing day out.

➜ Sycamore Gap may be no more but its saplings will live on throughout the country.

WALK 2

Breamish Valley Hillfort Trail
○○○

Enjoy expansive views and historical settlements on this wild circular.

Northumberland feels very different on this walk. It's wild, steeped in history and long enough for you to enjoy a good feed in Ingram Café afterwards.

It's possible to start this wander closer to Brough Law, but it's a shame to take you away from Ingram and the café. Instead, begin at Ingram Bridge and follow the road out of the village towards Bulby's Wood Car Park. There are facilities here if needed before the gradual climb to Brough Law hillfort. It's exposed most of the way up, but the view is worth it: the expanse of the National Park and Linhope Spout in the distance. Brough Law hillfort may be a ruin – and in the wind, this isn't a place to hang around – yet you can see the size of the original ramparts.

Turn left at the top and make your way to Ewe Hill and over the brow to Middle Dean Hillfort, which overlooks a dramatic ravine. A steep valley follows (your legs will be good for it), and Cochrane Pike and its four hut circles comes into view. Wether Hill is next on your list, with its remains of roundhouses.

START/END: Ingram Bridge Car Park, Ingram, NE66 4LT/ Ingram Cafe, Ingram, NE66 4LT
DISTANCE: 9.12km (5.67 miles)
GRADE: Moderate

⬆ Looking back towards Ingram.
➡ Brough Law hillfort.

The route here is a little sketchy in places – you're crossing burns and boggy fields, so try and stay on track – before you arrive at Turf Knowe, where archaeologists uncovered two Bronze Age burial cairns estimated to be 4,000 years old – almost twice the age of the hillforts. The path continues to Ingram Hill, the lowest-lying hillfort in the Breamish Valley. This site contains the remains of stone buildings, which were added long after it was built.

Down the hill, you reach the road into Ingram, but ignore the start point. Keep to the right and then turn left at the church to head into Ingram Café. You won't be disappointed.

Why not try these great walks...

DRAKE STONE AND HARBOTTLE: An 8km (5 mile) walk in Coquetdale that takes you up to the ancient Drake Stone and over to the ruins of Harbottle Castle.

HARESHAW LINN: Visit a spectacular waterfall located on this 4.8km (3 mile) walk within a Site of Special Scientific Interest (SSSI), designated for its rare ferns and lichens. There are more than 300 different types of mosses, liverworts and lichen here, as well as great spotted woodpeckers, redstarts, dippers, badgers and Daubenton's bats.

CAWFIELDS QUARRY CIRCULAR: A 5.6km (3.5 mile) circular from Cawfields to see the crags, Milecastle 42 and a fine stretch of Hadrian's Wall. The second legion built the milecastle here to protect the weak spot of Hole Gap.

Key Places

The rider...
Local accommodation is available for a variety of budgets. You can stay in an isolated shepherd's hut, a campsite, or enjoy higher-end hotels throughout the National Park. There is also a very popular youth hostel at The Sill. Outside the National Park, several towns offer cheaper places to stay, including Alnwick, a fascinating historic town.
www.northumberlandnationalpark.org.uk/visitor-info/where-to-stay

✦ The River Coquet at Rothbury.

A note to the reader: As you know, Northumberland National Park is one of the most sparsely populated in the UK. Therefore, I have taken the liberty of identifying gateway towns in this list, as well as those within the boundary.

Places to visit

Rothbury At the Park's eastern edge and on the picturesque River Coquet. A good base for exploring Simonside and the Cheviots. The high street has plenty of pubs, shops and cafés.

Wooler In the north-east and on the A697, this market town is known as the gateway to the Cheviots. It is home to the award-winning AD Gefrin Distillery and the town's annual Glendale Show takes place every August bank holiday and has been running for 130 years.

Bellingham Just off the A68, a perfect base for the Pennine Way, the Pennine Cycle Way and the Reivers Coast to Coast cycle route. Bellingham is home to Hareshaw Linn and has an annual show on the last Saturday in August. The 13th-century St Cuthbert's Church has a stone barrel vault designed to stop it from being burnt down by Border raiders. The Heritage Centre is also worth a visit.

Harbottle An ideal base for visiting the Drake Stone and 12th-century castle remains, which overlook the single street. The Star Inn is the community's hub – it's a village shop and information point too, and it offers wood-fired pizza in the courtyard. Just take my money!

Ingram A small hamlet in the Breamish Valley, in the shadow of hillforts and other remains. The café is a local enterprise that uses local produce and provides information.

Haltwhistle A small, picturesque market town that prides itself on being the Centre of Britain. It is the gateway to the central, most photographed section of Hadrian's Wall and the North Pennines National Landscape, which lies to the south.

Why not try...

Alnwick To the north-east, a bustling historic market town packed with pubs, restaurants and shops, as well as an amazing castle, Poison Garden and the simply brilliant Barter Books.

Holystone Visited off the B6341, this village has a little pool – Lady's Well – where St Ninian baptised early Christians. Holystone Burn Reserve is nearby.

Hexham On the south-eastern edge of the Park. Has Hexham House and England's first purpose-built prison, Hexham Old Gaol, dating back to the 1300s. Hexham Abbey was built in 674 and contains a crypt.

⬇ Barter Books in Alnwick. A must-see, do, key place, the lot – even if it is outside the Park boundary!

VISIT

Must Sees

Linhope Spout (NT 958 171) is a wild 18m (59ft) waterfall. It's encapsulated by a lush green gorge. The best way to approach is from Ingram, and parking on the grass verge on the left before the Alnhammoor track. It is then waymarked.

Another waterfall is at **Hareshaw Linn** (NY 841 854), a Site of Special Scientific Interest and home to red squirrels. A nice walk starts at NE48 2BZ.

Walltown Country Park ① (CA8 7HZ) is near the village of Greenhead. The visitor centre sells food and drinks and a small range of merchandise during peak times. Opened in 1876, Walltown Quarry was the largest 'whinstone quarry' on Hadrian's Wall and produced huge quantities of road chippings. It also has a serene lake, lots of trails and a Peace Garden. There is a Changing Places facility here and pathways have been updated to be wheel-friendly, making this a truly accessible way to visit the National Park.

Nearby is **Vindolanda** (NY 770 663), which has the only Roman milestone in Britain still standing in its original position. This was an important construction and garrison base and was built before the Wall. The accompanying museum is superb. www.vindolanda.com/roman-vindolanda-fort-museum

Brocolitia (NY 859 711) is the remains of a 3rd-century Roman temple. It was built by soldiers to worship a god from the Eastern Empire. Built in AD 200, it was rebuilt or refurbished four times.

Harwood Forest (parking at **Simonside Car Park** NE65 7NW) is family-friendly, quiet and packed with historic remains. A cairn was excavated here in the 1890s, and the stones from the central area were banked around the edge, revealing two cists, or chambers, beneath. A two-hour walk through the forest links up with Little Church Rock, an outcrop of fell sandstone hidden in the forest. It's also a great base for the Simonside Hills.

1

The 13th-century **Tarset and Dally Castles** can be found on a walk from **Greenhaugh Village** (NE48 1PP). The Park often runs annual guided walks to these strongholds, which were built when the area was under Scottish control.

High Rochester (NE19 1RB) is a small hamlet within the ruined ramparts of a Roman outpost called Bremenium. Two fortified farmhouses, also known as bastles, are used as houses here and feature walls that are around 1m (3.2ft) thick. The Rochester Relish is known as the last café in England. It is closed on Tuesdays and Wednesdays.

Nearby are the **Otterburn Ranges**, the 'wild heartland' of the Park. Walking in Otterburn Ranges is generally safe when adhering to the rules and guidelines, particularly respecting firing times and restrictions. Public access is permitted on designated tarmac roads, public footpaths and bridleways when red flags or lamps are not displayed, indicating that the ranges are not in use.

Cragside ❷ (NE65 7PX) is just outside the Park near Rothbury. It's billed as Britain's original smart home, and sits at the heart of a grand fantasy garden. It was the first home in the world to be lit by hydroelectric power, thanks to inventor and industrialist Lord Armstrong. The house is an 'Arts and Crafts mansion filled with Victorian inventions. www.nationaltrust.org.uk/visit/north-east/cragside

Must Dos

Walk in the footsteps of legions

Hadrian's Wall is a UNESCO World Heritage Site and an important attraction that crosses the southern end of the Park. The walk from the **National Landscape Discovery Centre** at **The Sill** (NE47 7AN) (www.thesill.org.uk) to **Steel Rigg** and **Crag Lough**, **Sycamore Gap** and beyond is vitally important to experience. The National Park does not shy away from the gravity of the monument, nor does it discourage visitors. The Wall was built in AD 122 after Hadrian inherited a spiralling empire. It was designed to keep various warring tribes apart and to secure the north-western border in the province of Britannia. Hadrian never got to see the project he commissioned. The Empire was sprawling, and when he came to Britain, he said he wanted a milecastle every mile and a turret in between. He then left! The Wall evolved along the route as the Roman Army updated its building techniques. At the very beginning, in Newcastle, sections are 3m (9.8ft) wide, but they reduce to 2.5m (8.2ft) further on to limit the amount of stone used. www.northumberlandnationalpark.org.uk/places-to-visit/hadrians-wall/steel-rigg/

You can visit **Walltown Country Park and Housesteads** to discover more about this amazing place. www.english-heritage.org.uk/visit/places/housesteads-roman-fort-hadrians-wall/

Learn and discover

The **Roman Army Museum** (CA8 7JB) is an immersive experience of life along Hadrian's Wall (www.romanarmymuseum.com). It has three galleries and is at the site of the Magna Roman Fort.

For something slower-paced, the **Heritage Centre in Bellingham** (NE48 2DG) is worth a visit. You can even have tea in a first-class carriage! www.bellingham-heritage.org.uk

⬇ Looking back at Hadrian's Wall as you head to Steel Rigg.

The Twice Brewed Inn has its own brewery, rooms, restaurant and planetarium.

See fortified homesteads

Tosson Tower (NE65 7NW) can be found on the south side of Great Tosson. It was built in the 14th or 15th century as protection against the bands of raiders who attacked the borderlands.

Star attraction...

Northumberland is England's most pristine dark sky. It is a **Gold Tier International Dark Sky Park** and, including the National Park, covers 1,481 sq km (572 sq miles) of starry skies. The Park brings several groups and businesses together to experience such amazing sights, but it's virtually impossible not to see the stars wherever you are. **The Sill**, **Walltown** and the **Twice Brewed Inn** are hotspots, but you can also enjoy experiences in the **Breamish Valley**, **The Star Inn** at Harbottle, **Hesleyside Huts** and **Kirklandlee**. www.northumberlandnationalpark.org.uk/things-to-do/discover-dark-skies/

Visit a cracking pub...

The **Twice Brewed Inn** has its own brewery, rooms, restaurant and planetarium ... the show-offs! It's in a place called Once Brewed, on the B6318 Military Road, and next to The Sill. People coming from the west will see Twice

↑ Ad Gefrin is a new distillery that offers whisky and gin as well as a museum of Northumbrian life.

↓ The spectacular entrance to Ad Gefrin.

Brewed as they approach, while those coming the other way will see 'Once Brewed'. It's thought that Twice Brewed's etymology comes from the fact that beer needed to be brewed twice because it wasn't strong enough – and most tales around the place follow a similar theme. One story centres on the Battle of Hexham (1464), where soldiers requested stronger beer to give them the fortitude to fight. It was twice brewed – and they won the battle! www.twicebrewedinn.co.uk

... and a distillery

Ad Gefrin (NE71 6NJ) in Wooler is a new distillery that offers whisky and gin as well as a museum of Northumbrian life. www.adgefrin.co.uk

See the Drake Stone

The Drake Stone (NT 921 044) is supposed to possess special healing powers. It was originally known as the Dragon Stone or Draak's Stone and was reputed to have been used by druids.

Not just walks

There are 1,100km (683.5 miles) of paths for walking, cycling and horse riding in the Park, so choices are good for a good day out. **Hadrian's Wall Path Trail** was created in 2003 and starts in Wallsend and ends at Bowness-on-Solway in Cumbria. The route can be broken down into sections, and public transport helps in exploring small chunks.

The **Sandstone Way** cycle route is a 193km (120-mile) mountain biking trail between Berwick-upon-Tweed and Hexham. It runs along the sandstone ridge in north Northumberland. www.northumberlandnationalpark.org.uk/things-to-do/get-active-outdoors/cycling/the-sandstone-way/

Woodlands

Just outside the Park boundary is **Kielder Water & Forest Park**. At 647.5 sq km (250 sq miles), it is the largest working forest in England. There are seven visitor centres, attractions and several mountain bike and walking trails, plus an observatory. It's also home to the largest population of red squirrels in England. www.visitkielder.com

Go wild ... very wild

College Valley feels like the wildest, least populated area of the National Park. The estate, which covers more than 4,856ha (12,000 acres), welcomes cyclists and walkers, but only 12 vehicles are allowed into its environs daily. It's pristine, with a variety of differing landscapes and habitats, including native woodlands, one of which contains 200 Collingwood oaks near The Bell on the western side of the College Burn. The site has the rocky gorge of Hethpool Linn, where you can play in the pools, as well as Iron Age forts and a history stretching back 7,000 years. There is a free car park at **Hethpool** (NE71 6TW). www.college-valley.co.uk

See the goats

The **feral goat herds** in the Cheviots pre-date present-day goat breeds and are living totally wild!

CAR-FREE TRAVEL

→ There are many ways to get around Northumberland National Park, and it is worth logging on to **www.northumberlandnationalpark.org.uk/visitor-info/travel/** to find out more.

→ The Hadrian's Wall Country Bus AD 122 runs every two hours for most of the day between Hexham Bus Station and Haltwhistle Rail Station via Hexham Rail Station, Acomb, Wall, Chollerford, Chesters Roman Fort, Housesteads Roman Fort, Once Brewed (for The Sill), Vindolanda, Milecastle Inn, the Roman Army Museum, Walltown and Greenhead. **www.gonortheast.co.uk/services/GNE/AD12**

→ From Newcastle or Carlisle, there are various Arriva (**www.arrivabus.co.uk**) and Stagecoach (**www.stagecoachbus.com**) buses, alongside Go North East (**www.gonortheast.co.uk**), which runs services into the National Park.

→ By rail, the Tyne Valley Line (**www.tvcrp.org.uk**) from Newcastle takes you into the southern part of the Park, with stations close to Hadrian's Wall. Key stations are located at Wylam, Prudhoe, Stocksfield, Riding Mill, Corbridge, Hexham, Haydon Bridge, Bardon Mill and Haltwhistle. **www.northernrailway.co.uk** and **www.scotrail.co.uk**

LAKE DISTRICT

BLENCATHRA
LATRIGG FELL
A66
KESWICK
AIRA FORCE
A591
BORROWDALE
ULLSWATER
BUTTERMERE
DERWENT WATER
GLENRIDDING
THIRLMERE
HAWESWATER
ENNERDALE
HELVELLYN
A592
GRASMERE
SCAFELL PIKE
AMBLESIDE
A593
BROCKHOLE VISITOR CENTRE
WAST WATER
ORREST HEAD
ESKDALE
TARN HOWS
RAVENGLASS
HAWKSHEAD
WINDERMERE
STAVELEY
CONISTON WATER
KENDAL
GRIZEDALE FOREST
A595
M6
A590
A6
M6

BARROW-IN-FURNESS

BUTTERMERE VALLEY

LAKE DISTRICT

DESIGNATED: 9 May 1951
SIZE: 2,362 sq km (912 sq miles), **HIGHEST PEAK:** Scafell Pike at 978m (3,209ft)
ANNUAL VISITOR NUMBERS: 18.11 million (2023), **POPULATION:** 38,993
OFFICIAL WEBSITE: www.lakedistrict.gov.uk

Of all our National Parks, the Lake District has the hardest balancing act. It was classified as a UNESCO World Heritage Site in 2017 for its 'Outstanding Universal Value' and 'cultural and/or natural significance which is so exceptional as to transcend national boundaries and to be of common importance for present and future generations of all humanity'. The Park's inclusion centred on three key criteria: the 'interchange of human values', being an 'outstanding example of a traditional human settlement', and the fact that it is 'associated with artistic and literary works of outstanding universal significance'. It brought recognition to an already world-renowned landscape, and it was hoped it would be an economic driver to long-term investment and sustainable tourism.

The Lake District is our most visited National Park, with more than 18 million visitors a year arriving to enjoy this special landscape – a perfect blend of high hills and glacial lakes – and connect to its communities and scenery. It's a managed landscape, too: hardy Herdwick sheep have shaped these hills, and this farming heritage is of utmost cultural importance. Honeypot places like Windermere are magnets for visitors, and that often leaves popular routes busy in peak season. The National Park Authority and its partners have worked hard to promote sustainable tourism, but it's hard to find a solution to the large number of private cars travelling along the narrow roads. These vital rural services are stress-tested by a large transient population but are paid for by local people. Without this influx,

➤ Family walks near Stanley Ghyll.

however, communities would struggle to survive.

Businesses are innovating and providing employment but have to consider their impact on a World Heritage Site.

The Lake District is also at the forefront of habitat and nature restoration. As the climate crisis bites, our land managers and landscapes are being asked to do more. Woodland covers just 13 per cent of the Park, and officials want to increase this number to 17 per cent by 2050. That means a change in land use in a place that has been intrinsically shaped by its agricultural processes.

In addition, there is the ever-present issue of dwindling resources. There are 16,510 archaeological sites and monuments recorded in the Park's Historic Environment Record, including 283 Scheduled Ancient Monuments, 1,779 listed buildings and structures and 23 Conservation Areas covering historic towns and villages. All need looking after, but finances are tight. Around a third of the National Park Authority's income comes from the Department for Environment, Food & Rural Affairs (Defra), some from grant funding and the rest from car parking fees and other commercial operations. 'Who Pays for the Lake District', a report commissioned by the independent charity Friends of the Lake District, suggested several alternative sources, including a 'congestion charge', as a way of boosting the coffers. There are no easy answers, especially in a National Park.

Millions of people feel a deep emotional connection with the place, driving many

✢ Did you know the Lake District has a coast? Head to Ravenglass to find out!

✦ Fine lush pastures near Ullswater.

examples of committed conservation. However, the thing that unites the National Park is its 'togetherness' and a desire to keep the place special. People are passionate because they believe in what the National Park stands for – the conservation and protection of wildlife, nature and cultural heritage, and the promotion of understanding and enjoyment. In partnership, amazing things are happening to improve habitats and local communities. Pioneering rewilding projects at Lowther and Wild Ennerdale are succeeding in creating a wilder, more diverse landscape, as is Cumbria Wildlife Trust's scheme to transform Skiddaw. Borrowdale's temperate rainforests were given National Nature Reserve status in 2024, and experts are working hard to look into sustainable transport to ease pressure on congested areas.

⬆ Ullswater from Gowbarrow.

➡ Not just lakes; a river near Dalegarth Falls.

As author, fell walker and passionate proponent of the Lake District Alfred Wainwright wrote: 'The fleeting hour of life of those who love the hills is quickly spent, but the hills are eternal. Always there will be the lonely ridge, the dancing beck, the silent forest; always there will be the exhilaration of the summits. These are for the seeking, and those who seek and find while there is still time will be blessed both in mind and body.'

The Lake District is a special place that brings people together in celebration of culture and landscape, and long may it thrive.

THE CHAMPION

Will Clark
○○○

Will Clark has been a Member of Lake District National Park Authority since 2021 and is a champion of Miles Without Stiles (accessible walking routes for everyone).

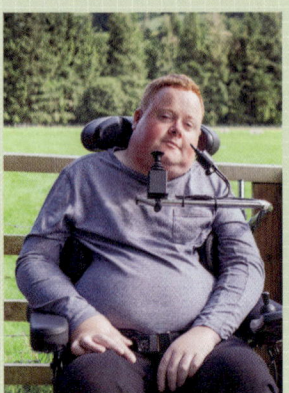

National Parks are for everyone. They were established to provide breathing spaces for all, recreation for the masses and economic stability for local communities. That ethos has been maintained throughout the Park movement and will continue, as new parks join the family in the future. Access, however, is still a moot point. If you don't have the means to travel to one of these special places, then these landscapes might as well be in another country. Minority groups, in particular, face barriers both economically and physically that many of us take for granted.

'National Parks have always been a big part of my life, particularly the Lake District,' Will says. 'I probably didn't realise it at the time, but I was very lucky to grow up in a B&B overlooking Grasmere, with woodlands at the back of my house. It was an extended back garden, and I spent hours there making dens and playing. When I went to Sheffield Hallam University, one of the main selling points was access to the Peak District. I spent a lot of time there. I then went to the Alps to work as a ski guide.

After a while, I came home and didn't really know what to do with myself. I got a job as a trainee manager at a local hotel, but I was still cramming in as much outdoor activity as I could. Then in 2012, at age 27, I was doing a local charity triathlon when a stick caught in the front wheel of my bike, threw me over the handlebars, and I broke the right side of my neck.' The C4 spinal injury means Will is paralysed below the shoulders. He says such an injury was a 'game-changer', but it didn't stop him from carrying on in the best way he could. It understandably took a bit of time – he worked with a mentor while he was rehabilitating in Middlesbrough who helped him see what life with a spinal injury could be like.

'He was an amazing person,' Will continues. 'He'd had a similar injury and was mentoring me through mine. He called me one day from the top of one of the two main accessible fells in the Park to catch up. That was massive for me because he was effectively saying that while things had changed, like him, I could still live a busy life and get back up on the fells. I knew life would be different, but I never quite appreciated what was still possible.

I didn't just want to do nothing, so I started to take on some voluntary work. I met Tim Farron (Liberal Democrat MP for Westmorland and Lonsdale) a few times, and he convinced me to stand as a County Councillor. I had no idea what it meant, but I wanted a new challenge and to help people, and I knew I couldn't sit at home all my life. From there, an opportunity arose to become a Member of the National Park, and it has been a great experience.'

In his time as a Park Board Member, Will has been championing Miles Without Stiles routes and other projects in the Lake District to show access doesn't have to be a barrier. He also spoke at the National Parks Conference in Newcastle in 2024 about life with a spinal injury and his work championing access.

'The conference was good because it showed every Park how to make their areas more accessible to all minority groups,' he continues. 'We know that some things are difficult to change, but others are relatively simple. Look at kissing gates, for instance. If you just move a couple of slats here and there, then you can put in a gate, and you have a route that is usable for all. The Lake District has taken this on and not only introduced more routes but also invested in keeping them maintained.'

Not every route up the highest mountains can be accessible, but balance can be achieved with good planning, partnerships and landscaping. LDNPA, in partnership with Keswick Town Council, worked incredibly hard to make the path up to Orrest Head, which used to be inaccessible, a possible option for all. The new route provides quality access, maintains the ethos of National Parks welcoming all, and above everything, it looks great too!

'There was some opposition to changing that path as it meant removal of the dramatic steep steps,' Will says. 'Orrest Head offers a stunning panoramic view and is just a short walk from Windermere Station. It kindled Alfred Wainwright's love with the Lake District and set him on the journey to writing his *Pictorial Guides to the Lakeland Fells*; guidebooks that have inspired and influenced generations of walkers. Everyone should be able to experience that. The multi-user trail from Keswick to Threlkeld is also fantastic, one of my favourites, but it also had opposition at the time. There's only so much a National Park can do to please everyone, and budgets are tight.

The one thing I would like to change is the provision of big accessible toilets. We have two Changing Places toilets on the side of Lake Windermere, but we know we could do more. They take up a lot of room, but they would open the Park up to more users.'

Most of our National Parks now offer Miles Without Stiles routes – there are 50 celebrated on the Lake District's website – and Will has proven there are other means of getting around too, albeit with a little help. He was pushed up to the top of Helvellyn, all 950m (3,117ft) of it, by a team of 50 people to help raise money to improve Ambleside and Grasmere's parks.

'That was a great day,' Will adds. 'Lots of brilliant local people came out to help, but honestly, we couldn't have picked a day with worse weather in July! We didn't see a thing all the way up and at the top. That mountain might not be accessible without a little help, but Latrigg near Keswick is. There's a fine view of the northern fells up there, and it's a relatively short trip from Keswick. I'd like to paraglide from there soon; that's a goal.'

> **Will's favourite thing to do in the Lake District:** 'I live in the middle of the Park, and there are so many options. Before my accident, it would have been a case of me chucking on my trainers and going for a run or jumping on the bike. Now, it's obviously a bit more restrictive, but there's a lot to do. We have a great accessible sailing club here, and I have attempted to sail the length of Windermere. Sadly, the weather put an end to that, but I'll be having another go soon.'

Lake District

FACTS AND QUIRKS

The Poets

Wordsworth, **Coleridge** and his brethren may have brought their love of the Lakes' landscape to the masses through their poetry and prose, but the writers didn't have it all their way. **Wordsworth's sister, Dorothy**, accompanied him on many journeys, jointly inspiring the Romantic movement, and she encouraged her friend Mary and Mary's maid Agnes. Renowned author and hillwalker Ronald Turnbull writes that 'Dorothy was mentioned as "—" in one poem that depicts one of their walks, and later in *Guide to the Lakes*, Wordsworth attributed her ascent of Scafell Pike to none other than – himself. In later editions, that was updated to 'a Friend' (of unspecified gender).'

All were prolific hillwalkers but didn't get the recognition others received, much like Mrs Smith of Coniston, who was a linguist and big fell walker. Turnbull writes: 'Thomas Wilkinson's *Tours to the British Mountains* (1824) mentions Mrs Smith of Coniston and her two daughters, right at the start of the century, heading up Helvellyn without a guide, and in winter conditions too.'

Rocks, fells and furry faces

In Borrowdale, the **'Borrowdale Volcanics'** are very hard lavas formed by eruptions 450 million years ago. They make up the highest mountains of Scafell, Helvellyn and the Langdale Pikes. The Park says: 'These peaks are not the remains of the original volcanoes – they are the harder volcanic rocks that have withstood erosion'.

Part of the Lake District's appeal is its clipped and neat fells, in contrast with the sharp craggy mountains and glacial lakes. The **Herdwick sheep** has shaped this Park and is noted in its UNESCO World Heritage Site citation. It's thought there are around 50,000 Herdwicks in the Park, with 95 per cent of these living within 24km (15 miles) of Coniston. Their smiley faces can be seen across the landscape, and genetically, they are more than 10,000 years old. They heft to the landscape and therefore could be classed as wild.

Myths, memories and tasty morsels

Like its Yorkshire Dales neighbour, the Lake District is crisscrossed by **corpse roads**: routes and trackways rural communities would use to transport their dead to the nearest consecrated burial ground. Wasdale to Eskdale was a busy route, and many have tales of ghostly happenings. On Souther Fell, there have been **'confirmed' sightings of a 'spectral army'**. On Midsummer's Day in 1745, marching troops, cavalry and carriages were seen travelling along the summit ridge. Apparently, 26 sober and respected witnesses swore on oath that their tale was true.

Not related to the above … the **Biggest Liar in the World** is elected every November after a competition in The Bridge Inn, in the Wasdale Valley.

Graphite was mined in Seathwaite and was used to make **the first pencil**. Francis Coulson also created the **first sticky toffee pudding** in the 1970s. The recipe contains fig and sponge with toffee, but the true mixture is a secret.

WALK 1

Blencathra

○○○

Take on old Saddleback on this classic climb.

Blencathra is a huge hunk of a mountain, standing at 868m (2,848ft), and imposing from all around. It is a fine introduction to the Lakeland Fells, offering amazing views and a relatively simple challenge for even the smallest of legs – weather permitting, of course.

The hill has six separate ridges, and that affords several different routes to the summit; from the downright frisky to the straightforward. This walk starts outside Dam Mire Wood and treks along a quiet road before cutting up the hill, through bracken, to the switchbacks on Blease Fell.

The views are impressive back to Keswick and beyond before, after seemingly an aeon of aching quad muscles, Knowe Craggs appear on your right. Blencathra can often be in cloud, so it is important to stick to the track until you arrive at Hallsfell Top. It is possible to take Hall's Fell Ridge back to the start of

START/END:
Threlkeld, CA12 4SA
DISTANCE: **10.3km (6.4 miles)**
GRADE: **Moderate**

⬆ The view from the upper crags of Hallsfell Top.

this walk, but it is a serious undertaking with some significant scrambling.

Back at the start, it is worth heading into the 2ha (4.9 acre) Dam Mire Wood, which was gifted to the Friends of the Lake District by resident Professor Mike Hambrey. It has a circular path, and the charity has planted more than 1,000 trees and 300 new wetland plants to diversify its special habitat.

A note to the reader: Threlkeld is a small village with very limited parking, but it's well served by buses running every 30 minutes, seven days a week from Keswick. For more on car-free travel, see page 45. Alternatively, there is a pay and display car park on the side of the A66 next to the Cricket Club (CA12 4TZ) and another car park at the LDNPA (CA12 4TT).

Be Lake District Kind and follow the Countryside Code to help care for the landscape, wildlife and to keep people safe. www.lakedistrict.gov.uk/visiting/plan-your-visit

↓ The view on the way up Saddleback.

WALK 2

Keswick to Threlkeld

○○○

A delightful Miles Without Stiles walk along the River Greta gorge.

Originally damaged by Storm Desmond (2015), this route has been reopened as an accessible trail and is designed for all levels of mobility.

It follows the route of the old Keswick to Penrith Railway and weaves its way over the River Greta on some of the original Victorian railway bridges, as well as those rebuilt following the storm. It is well signposted with information panels and seats.

START/END: Opposite the old Keswick Station, CA12 4NP
DISTANCE: 10km (6.21 miles) (5km/ 3.1 miles each way)
GRADE: Easy

This is a pleasant meander for the whole family that ends near Threlkeld, where, for just another 0.75km (0.5 miles), you can visit a couple of pubs and a coffee shop.

Alternatively, you can go right before the last bridge to follow a route to Threlkeld Quarry, a farm shop and a museum.

This part of the route isn't suitable for all wheelchair users.

Why not try these great walks...

THE ULLSWATER WAY: A 32km (20 mile) yomp that goes around the whole of Ullswater. It can be started at any point along the route and takes in several beautiful villages, as well as Aira Force. There's also the option to split the full distance into sections by walking, catching a boat or grabbing the bus.

HIGH STREET FROM HAWESWATER: This 13km (8 mile) circular from Mardale Head climbs Kidsty Howes and Kidsty Pike before arriving at the 828m (2,717ft) cairn at Racecourse Hill. With amazing views of Blea Water, it descends via Mardale Ill Bell and returns via Nan Bield Pass.

GALAVA FORT AND AMBLESIDE: A lovely 4.4km (2.7 mile) lakeside and town walk around Ambleside to the Roman Galava Fort.

Key Places

The rider...
The Lake District has a vast range of accommodation for a variety of budgets. B&Bs, guesthouses and hotels are available, while it has a strong youth hostel (18 in total) and bunkhouse network, alongside a multitude of caravan and campsites. www.lakedistrict.gov.uk/visiting/where-to-stay

Places to visit

Keswick A natural hub for the northern Lakeland Fells with its own unique character. It's packed with outdoor shops, cafés and pubs, as well as a quirky pencil museum. Latrigg Fell at 368m (1,207ft) is close by and is accessible for all. Skiddaw is to the north and Derwentwater to the south. Tourist information is available at Moot Hall.

Windermere The ubiquitous destination, along the busy A591. The lake is 18km (10.5 miles) long and offers all kinds of watersports, surrounded by stunning natural beauty. Enjoy a boat trip, walk along the shore, or take in the many tea rooms and restaurants. The accessible walk from Windermere to Orrest Head is a must for the view alone.

Grasmere A quaint village that houses Wordsworth's grave in St Oswald's churchyard, a medieval place of worship built on a 7th-century site. A great base for exploring Grasmere Water, which is popular for wild swimming and rowing. You can also buy Grasmere Gingerbread,

Moot Hall in Keswick.

which was invented by Sarah Nelson in 1854.

Ambleside At the northern end of Windermere, this popular market town has many great features, including its own Roman Galava Fort, the Armitt Museum – a gallery and reference library celebrating the history of the area – and Zeffirellis, an independent music and cinema venue. A spectacular waterfall can be found at Stock Ghyll Force.

Coniston Water Smaller than its neighbours, with exploration possible via boat, bike and steam yacht gondola. The Old Man of Coniston, with its mining remains, and Dow Crag, as well as the serene Tarn Hows, are nearby.

Why not try...

Staveley Close to Kendal, this small village is on the south-east boundary of the Park, near the Kentmere Valley. A Miles Without Stiles route runs alongside the river.

↑ Surprise View is worth a detour from Keswick.
↓ The majestic Tarn Hows, near Coniston.

Glenridding Said by some to be the gateway to the Lakes, this village is at the foot of the Kirkstone Pass, right next to Ullswater.

Hawkshead Has connections to William Wordsworth and Beatrix Potter. Cobbled streets add to its charm, while the church at St Michael & All Angels has been in place for more than 800 years – the present building dating to 1490. There are good options for bike hire available here.

VISIT

Must Sees

Brockhole (LA23 1FF) is the Lake District Visitor Centre on the shores of Windermere. There is plenty to do for all the family, including archery, golf and an adventure playground. www.brockhole.co.uk

It feels unfair to choose a must-see lake in a National Park whose very raison d'être is its great waters. There are 16 lakes in the Park, or 17 if you include Brothers Water, which is a tarn. However, there's only one *official* lake – **Bassenthwaite Lake** (NY 225 271) – as it is the only one to have lake in its name. The rest are waters or meres.

Windermere (NY 387 000) is England's largest and deepest lake at 14.8 sq km (5.71 sq miles) and 74m (242ft), respectively.

Derwentwater (NY 260 208) and **Buttermere** ❶ (NY 181 159) are favourites, as is **Haweswater Reservoir** ❷ (NY 485 148), for the fantastic work the RSPB is doing to bolster species such as ring ouzels.

Borrowdale has genuine Atlantic rainforests and is a National Nature Reserve (NNR). The Borrowdale Oakwoods are one of England's largest remaining pieces of temperate rainforest, which once spread from the north of Scotland down the west coast of England, Wales and Ireland. It was given NNR status in May 2024 and is looked after by the National Trust. The first part of the reserve is 721ha (1,782 acres). The NNR is best visited from the **Bowderstone Car Park** (CA12 5XA).

Castlerigg Stone Circle ❸ (NY 291 236) is described as 'the most atmospheric and dramatically sited of all British stone circles, with panoramic views and the mountains of Helvellyn and High Seat as a backdrop'. It is thought to have been built in 3000 BC, potentially one of the earliest in the country.

Ennerdale ❹ (CA23 3AS) is the site of a rewilding transformation as it moves from spruce to native broadleaf woodland. The Wild Ennerdale Partnership is allowing the landscape to evolve naturally by reducing human intervention and is realising great results along the River Liza. There are two car parks on either side of the Ennerdale Lake – Bowness Knott to the north and Bleach Green to the south. www.wildennerdale.co.uk

Amazing waterfalls can be found at **Aira Force** ❺ (NY 399 205) and **Stanley Ghyll Force** ❻ (SD 174 995). The former sits in an 18th-century pleasure ground and has fine oak woodland trails and huge trees. Stanley Ghyll feels like it's part of a jungle, with ferns, mosses and liverworts lining the trail up to the 18m (60ft) waterfall.

Near the beginning of the trail is **Dalegarth Falls** (NY 178 001).

6

Must Dos

Be inspired...

The Lake District has some of the highest mountains in England – from **Scafell Pike** (NY 215 072) at 978m (3,209ft) to **Catstye Cam** (NY 348 158) at 890m (2,920ft). There are 214 fell tops classed as Wainwrights, and summiting them all is a challenge in its own right. The Park has a staggering 3,200km (1,988 miles) of rights of way!

The **Fairfield Horseshoe** is a classic circular walk, stretching 16.4km (10.2 miles) from Ambleside and 'bagging' eight Wainwrights in the process. It's strenuous, and can be challenging, but is a real rite of passage. **The Old Man of Coniston** (SD 272 978) has remnants of old copper mines and offers extensive views from its summit at 803m (2,633ft).

There are plenty of low-level routes, too. A walk around **Tarn Hows** (SD 331 999) is as fine as any lakeside walk in the country, while the accessible route up **Orrest Head** (SD 414 993) from Windermere offers a panoramic view that kindled Wainwright's love of the Lake District.

... and then grab a beer

The Wasdale Head Inn (CA20 1EX) is the home of British rock climbing. In Keswick, several pubs have been included in the Campaign for Real Ale's (CAMRA) *Good Beer Guide* – the **Fox Tap Bar** (CA12 5BY) at Keswick Brewery (www.keswickbrewery.co.uk), **The Wainwright** (CA12 5BZ) and **The Dog and Gun** (CA12 5BT) – which also sells homemade Hungarian goulash. Other favourites include the **Golden Rule** (LA22 9AS) in Ambleside, which is at the bottom of the 'struggle' that leads to Kirkstone Pass, and the 16th-century **Black Bull Inn** (LA21 8DU) in Coniston.

◤ Eyeing up the high street from Haweswater.

◆ A wander around Tarn Hows is as good as any in the country.

Visit the coast

The Lake District's boundary skirts the west coast of Cumbria from Silecroft to **Ravenglass** (CA18 1SQ). This is the Park's only coastal village and is on the estuary of three rivers – the Esk, Mite and Irt. It's a remarkable place, a far cry from the mountain scenery close by. It has two pubs, the narrow-gauge heritage Ravenglass and Eskdale Railway (www.ravenglass-railway.co.uk), and a Roman bathhouse – Walls Castle. It is also where two World Heritage sites overlap.

The **Ullswater Steamers** have been running for more than 160 years, offering scenic heritage tours over Ullswater. www.ullswater-steamers.co.uk

There is also a heritage railway at **Haverthwaite Station** (LA12 8AL) near Newby Bridge. Established in 1973, The Lakeside & Haverthwaite Railway hauls traditional 1950s carriages along a 5.1km (3.2 mile) long track to Lakeside Station, where connections are available with Windermere Lake Cruises.
www.lakesiderailway.co.uk

Fancy a scramble?

The best scrambles, from the easy to the most difficult, can be found in the Lakes. Some are family-friendly, while others will need expert support. **Jack's Rake** (NY 285 078) is a grade 1 scramble – one of the most popular in the country – while **The Bell** (SD 288 977) is a quick wander from the **Walna Scar Car Park** (LA21 8HD). For more challenging routes, the grade 3 **Pillar Rock** (NY 171 123) is at the head of Wild Ennerdale – not for novices – while **Giant's Crawl** at **Dow Crag** (SD 264 977) near Coniston is difficult and only for those with rock-climbing experience and route-finding ability.

↑ Taking flight on the quiet coastline.

→ Warnscale Head Bothy.

For a guided experience, the slate mine at **Honister** (CA12 5XN) offers via ferrata – both classic and extreme – mine tours, canyoning and more. www.honister.com

Into the woods

Whinlatter Forest offers walking, running and cycling trails, an adventure play area and a Go-Ape course. (www.forestryengland.uk/whinlatter) **Grizedale Forest** is a great place to see red deer and red squirrels. There are trails for bikes and horses, a Go Ape course and a family-friendly campsite. www.forestryengland.uk/grizedale

Stay in a bothy

If you can cope with a resident mouse that likes stealing your food, then a night in **Warnscale Head Bothy** (NY 204 132) could be for you. This 18th-century mine cottage is a shelter for walkers, with fine views over Buttermere, and close to Haystacks. Bothies bring people together in a confined space, with an ensemble of stories, whisky and, hopefully, some wood for the fire. Warnscale is certainly small – realistically, room for three on the wooden shelves near the walls and perhaps one or two on the floor, if you remember to leave your foodstuff higher up. It's important you leave no trace, carry your rubbish out and bring a tent, as the bothy is often full. You won't get it to yourself, but the front door's inscription reads, 'all friends of wild places are very welcome'. www.warnscalehead.wordpress.com

Visit a museum

There are more than 30,000 exhibits at the **Lakeland Motor Museum** (LA12 8TA), which is open daily until 4.30pm (www.lakelandmotormuseum.co.uk). The Park has a variety of other museums too, including Keswick Museum, Ruskin Museum, Brantwood and Dove Cottage.

CAR-FREE TRAVEL

➜ Public transport information for most of the places and experiences in the Lake District can be found at www.lakedistrict.gov.uk. Simply search your desired location, and you can find the best way to get there. Buses are available from Keswick for Blencathra, for example, and there is an open top bus service every half-hour from Keswick to Borrowdale.

➜ Buses run throughout the year in the popular valleys, including Borrowdale, Langdale, Grasmere and Coniston. Core services include the #555 through the heart of the Lake District, #599 Bowness to Grasmere and X4/X5 Penrith to Keswick, Cockermouth and Workington. There are also open-top bus tours (www.stagecoachbus.com and www.traveline.info). A free Wasdale shuttlebus also runs from mid-April until late September.

➜ Stagecoach offers combined bus and boat tickets, meaning you can enjoy a cruise on either Windermere (www.windermere-lakecruises.co.uk), Ullswater (www.ullswater-steamers.co.uk), Coniston (www.conistonlaunch.co.uk) or Derwentwater (www.keswick-launch.co.uk). Each lake has passenger boats with multiple stops. www.nationaltrust.org.uk/visit/lake-district/steam-yacht-gondola

➜ The West Coast Main Line runs trains to the east of the Lake District, connecting Oxenholme, Penrith and Carlisle. Direct trains run from Manchester to Windermere while local trains from Oxenholme call at Kendal, Staveley and Windermere. There is also a route following the Cumbrian coastline. www.thetrainline.com

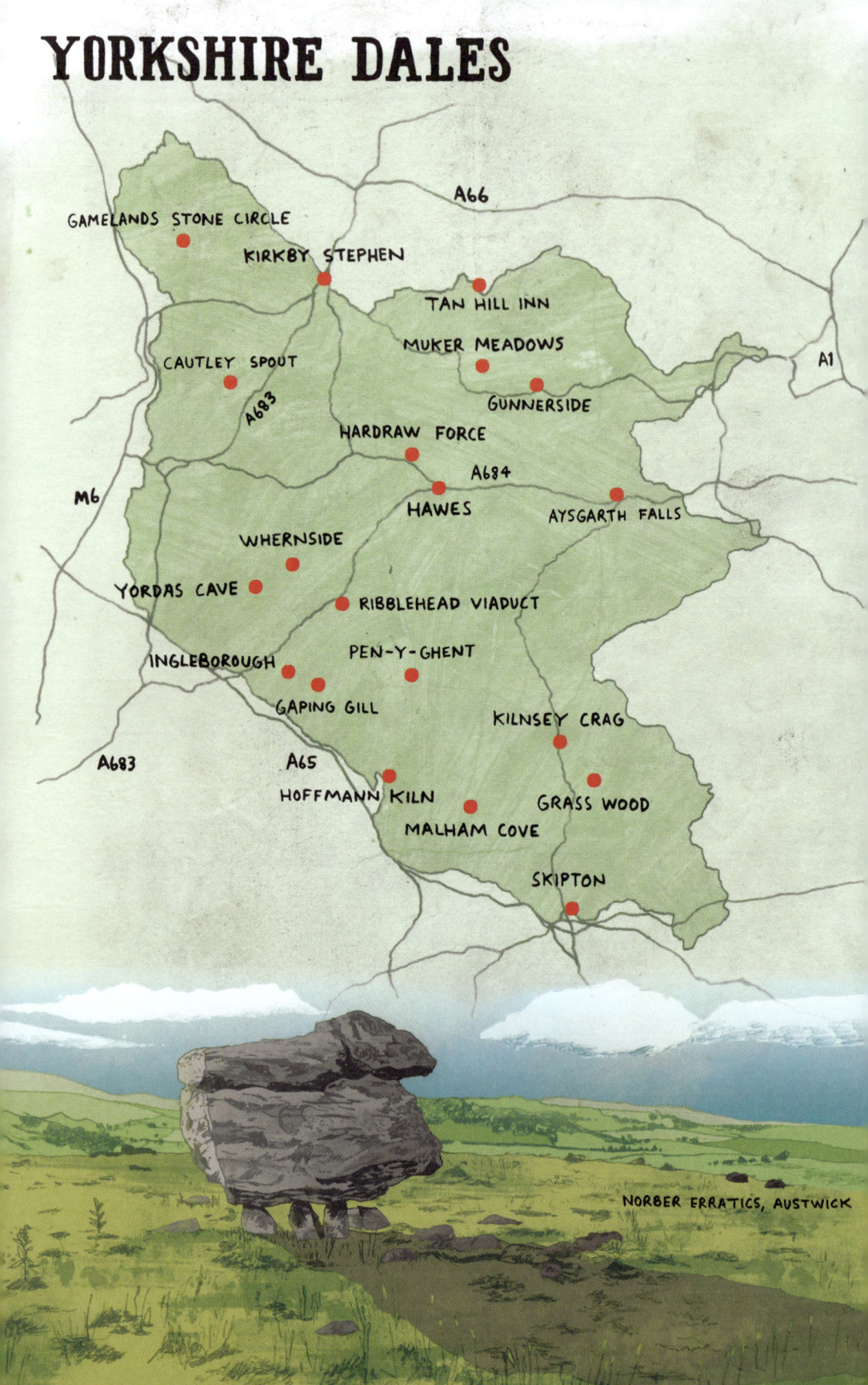

YORKSHIRE DALES

DESIGNATED: 16 November 1954
SIZE: 2,179 sq km (841 sq miles), **HIGHEST PEAK:** Whernside at 736m (2,415ft)
ANNUAL VISITOR NUMBERS: 5.09 million (2023), **POPULATION:** 22,798
OFFICIAL WEBSITE: www.yorkshiredales.org.uk

Force, gorge and crag are words that evoke meaning, a way of describing the landscape. They reflect human interaction with place and how language is passed through history to show the impact of nature and geology. Scaur may have now been shortened to scar, but the original dialect has a somewhat melodic note to it. Indeed, Hardraw Force, England's largest single-drop waterfall, falls some 30m (100ft) over its Scar, and local brass bands use this natural amphitheatre to create a wall of sound. A rather apt correlation...

A lifetime of love for landscape is how I became addicted to the Yorkshire Dales. My first forays into the Park were in an A-Reg Ford Escort, violently shaking as it accelerated up the M6, the radio being turned up to drown out the noise. It was a military operation, leaving home early, butties and snacks in tow, but always stopping at the services for a brew before undertaking a walk or visiting some kind of cave. Many people remember the Dales with the same misty memories – childhood holidays, rolling landscape, sheep, limestone, peaks and walls.

The Dales hasn't changed much since I spent my early days in the village of Dent on the western side of the Pennines – its close-knit cobbled streets resembling a film set and something out of a bygone era – playing in the river, climbing trees and getting into trouble. It didn't change when I was let off the leash a bit more, and now, although this National Park is certainly busier, it's still the same place. The landscape has barely altered, and

➜ Norber Erratics near Austwick.

that warm welcome I remember so well is still there; Dales' people are some of the friendliest around.

The Yorkshire Dales was designated in 1954 in recognition of its extraordinary natural beauty, the diversity of its wildlife habitats, its rich cultural heritage and its fantastic opportunities for outdoor recreation. It is also one of the more distinctive places in terms of its array of varied landscapes. In the south, there are the iconic peaks of Ingleborough, Pen-y-Ghent and Whernside, vast areas of limestone pavement and the epic showcaves in Clapham and at White Scar, just outside Ingleborough. As you head north into Swaledale and Wensleydale, it becomes more rolling and wooded. Grass Wood is an ancient woodland just outside Grassington, and in Muker you can visit hay meadows that are still traditionally managed, using techniques sadly in the rearview mirror as farms intensify. These Dales are 'managed', carved and manipulated by rivers as well as long-gone industries such as lead mining. Travelling further 'upwards', it becomes more sparse, with open moors, isolated villages and pubs (more of that later), and the Westmorland Dales to the west, which has its distinctive character. This area was added to the Park in 2016, making it 2,179 sq km (841 sq miles) in total, alongside landscapes near Kirkby Lonsdale, such as Barbon and the Casterton Fells. Different outlooks, different challenges, but the same welcome.

The picture is bright, lavish and bountiful; this is an open place where you can walk along a river in the morning, visit a pub that probably hasn't changed for more than 100 years, climb in the afternoon, and then enjoy some traditional Dales folk music later. Cycling is a must-do, the Buttertubs pass out of Hawes a challenge for many as it was for the Tour de France in 2014, and while the walks may not be as dramatic as in Eryri (see page 193) or the Cairngorms (see page 249), for little effort you can see cloud inversions from many of the peaks. Some of the best caving in the world can be found here, too. The public can be winched down Gaping Gill and its 98m (322ft) main shaft – and for the more iron-willed, there are more than 90km (56 miles) of passage to

← Woodland near Beamsley.

↑ Dentdale.

be explored in the Three Counties System. It is possible to enter a cave in Yorkshire, pass under Lancashire and come out, tired and wet, in Cumbria.

There are challenges, of course, and having spent the majority of my life working in and visiting the Park, these have become even more stark. The honeypot sites of Horton-in-Ribblesdale, Malham and so forth are ever busier, and the pressure to manage the expectations of visitors and the local population is ever higher. This Park sits squarely in the middle of those who want to keep it as a living museum (this is one of the most worked landscapes in the country) and those who want it to welcome development and 'modernise'. The brain drain to Leeds and other urban centres is high, as finding employment in this region, especially as a young person, can be difficult. Getting around is also a challenge, despite concerted efforts to ensure rural bus services survive, and regular trains continue along the Settle-Carlisle Railway, crossing the spectacular Ribblehead Viaduct.

This is a Park that understands its purpose and its qualities. A working landscape consisting of salt of the earth people who, despite all the problems in the world, just want to do the right thing. And you know what … those areas that are busy in the height of summer? Take a walk around Kingsdale near Ingleton, and most of the time you won't see anybody else. The same can be said for Ravenstonedale. Delay your walk up any of the Three Peaks, Buckden Pike or Simon's Seat, and you can have it to yourself. Swim in rivers off the beaten track, enjoy a saunter through Grass Wood at dusk, and you will soon see for yourself why this Park is in my heart.

And I've not even mentioned cheese…

THE CHAMPION

Neil Heseltine
ooo

Neil Heseltine farms 500ha (1,235 acres) in Malham, one of the most iconic and visited villages in the Park. He is the former Chair of the Yorkshire Dales National Park Authority and National Parks England.

If there is anything Dales' farmers are passionate about, it's their livestock and the landscape they work in. Hill farming is king, but it's a lifestyle under threat because of environmental and economic challenges. Neil was a dyed-in-the-wool sheep farmer – managing a flock of around 800 sheep at Hill Top Farm – until 2012 when, alongside his partner Leigh Weston, he opted to scale back for a better quality of life and a healthier bank balance. It had positive impacts on the Dales environment and led him to be a champion for nature-friendly farming.

"My grandparents moved to Hill Top in the 1950s, and my parents bought it 30 years later. It was on my mum's side of the family long before that too. You could say farming was in my blood, but I wasn't always about agriculture, and it wasn't always what I was going to do. It just seemed to happen, as I never really had any thoughts of doing anything else. I went away to agricultural college and worked on a farm in Northumberland. I then played rugby semi-professionally for the best part of a decade, worked on local farms, did some milking and sold animal feed. I met Leigh and returned to the farm full-time after the 2001 Foot and Mouth outbreak.

In 2003, as part of the Limestone Country Project, we introduced 19 Belted Galloway heifers and a bull. The idea was that different grazing practices would help regenerate some of the habitats in the National Park. Before then, subsidy pay was based on "headage"; the more sheep and cattle you had, the more subsidy you could claim. The result was a higher concentration of sheep grazing in the uplands, and this meant the decline of flora and fauna, as well as biodiversity, in those pastures.

That programme taught us a lot. It made us begin to understand how grazing affected the biodiversity of those pastures. After a while, we started to reduce our flock and increase cattle numbers. We had no real concern about reducing sheep because we knew they weren't making us any money. Having fewer sheep and lowering our cost structure resulted in us making a bit of a margin. As we continued to learn about land management and biodiversity, it became more important to us. It is on par with the food we produce, whether that is beef, lamb, or even wool.

What we have tried to create is a far greater balance between our production and the biodiversity on the farm. Having less stock and a different grazing system has allowed us to have more free time. We feel we have a better balance between production and our environmental impact and are getting a better work-life balance too.'

When Neil and Leigh made the change, Hill Top was a pioneer, and they weren't afraid to own their story. Making the connection between farming, nature and the food we eat is important to them both, and they use social media to not only highlight what they do but champion nature-friendly practices within the wider farming community. Check out @hilltopfarmgirl on Instagram to see for yourself. Several other farms in the Dales followed their lead in later years.

'I think what we did was to go back to traditional hill farming. What we are doing is more akin to what farmers were doing in the 1960s and 70s. People say we are progressive in our farming, but I would say we are regressing, going back to what it used to be. When you make decisions – and a big one like we did, despite all the evidence – you do wonder if you've done right or wrong. At certain times of the year, I would have been stressed dipping and clipping gimmer lambs, ready for market. As a farmer, those events are something you aspire to. You want to produce much better lambs, and the people who do that and do it to the "top end" are extremely skilful.

We've achieved things here that I never expected, and both Leigh and I are proud of it. We enjoy having people here to show them what we have done and work with local charities and the Park to bring groups – from school children through to asylum seekers and refugees – to enjoy this special landscape. We feel privileged to farm here.

Our farming system delivers environmental benefits and puts food on people's tables. I would like farmers to follow what we have done, but I know from experience it is difficult to change. We need to take people along with us to show that this kind of management is not only going to be beneficial for climate and nature, but it's also going to be beneficial for farming and farmers.

Two of the biggest issues facing the globe are climate change and biodiversity decline. I think we can turn that into revenue for farming if we grasp the nettle. We must do so not just for the uplands but across the country. We can turn that into a real positive for this industry and its community, but we must take that opportunity.

I don't think that change is something we should fear; it is something that has happened in this landscape for centuries. I am excited about it as it creates an opportunity for farming to find a way of putting carbon back into the soil. I suppose the way we are farming at Hill Top would be some people's version of rewilding. We're using stock to manage the land, increase biodiversity and are moving away from mechanisation.

The most important thing is we must involve people in managing the land. I think the cultural heritage we have as farmers and our part in the community as farmers is important – and I know we can make a difference.'

Neil's favourite thing to do in the Dales: 'I'd be in Littondale, just going about my farming life.'

Yorkshire Dales | 51

FACTS AND QUIRKS

Dales on film

Malham Cove (SD 896 641) is one of the most popular places in the country for film and TV crews, and it's easy to see why! Many people will remember a helicopter sweeping over the 70m (230ft) limestone cliff for the Barrett Homes ad, and in more recent times, it has appeared in *Harry Potter and the Deathly Hallows: Part 1* (2010) and the 1992 version of *Wuthering Heights*, while in 1951, Bette Davis' *Another Man's Poison* featured Malham village and Malham Tarn. The limestone pavement at the top of the Cove is part of *Slipstream* (1989) as a microlight chases Bob Peck.

Hardraw Force and Aysgarth saw regular visits from the cast and crew of *Robin Hood: Prince of Thieves* (1991). Robin of the Hood, as Marian describes him, and played by Kevin Costner, bathes in the waters underneath the 30m (100ft) waterfall after daubing himself in manure to get into a castle. (It's not Costner's backside on camera in the plunge pool but rather a body double's, and a no doubt cold one at that). At the upper Aysgarth Falls, Costner meets what would later become Robin's merry men and takes an unfortunate dip after being tripped up during a heist. These falls were also a haven for Wordsworth and JMW Turner. Wordsworth and his sister, Dorothy, visited while they waited for their coach horses to be changed, and Turner sketched them on a tour of the north.

All Creatures Great and Small is home to scenes from Askrigg, Swaledale, Arkengarthdale and Langthwaite as well as, more recently, Grassington.

Local legends

If you get **married in Askrigg**, remember a knife ... or some change! Local children will tie the church gates together with baler twine. It's then up to the best man to pay off the mischievous kids before he is allowed to cut the gates free.

The Burning of Old Bartle takes place at West Witton on the first Saturday and Sunday after St Bartholomew's Day. In the evening, after a day of fell running and other festivities, an effigy known as 'Old Bartle' is taken through the village before it is burnt. During the wander, an ancient verse is chanted, depicting 'old Bartle', which some speculate could be St Bartholomew or a sheep rustler.

In Bainbridge, the **blowing of the forest horn** takes place at 9pm between 28 September and Shrove Tuesday. It's a practice likely to date from when Bainbridge was the administrative centre of the Forest of Wensleydale, with the horn sounded to guide travellers to safety.

Outside the porch of Dent's 12th-century St Andrew's Church lies the **gravestone of George Hodgeson**, who died in 1715 aged 94. He was said to drink a daily glass of sheep's blood as a tonic. After his death, villagers claimed he kept appearing around the village. One farmer shot a black hare and followed the blood trail to George's door. Peering through the window, he said he saw George tending a shotgun wound. Alarmed, locals exhumed the body, reburied it, and drove a brass stake through his torso. The top of that stake is still visible in the gravestone.

Wensleydale cheese is best served on fruitcake.

WALK 1

An Ingleborough epic!

A challenging circular that takes in the iconic hill, Gaping Gill, Trow Gill and vast limestone landscapes.

If you're looking for an introduction to the breathtaking and varied landscape of the Yorkshire Dales, then this walk is for you. At around 24km (15 miles) in distance, it begins in the hamlet of Horton-in-Ribblesdale before crossing the historic Settle-Carlisle Railway and gradually climbing to the 723m (2,372ft) summit of Ingleborough. It's a well-defined route that will suit hikers who are keen to test themselves over a longer distance while not being confined by a particular timeframe.

Rising out of the station, limestone pasture and farmland are quickly surpassed by a more rugged landscape before Ingleborough appears. Once on the summit, 360-degree views encompass the entire Lake District and beyond. You then drop down into Clapham, passing the staggering Gaping Gill – where Fell Beck falls into a chamber that is as large as York Minster – before moving to the collapsed cavern of Trow Gill and Ingleborough Cave.

The path levels out somewhat and becomes more of a stroll as you walk along Ingleborough's Nature Trail and among the plants of renowned

START/END:
Horton-in-Ribblesdale National Park Car Park, BD24 0HF or Horton-in-Ribblesdale Station, BD24 0HL
DISTANCE: 24km (15 miles)
GRADE: Challenging

↑ Trow Gill.

Yorkshire Dales | 53

botanist Reginald Farrer. Historic Clapham village follows before you take to a green lane to skirt around another side of the hill. Here, the land is green, lush and inviting, and there's even time to take a slight diversion to the Juniper Gulf pothole before tracing your route back to Horton-in-Ribblesdale.

This route is best done in winter as the sharp cold is contrasted by clear skies, but you'll need adequate winter skills and equipment at Ingleborough summit. In summer, you should attack this hike in the morning, as towards the end of the day the route down is popular with Three Peaks walkers – those attempting the famous challenge that takes in this mountain, Pen-y-Ghent and Whernside.

← Looking towards Ingleborough.

WALK 2

Aysgarth Falls & Freeholders' Wood

The three-stepped waterfalls at Aysgarth have been a tourist attraction for more than 200 years.

This accessible walk is an ideal rainy day wander and has the bonus of a fantastic café and facilities at the National Park Centre. In Aysgarth itself, there are more pubs and places to stay too. The opening third of the amble – a Miles Without Stiles route – runs through Freeholders' Wood and has some great views of the middle falls.

This is a nature reserve with ancient semi-natural woodland and a hazel coppice – best seen between March and June for its beautiful flowers. You could also be lucky and meet a dormouse; the rare and secretive small mammal was reintroduced here in 2008.

Seventy steps take you to the lower falls – dramatic in flood – or you can continue a further 1km (0.6 miles) along an unsurfaced grass route. There are also different routes through the woodland itself.

START/END: Aysgarth National Park Centre, DL8 3TH
DISTANCE: 2.5–3km (1.5–2 miles)
GRADE: Easy

→ Aysgarth Falls.

Why not try these great walks...

THREE PEAKS OF YORKSHIRE: Tackle Pen-y-Ghent, Whernside and Ingleborough on a challenging 38.6km (24 mile) round trip.

GRASSINGTON TO HEBDEN: This 6.5km (4 mile) walk begins at the National Park Visitor Centre, in the village of Grassington. It offers fine views without straying far from the nearest facilities. Quickly and gently rising above Grassington, it passes over stiles through woodland and hay meadows to the pretty village of Hebden.

MUKER TO KELD: A gentle 6.5km (4 mile) circular through hay meadows and mining remains with amazing views across Swaledale.

↑ Malham Cove.

Key Places

The rider...
Plenty of accommodation is available with B&Bs, pubs, guesthouses, hotels and campsites, all varying in price depending on the season. Well-equipped campsites are available in Dent for the Dales Way, while the youth hostel in Hawes lets private rooms, camping and cabins, and the whole hostel.
www.yorkshiredales.org.uk/plan-your-visit/where-to-stay/accommodation-search/

Places to visit

Hawes On the A684 between Ingleton and Leyburn is Hawes, a historic market town. It's a busy but charming thoroughfare with a market on a Tuesday. There are several historic pubs and the Wensleydale Creamery, which offers tours and free samples. Ideal for walks to Hardraw Force and Semerwater.

Grassington *All Creatures Great and Small* location, which was granted market town status in the 13th century. Although stalls on the small cobbled square disappeared some 600 years later, the Dickensian festival each Christmas reignites those past days. Grassington has cosy cafés and shops, as well as a folk museum and National Park Centre. Linton Falls is just a short walk away, as is Grass Wood, an ancient woodland.

Kirkby Stephen When the Park expanded in 2016, it welcomed an already Dales-esque town in Kirkby Stephen. Nestled in the Upper Eden Valley, right on the edge of the Park's northernmost claim, it has historic buildings, cobbled yards and the church of St Stephen, known as the 'Cathedral of the Dales' because of its 'size and elegance'. Nearby is Pendragon Castle, allegedly founded

← Hardraw Force.

↓ Linton Falls.

Victoria Hall, the oldest music hall in the world, opened in 1853. A great base for the Settle-Carlisle Railway.

Ingleton An alternative starting point for the Three Peaks. The Waterfalls Trail includes the stunning Thornton Force, while White Scar Cave is nearby.

Leyburn Ideal for exploring the quieter areas of Wensleydale. Do not miss the Forbidden Corner! It's billed as 'The Strangest Place in the World' with its labyrinth of tunnels, chambers, follies and surprises created within a garden in the heart of Tupgill Park.

by Uther Pendragon, the father of King Arthur, and the site of a Roman fort built as a stopping-off point between camps at Bainbridge and Brough. Less than a few kilometres away is Smardale Gill Nature Reserve, set in the backdrop of the steep gill. It has species-rich grassland with 6km (3.7 miles) of level walking.

Malham Incredibly busy all year round but a must-see because of the delicate waterfall at Janet's Foss, dramatic Gordale Scar, Malham Tarn and Malham Cove. The circular walk is around 10.5km (6.5 miles) but can be broken down into sections.

Skipton This market town has recently earned the moniker of 'Little Ibiza' due to its burgeoning bar scene. It's a sum of its parts; a classic cobble-lined town with side passages revealing hidden pubs and shops. The Leeds and Liverpool Canal is nearby, atmospheric alongside locks and peaceful meanders away from the main strip. At the top of the main street is Skipton Castle, with origins of more than 900 years old.

Why not try...

Settle Market town on the outskirts of the Park in the south. Features Settle

Must Sees

Ribblehead Viaduct ① (SD 758 794) is an eerie piece of Victorian architecture that supports the weight of the historic Settle-Carlisle Railway. Construction began in 1869 and was completed in seven years, with around 6,000 men working across the 117km (73 mile) route. Evidence of the construction is all around, including the site of a smallpox hospital, brickworks and an inspection pit. Brickworkers were housed in a shanty town on the moor called Sebastopol – named after the Crimean War siege of 1855 – with Inkerman, Jericho, Jerusalem and Belgravia nearby. Hundreds of navvies died on the construction due to accidents and smallpox.

Bolton Castle ② (DL8 4ET) is one of the best-preserved castles in the British Isles. Building began in 1379, and it took 20 years to complete. This isn't an ordinary tour around a castle – there's falconry, wild boar feeding, archery and medieval games. www.boltoncastle.co.uk

Bolton Abbey ③ (BD23 6EX) is set in 12,140ha (30,000 acres) of rolling countryside. Remains of a 12th-century priory overlook the River Wharfe, which can be crossed via stepping stones. The existing church is impressive, as is Strid Wood – an ancient woodland. www.boltonabbey.com

Gamelands Stone Circle (NY 640 082) stands at the base of Knott Scar, about halfway between Orton and Raisbeck. The 33 stones create an oval shape of 44.5 x 37.5m (146 x 123ft), and artefacts have been dated from between 1800 and 1400 BC.

Great Asby Scar (NY 656 097) rivals any of the limestone pavements in the southern part of the Dales! It is part of a scar that covers around 11 sq km (4.25 sq miles). It also contains Castle Folds, a Romano-British walled settlement that was used as a summer shelter, called a shiel. Sunbiggin Tarn is nearby.

Muker's meadows ④ (SD 910 983) are best visited between late May and early July on a circular walk from the village to Keld. The walk also has mining remains, and the tranquil Kisdon Force ⑤ (NY 898 010).

Cautley Spout (SD 681 975) is England's highest cascading waterfall, above ground. Cautley Holme Beck travels some 200m (656ft) down the fells.

Semerwater (SD 919 871) is best visited if you approach Bainbridge on the A684. Legend states it was once a prosperous city. There's a tale of an old man who came to the city in search of food and drink. He knocked on every door, being rebuked each time before he found a welcoming 'hovel' where a poor couple pitied and took him in. After enjoying the couple's hospitality, the old man turned to face the town and said: 'Semerwater rise! Semerwater sink! And swallow the town, all save this house, Where they gave me meat and drink.' Immediately, the waters of the lake rose and flooded the area, drowning its citizens but saving the couple who took him in. It is the second-largest natural lake in the Park after Malham Tarn and is around 0.8km (0.5 miles) long.

Must Dos

Eat...

The **Yorkshire Dales Cheese Festival** is held annually every autumn. Businesses host events with menus and tastings to mark the occasion. The park produces a map of the festival: www.yorkshiredales.org.uk/things-to-do/whats-on/shows/cheese-festival/

At **Curlew Dairy** (DL8 4DB), you can enjoy Yoredale, a smooth and buttery traditional small batch Wensleydale cheese. At the **Courtyard Dairy** near **Settle** (LA2 8AS), you'll find everything you need if you're a cheese addict – and a restaurant as well as a small outlet selling wine.

Town End Farm Shop in **Airton** (BD23 4BE) sells local produce such as homemade Yorkshire chorizo, a Spanish-inspired paprika-flavoured fermented sausage. Keep an eye out for **Yockenthwaite Farm's** award-winning granola, while the **Game Cock** at **Austwick** (LA2 8BB) has a bakery and pub with a French twist.

... and be merry

Tan Hill Inn (DL11 6ED) is famous for being the highest pub in England at 528m (1,732ft) and for punters being locked in for days when the snow descends! It dates back to the 17th century, and as well as being a focal point for tourists, it is a beacon of safety too. Set on the Pennine Way, it's a welcome sight on the 431km (268-mile) journey from Edale to Kirk Yetholm. Plenty of people have camped around its grounds, and once upon a time you could stay within the confines of the snow plough. Camping is welcome (there is a charge), and you can also book in for breakfast. Readers of a certain vintage will recall Ted Moult's 'Fit the Best, Everest' ads being filmed here!

Fetes and shows

Held every May, **Austwick's Cuckoo Festival** celebrates the spring visitor, which is seen as a sign of warmer times. A tale says that the people of Austwick were so pleased to see a cuckoo nesting in a tree that they built a wall around it in the hope of keeping it there. They believed if it stayed in the village, they would keep the balmy temperatures all year round. Sadly, the wall they constructed wasn't high enough, and it simply flew away.

⬇ Tan Hill Inn.

↠ An icy Pen-y-Ghent.

In Ingleton is the **1940s Weekend**, which celebrates 'old-time' nostalgia. The village is turned over to the atmosphere and poignant history of wartime in July each year.

Malham Show is a real tourist attraction and has all manner of events including sheepdog demonstrations, Punch and Judy, fell faces, drystone walling competitions and a lot more. It's held every August. **Kilsney Show** has been running since 1897 and is held on the Tuesday after the August bank holiday. Its remit is to promote and showcase farming in the Yorkshire Dales – and it features the famous crag race where runners tackle the western side of Kilnsey Crag. It's an impressive sight watching athletes of all ages and abilities take on the almost vertical challenge!

The annual **Settle Flowerpot Festival** runs over the summer. More than 150 installations appear around the streets of the town, with several thousand flower pots used to create diverse and entertaining exhibits. **Kettlewell** hosts a Scarecrow Festival along similar lines in August.

Adventure on the Dales

The Dales has 2,628km (1,632 miles) of footpaths and 618km (384 miles) of bridleways.

The **Three Peaks Challenge** starts from **Horton-in-Ribblesdale** (BD24 0HF) and climbs Pen-y-Ghent, Whernside and Ingleborough. It's a 38.6km (24 mile) route that is supposed to be completed in 12 hours. The annual fell race runs the same route, with a record time of 2 hours and 46 minutes. The **Three Peaks Cyclo-Cross** starts at Helwith Bridge and is billed as the 'toughest and biggest Cyclo-Cross event in the UK'. Riders will race for 61km (38 miles); around 27 of those on the road, more than 32 'off' it including 6km or so when they have to carry their bike. It adds up to around 1,524m (5,000ft) of ascent.

The **Swale Trail** is aimed at aspiring young mountain bikers and families who want to ride together. It's a valley bottom route 20km (12 miles) in length, 70 per cent on unsurfaced tracks. www.cyclethedales.org.uk/route/swale_trail/

Parts of the **Pennine Way** and **Coast-to-Coast** paths also cross the Dales.

Learn

The **Dales Countryside Museum** (DL8 3NT) is a great place to see the Dales and the people who have lived and worked here for thousands of years. www.dalescountrysidemuseum.org.uk

The 19th-century **Old Gang Smelt Mill** (DL11 6PR) can be visited via an up to 8km (5 mile) Miles Without Stiles route.

Hoffmann Kiln (BD24 9NU) is located off the main road between Langcliffe and

Stainforth. Walk around the interior of the huge lime kiln!

Wonders, woodlands and wildlife

Freeholders' Wood (SE 013 816) in Aysgarth and Grassington's **Grass Wood** (BD23 5FA) offer lonely walks in outstanding woodland. Near Hawes, you can find red squirrels at **Mirk Pot** (SD 828 863), and they'll even let you feed them if you're lucky!

Hoffmann Kiln.

The Little White Bus operates a book-in-advance service throughout the year from the Dales Countryside Museum.

In autumn, salmon can often be seen leaping on their final journey upriver to their spawning grounds at **Stainforth Falls** (BD24 9PQ).

The **Dark Skies Festival** is held annually over 17 days during February and March. Great spots for stargazing include four Dark Sky Discovery Sites – Hawes and Malham National Park Centres, Buckden National Park Car Park and Tan Hill Inn. www.yorkshiredales.org.uk/things-to-do/whats-on/shows/dark-skies-festival/

Caving – for the adventurous and not so...

In the south-west, there are more than 90km (56 miles) of passage to be explored in the Three Counties System – meaning it is possible to enter a cave in Yorkshire, pass under Lancashire and resurface in Cumbria. It's a system still being pushed, and while access is difficult because of its nature, there are still caves that can be visited nearby.

Yordas Cave (SD 705 791) was opened as a showcave in the early 1800s and can be visited from the road to Dent from Ingleton. Take a head torch and hard hat, and after walking down the steps, enter the Great Hall. On the right is the

---

CAR-FREE TRAVEL

➜ Regular train services are available along the Settle-Carlisle Railway, which takes you over Ribblehead Viaduct and into Ribblehead and Horton-in-Ribblesdale. Ideal for the Three Peaks if you time it right. www.northernrailway.co.uk/travel/timetables

➜ The Yorkshire Dales Explorer train service runs every Saturday from Rochdale via Manchester Victoria, Bolton, Blackburn and Clitheroe to Settle, Horton-in-Ribblesdale and Ribblehead. https://communityraillancashire.co.uk/yorkshire-dales-explorer-timetables/

➜ Regular services also operate into Skipton, and leisure steam trains run on the Embsay & Bolton Abbey Steam Railway. www.embsayboltonabbeyrailway.org.uk

➜ Bus services are available across the Dales but are dependent on the season. The #874 runs from Wetherby to Buckden, taking in Bolton Abbey, Grassington and Kettlewell on Sundays and bank holidays. www.dalesbus.org

Bishop's Throne and the wonderful Chapter House waterfall.

Long Churn Caves (SD 775 756) is a place for novices to learn skills when accompanied by an experienced caver or guide. **Great Douk Cave** (SD 747 770) in Chapel-le-Dale is also great to explore. The Council for the Northern Caving Community released a self-guide sheet: www.cncc.org.uk/publications/

For most cavers, there isn't a more iconic pothole in the world than **Gaping Gill** (SD 751 726). Impressive above and below ground, Fell Beck meanders along the hillside until it plunges 98m (322ft) into an open chasm. The pothole was first bottomed in 1895 after several previous attempts inched closer to its floor. Subsequent explorations have found more than 15km (9 miles) of passage and a link – now blocked – to Ingleborough Cave down the valley. For those who aren't experienced cavers, you can be winched down the shaft in a boson chair courtesy of volunteers at Craven Pothole and Bradford Pothole clubs. These events occur around the spring bank holiday and in mid-August. To visit, simply walk up from Clapham, along the nature trail, and follow the route to the open pot. It's popular, so be prepared for a long walk and long wait. The price is £30 and must be pre-booked. You can find out more at www.cravenpotholeclub.org and www.bpc-cave.org.uk.

For a gentler way of exploring, there are three showcaves in the Dales – **Ingleborough Cave** (LA2 8EE) near Clapham, **White Scar Cave** (LA6 3AW) near Ingleton, and **Stump Cross Caverns** on the road to Pateley Bridge from **Grassington** (HG3 5JL).

⬆ The magnificent Main Shaft of Gaping Gill.
⬇ Great Douk Cave.

NORTH YORK MOORS

SANDSEND BEACH

NORTH YORK MOORS

DESIGNATED: **28 November 1952**
SIZE: **1,436 sq km (554 sq miles)**, HIGHEST PEAK: **Round Hill at 454m (1,490ft)**
ANNUAL VISITOR NUMBERS: **8.97 million (2023)**, POPULATION: **22,935**
OFFICIAL WEBSITE: **www.northyorkmoors.org.uk**

Let's be honest: moorland can be seen as scary, and those travelling through the North York Moors to the coastal hotspots of Whitby and Robin Hood's Bay might feel similar too, but they are missing so much. Take time to discover and savour them, and you'll see why the North York Moors are a rich, diverse misunderstood landscape.

They contain one of the largest expanses of heather moorland in England and Wales, covering an area of more than 44,000ha (109,000 acres) or around one-third of the National Park's boundaries. This is a vital habitat for merlin and golden plover, being a European Special Protection Area for both species, and the area is an internationally renowned haven for ground-nesting birds. It is home to the most northerly colony of the Duke of Burgundy butterfly in Britain, and the southernmost place for the dwarf cornel (creeping dogwood). The landscape and

↓ The North York Moors are a working landscape with heathland, moorland and wooded habitats intermixing with agriculture.

its climate create a special, unique ecosystem.

Woodland and forests cover about 23 per cent of its environs, and the North York Moors contain one of the largest concentrations of ancient and veteran trees in northern England. From the mixed woodland of Dalby Forest and its world-class UCI mountain bike trails to the nooks of Arncliff, it rivals that of the New Forest and the ancient woodlands in Dartmoor for variety. These areas are protected, cared for and loved.

The North York Moors also has big skies, the size of sky you'd expect to see cruising down a highway in the USA. The Hole of Horcum is colossal, with views stretching beyond the norm. Sutton Bank, on its westerly border, is considered the finest view in England – and is a steep climb that has ruined the confidence of many an HGV driver, and a fair few clutches too. In December 2020, the National Park was also designated as an International Dark Sky Reserve, along with the Yorkshire Dales, one of only 24 in the world (as of 2026). At a combined area of 3,615 sq km (1,395 sq miles), it represented the largest area in the UK and one of the biggest in Europe to be simultaneously designated – and it's easy to see why. The night sky is incredible, with thousands of stars waiting to be seen in an area largely free of light pollution. Support for the designation came from more than four-fifths of the population, and local businesses have worked together to

← Discover special woodland trails.

→ Bank Top in Rosedale.

welcome many from all over the world to see the natural wonders above our heads.

The coastline possesses no heirs and graces; it's in-your-face rugged. Robin Hood's Bay is postcard-friendly and popular too, but beyond are just-as-pretty villages and sea to be dipped in. You can discover fossils and dinosaur footprints at Runswick Bay, Ravenscar and Saltwick Bay and see whales on special tours from Staithes. Whales … in Yorkshire!

Above all, the North York Moors is a friendly place. There are 105 settlements across the National Park, and each has been captured in a one-minute video – a monumental task put together by the National Park to show its love for its communities. They're a plea for protection, a display of quirkiness and beauty, but they demonstrate just how good local people are. This is an open place, in both heart and landscape. No one takes a back step; it's a warm hug of a welcome, but honest too. This National Park that knows what it is and what it does well.

And don't get me started on the food portions!

↑ Rievaulx Abbey.

← The North York Moors coastal view towards Robin Hood's Bay.

THE CHAMPIONS

Jackie & Ian Berry – Town End Farm, Appleton le Moors

○○○

Jackie and Ian Berry are owners of Town End Farm guesthouse, a converted Grade II listed barn and buildings in Appleton le Moors.

A lot of people dream of leaving the rat race and running a small guesthouse somewhere in the countryside – endless days of walking, scenery and pub lunches as you see out your retirement in peace and comfort. That was the plan for Jackie and Ian Berry, a midlife crisis eventually leading them to the North York Moors and Town End Farm. Yet, instead of buying a sleepy B&B in a quaint village, they opted to completely renovate a run-down property and create a venue capable of taking in around 14 people, with modern, high-end comforts.

> Ian says: 'We'd had enough of the corporate nonsense and thought long and hard about doing something different. We loved the idea of a big project like this, and after talking it through, we thought what was the worst that could happen. Town End Farm just fitted what we needed. It's fair to say we hadn't understood what the North York Moors were all about until we moved here. We hadn't appreciated the variety: the big skies, coast, woods and forests. It is very diverse.'

When the couple arrived in Appleton le Moors, there was a lot to do. The house and barns had been on the market for some time, and there were major building works required that had put off potential buyers. They also had to navigate through a minefield of planners, conservation officers and bat surveys, but they eventually got the go-ahead in 2014. Ian managed the project and did a fair bit of the work himself, while Jackie continued to commute to Hull.

She says: 'I think all the farmers in the village thought I was nuts because I was travelling that far, but we had to make it work. It made it slightly less scary that we had a salary coming in. It was a big task to get this place right because we didn't want to rip it apart and turn it into a box. We wanted to be sympathetic to its character, and I think we've managed that. We also knew that we didn't want to go down the B&B route. We spoke to some friends who gave us the lowdown on what it's like, and they were really honest. We felt we would be tied to the place all the time if we operated a B&B, and that didn't suit what we wanted. We're here for our guests and whatever they need, but they don't want to see us, do they? It gives us the freedom to go off walking when it's a nice day.'

Town End Farm focuses on providing luxury accommodation and other services that connect people to the local area. They have produced a digital guide that demonstrates the best of the North York Moors, and includes local walks, where to go out and what local businesses offer. They will also suggest where to get off the beaten track and where to enjoy a unique experience.

'That connection is important to us; a lot of businesses here are doing great things, and we want people to enjoy that,' Ian continues. 'If our guests want a dinner party, we connect them with a local chef. We've found that since the pandemic, people want to push the boat out a little more and spoil themselves. Our chef will come in, cook a fabulous meal and do the cleaning up. You can see why people would want to do that.'

Town End Farm's clientele ranges from families celebrating big birthdays and anniversaries, people enjoying walking and cycling breaks, to yoga groups and the occasional hen party. They have also welcomed Dementia Adventure, a charity that supports a more active and fulfilling life for everyone living with the condition.

Jackie adds: 'We enjoy being in this community and have worked hard to be a part of it. We were upfront and honest about what we were doing from the very start. When we were getting closer to the end of the project, we held an open house and invited them in. I also volunteered Ian for lots of things around the village, and we also forced ourselves to go out regularly to chat with everyone in the local pub. A tough job, I know. It was great to discover what the village was like, and it didn't take us long to find out that it was an amazing place with the friendliest people. A lot of people helped us to get this project to where it is now.

One time, one of our guests asked if there was a field they could do some archery in. We had a chat with the farmer next door, and he got his tractor out, got one of his big round hay bales and dropped it in a field for us. That wouldn't have happened if we hadn't made sure we were part of this special place. During the pandemic, I think we caffeinated the whole village! We provide coffee for our guests from a local supplier, so during that time, Ian would put out an email every month to see what people wanted. We just charged the wholesale price and helped the village out in a little way at a time of crisis. It's been absolutely fabulous being here, and we definitely made the right choice.'

You can follow Jackie and Ian's journey at www.townendfarm.org.uk and @town_end_farm_long_barn on Instagram.

> **Jackie and Ian's favourite thing to do in the North York Moors:** 'We would take a walk from Rosedale. You can walk along the old railway lines to an area where the mines used to be. We've taken pictures of shooting stars there at night. You can then walk down to Rosedale Abbey and have cake at Graze on the Green. Then there's a fabulous goat's cheese dairy just a short walk away.'

Mysterious moorlands

In late 2022, I saw a video clip of British cryptids – animals that some people believe may exist in the wild but are not recognised by science. One of these apparitions was sighted in the National Park and was called the **Yorkshire Yeti**. *British Cryptids: Yorkshire Yeti* was released in 1974 but only seems to have been 'shown at schools or languished in public libraries'.

Boggle Hole near Robin Hood's Bay was the home of boggles, also known as hobgoblins. They lived in 'hob holes', and locals would take their ill children there to be cured. Later, it was also a smuggler's hideout.

Nan Hardwicke was apparently a bona fide witch. People claimed to have seen the devil coming out of her small cottage in Danby, while others say two of her sister witches flew out of the door. After dusk, she would transform into a hare and have to flee from hunters.

Hart Hall in Glaisdale was haunted by a hob, a good spirit that would help with a long day's work in the farm's fields. But it took flight when farm workers offered it a gift, an easy way to offend a good spirit.

Byland Abbey is also said to have a ghostly presence after an anonymous monk wrote about them in 1400. According to English Heritage, they are 'generally people from the community who have died with the stain of unforgiven sins on their souls, or who still need to right some wrongs. The ghosts cannot get to heaven until these issues have been resolved, so they rise from their graves to seek help from the living. The sins in question tend to be relatively mundane. Story IX tells of a ghost whose crime is 'a matter of a sixpence'. In Story VI, the ghost of a canon of Newburgh Priory is tormented for stealing silver spoons. In Story VII, a hired hand is punished for overindulging his oxen, feeding them on his master's stolen corn.'

Gormire Lake could be bottomless according to legend, but when you do reach the bottom (is it really bottomless then?), it is the entrance to hell. There could also be a submerged village there.

Fruit, frightening roads and film

The oldest surviving **Gooseberry Show** in the country, established in 1800, is held at Egton Bridge. Entrants try to win the heaviest gooseberry competition, which is measured in drams and grains. Winners usually weigh in at 33 drams (the size of a golf ball!), but in 2025, a new record was set at 36 drams, 24 grains, or around 65.59g (2.3oz). www.egtongooseberryshow.org.uk

Chimney Bank in Rosedale goes head-to-head (or is it bumper-to-bumper) with Hardknott Pass in the Lake District for being the steepest road in England. It has a gradient of 1 in 3 ... not for the fainthearted, whatever the weather.

TV series *Heartbeat* and *Harry Potter and the Philosopher's Stone* (2001) were filmed at Goathland. The village was also a popular mini spa town in the 19th century because of the 21m (70ft) Mallyan Spout.

WALK 1

Levisham Moor, Hole of Horcum & Skelton Tower

◊◊◊

A classic moorland circular with breathtaking views.

The North York Moors possess big skies and grand views. This wander allows you to see stunning vistas while enjoying a little of the National Park's archaeological past and inspiring bowl-shaped valley. Starting from the car park and safely crossing over the road, you circumvent the Hole of Horcum, a hollow created by water undermining the steep slopes. It is 120m (400ft) deep and 1.2km (0.75 miles) across and looks different every time you stop to view it. The route takes you past an Iron Age dyke before arriving at Dundale Pond. Here, you turn right and pick your way down to Skelton Tower to see the North Yorkshire Moors Railway heritage line below.

Retracing your steps, you arrive at Dundale Griff, an oak-wooded ravine that is far away from the expansive views experienced earlier. It's a quiet place to reflect ... well, it was until the Lockton Limping fell race came running through – a challenging 11.2km (7 mile) race across the landscape.

Towards the bottom the route crosses a small stream into the base of the Hole of Horcum, with sweeping banks around. The walk back to the top is taxing but more than worth it. Legend says this feature was formed when Wade the Giant got upset during an argument with his wife and scooped up a handful of earth to throw at her. It may have been catching, as there were a few cross words from a couple of walkers as they climbed up the path, but nothing too serious!

This walk can be done all year round, but does get busy at weekends. There are lots of alternative routes in the area for less crowded paths. You can get the Coastliner bus to the Hole of Horcum Car Park.

START/END: Hole of Horcum Car Park, Lockton, YO18 7NR
DISTANCE: 11.2km (7 miles)
GRADE: Moderate

⬆ The Hole of Horcum is a dramatic basin, viewable on a circular walk.

WALK 2

Sutton Bank & Garbutt Wood

The finest view in England? James Herriot thought so.

Sutton Bank National Park Centre is a hive of activity for cyclists, walkers, runners and everything in between. Right at its heart, alongside the well-equipped visitors' centre, is a kids' bike trail where very young children can practise their skills in safety. Yet, within a couple of minutes, you're completely alone on an accessible tramper trail to 'The Finest View in England', according to vet and author James Herriot. The view is huge, and it is easy to see why he liked it so much. The route back is just beyond this point, a pleasant meander through Cliff Plantation, back to the Centre.

START/END: Sutton Bank National Park Centre, Sutton Bank, Thirsk, YO7 2EH
DISTANCE: 4.5km (2.8 miles)
GRADE: Easy/Moderate in places

Our walk continues along the Cleveland Way, a 175km (109 mile) National Trail from Helmsley to Filey Brigg, before dropping down through a sweet chestnut-lined wooded valley to Garbutt Wood Nature Reserve. This managed woodland is best visited in May and June, according to Yorkshire Wildlife Trust, with Whitestone Cliff, also known as White Mare Crag, on your left and Gormire Lake on your right, adding to the atmosphere.

The route rises steeply in places to Great Relief Pot – a small cave entrance with a heck of a draught – before returning to the view and the Centre. A gem of a walk.

➜ Heading down to Garbutt Wood.

⬇ The best view in England?

Why not try these great walks...

LYKE WAKE WALK: A notorious 64.4km (40 mile) challenge walk across the North York Moors from Osmotherley to Ravenscar. The walk's emblem is a coffin. Good luck with that one!

ST AELRED'S PILGRIM TRAIL: A 66km (41 mile) pilgrimage route linking the 12 churches of Upper Ryedale and Helmsley with Rievaulx Abbey. It is accessible to walkers, cyclists and horse riders.

FARNDALE WILD DAFFODIL WALK: An accessible Miles Without Stiles route, 5.95km (3.7 miles) long, that follows the River Dove from Low Mill to Church Houses and back.

↑ Sandsend … why travel to Robin Hood's Bay when this is up the road?

Key Places

The rider…
B&Bs, pubs, guesthouses, hotels and campsites all vary in price depending on the season. Just outside the National Park is Kirkbymoorside – an ideal base for exploration. The North York Moors is also a coastal National Park, and although Whitby is outside its boundary, it has a variety of places to stay, but usually at the higher end of budgets. www.northyorkmoors.org.uk/visitor-information

Places to visit

Rosedale Abbey A beautiful and historic village at the base of Chimney Bank, a 1:3 gradient road. It was a small hamlet until 1830 when a new church, mill and stone bridges were built due to the increase and wealth brought by ironstone mining. The village celebrates its past with historic walks in all directions, and has the best cake in the area (a big call…) at Graze on the Green. Gillies Jones – an artisan glassmaker – plies its trade in the village, while a tasty goat's cheese dairy is just a short walk away. The village also has a large caravan park with pods and pitches.

Appleton le Moors Off the beaten track, this is a one-road village, medieval in layout, with a fine pub – The Moors Inn – attracting people from all around. The reading room is quaint, and next door is a pinfold, which was restored in 2018 after being present since the 17th century. Local woodlands are explorable, an oasis away from the busy A170. The Grade I

Christ Church and the rose window.

Christ Church at the top end of the village has an ornate rose window.

Sandsend The seaside village of Robin Hood's Bay and town of Whitby are classic destinations in this area. They are busy all year round, whatever the weather, and that's understandable, considering the coastline is wild and breathtaking. Whitby's fish and chips are award-winning, too. Just a few minutes up the coast is Sandsend, a small coastal village with an equally stunning coastline and quaint local eateries. The Mulgrave Estate has holiday cottages just a few metres from the coast, and the Wits End Cafe is excellent.

Danby This village is in the Esk Valley and has several historic sights. Danby Castle stands on an escarpment spur above the village and was home to Catherine Parr before she became the sixth wife of Henry Vlll, while up the road in Ainthorpe is The Fox and Hounds Inn, which dates back to 1555. The North York Moors National Park Centre, Danby Lodge is a must-visit, too.

Helmsley A busy little hub on the A170 and the National Park's only market town, it was granted market status in 1191. It has a medieval castle and walled garden as well as shops and cafés. Nearby is the National Centre for Birds of Prey. Helmsley is also the start of the Cleveland Way, a National Trail to Filey Brigg.

Why not try...

Kirkbymoorside Just outside the National Park, with plenty of character alongside four pubs, cafés and restaurants to suit your budget and taste.

Pickering One of the area's oldest towns and just on the edge of the National Park. It's a busy place with a motte and bailey castle built in 1069 and the North Yorkshire Moors Railway, which was saved by volunteers in 1973.

Grosmont A gem that feels indebted to its industrial past but is now a pleasant but peaceful village in the Esk Valley. Like Pickering, it has a real rail heritage, as steam trains run frequently. The village shop is Britain's oldest retail cooperative, established in 1867.

⬇ Helmsley is a beautiful and quiet market town.

Must Sees

Located in Helmsley, **Duncombe Park** (YO62 5EB) is a historic estate with gardens and a nature reserve. It opens seasonally from April and can be visited all week except for Saturdays when the garden closes. There is a reasonable entry fee to the gardens, which also have trails and orienteering courses. www.duncombepark.com

The Church of St Mary in Lastingham ❶ (YO62 6TL) is thought to contain the oldest Norman crypt in the world. The first building here was a wooden monastery founded in 654 by St Cedd of Lindisfarne. A stone church followed in 725, while the earliest parts of the current church, including the crypt, date from 1078. The eerie crypt is found by walking down the steps in the centre of the church. It was built to house the bones of St Cedd and has been used as a place of worship ever since. The temperature changes, as does the atmosphere, as you descend into the mysterious place, which houses several artefacts, including a 9th-century Saxon crosshead. It is the only crypt in Britain with a nave, aisles and chancel.

Arnecliff Woods ❷ (NZ 787 049 and NZ 780 044) are tranquil areas of woodland with a historic past. There is a trod in the eastern wood, a route for monks to walk between Whitby Abbey and Guisborough. Clogs were also made by hand here because of the generous amounts of coppiced beech, alder and ash. The woodlands can be visited as part of the Esk Valley walk from Lealholm and the Coast to Coast National Trail.

'Everywhere peace, everywhere serenity, and a marvellous freedom from the tumult of the world' is a fine description of **Rievaulx Abbey** ❸ (YO62 5LB) by Aelred, the monastery's saintly abbot from 1147 to 1167. It was founded by 12 monks of the reforming and austere Cistercian Order in 1132. They wanted to return to the basic principles of monasticism, and by the 1160s, it contained 640 men who dedicated their lives to God. English Heritage preserves its remains and, as a result, it isn't cheap to visit, but there is a museum of artefacts, a visitors' centre and a café. Book ahead to save 15 per cent: www.english-heritage.org.uk/visit/places/rievaulx-abbey

James Herriot said the view from **Sutton Bank National Park Centre** (YO7 2EH) was the finest in England (although he did say a similar thing about the view at Crackpot Hall above Muker in the Yorkshire Dales). The centre is packed with trails and walks and is the perfect place for cyclists, with a repair shop and cleaning facilities. There's an eatery, while a project called Raiding the Bank is using community research and archaeological excavations to investigate historical moments. Sutton Bank has two Trampers (all-terrain mobility vehicles) and a Changing Places toilet (accessible toilet for those with further care needs). www.northyorkmoors.org.uk/suttonbank

Scaling Dam Reservoir (TS13 4TR) might be humanmade, but that doesn't detract from its charm. There are places to walk and fish and several watersports accessible to the public. It's located between Guisborough and Whitby, directly off the A171.

Dalby Forest ❹ (YO18 7LT) on the

A169 from Pickering to Whitby is a paradise for cyclists! It's packed with things to do, such as Go Ape treetop adventures, a huge playground for kids, and lots of trails for walkers and cyclists alike. The bike trails range from the easy, ideal for everyone, to the UCI World Cup trail – a 6.4km (4 mile) extreme world-class route.
www.forestryengland.uk/dalby-forest

Cawthorn Roman Camps (SE 782 896): This 2,000-year-old military camp has an accessible viewing platform and can be visited via an accessible Edge of Empire trail of around 1.6km (1 mile). The site was thought to be a group of military practice camps, but after investigation, it was found to include three military fortifications.

There are around 1,500 boundary stones and crosses in the North York Moors. **Lilla Cross** (SE 889 986) is one of the oldest Christian monuments in England, dating from AD 626. It stands on Lilla Howe, a round barrow.

Must Dos

Experience a genuine dark sky

Light pollution from street lamps and other sources means we very rarely see the real darkness of the sky and the wondrous nature of our stars. Thankfully, the North York Moors is one of six UK National Parks to have been awarded **International Dark Sky Reserve** status. It celebrated the 10th anniversary of its February Dark Skies Festival in 2025; each Festival has around 100 events, provided by more than 20 different businesses over two weeks while a smaller Fringe Festival runs every October. Events include stargazing, night walks, astrophotography, yoga and mindfulness sessions, stay-and-gaze packages, and children's daytime activities such as trails, crafts and bat box making. The National Park places significant focus on making sure the events are affordable and for the family. www.darkskiesnationalparks.org.uk/north-york-moors-events

At **Dalby Forest** there are also telescopes run by the Scarborough & Ryedale Astronomical Society, as this is a dark skies hotspot. www.scarborough-ryedale-as.org.uk

Take a hike

There are 2,268km (1,408 miles) of Public Rights of Way in the National Park, so finding a walk isn't difficult. The National Park promotes several routes on its website, some with public transport use and a strong message to share with care. www.northyorkmoors.org.uk/share-with-care

If you want more of a challenge, then walk the **Cleveland Way** or at least some of it. The 176km (109 mile) route forms a horseshoe around the North York Moors, starting in Helmsley and finishing in Filey. www.nationaltrail.co.uk/en_GB/trails/cleveland-way/

The River Esk, which flows from the moorland tops to the North Sea at Whitby, is one of only seven rivers in England to contain the freshwater pearl mussel. The **Esk Valley Walk** is a 60km (37 mile) walk that traces the source of this river

↑ Robin Hood's Bay.

from Castleton to the coast at Whitby. It's waymarked with a leaping salmon and passes through Danby, Lealholm, Glaisdale, Egton Bridge and Grosmont.

Get high-ish

While not having the peaks of its Yorkshire Dales neighbour, it's possible to climb high in the National Park and enjoy some great views. **Round Hill on Urra Moor**, at 454m (1,490ft), is the highest point in the North York Moors, while Roseberry Topping, the most iconic hill in the North York Moors and therefore the busiest, is 320m (1,050ft). The National Park is working with the National Trust to restore the paths for people and nature. Restoration of the first and most direct path up to the top is complete, with the remaining routes expected to be completed by 2027.

Experience culture

There's a long tradition of **folk music** in Robin Hood's Bay, and the village holds a festival every year to celebrate its rich heritage. The Folk Club hosts regular musicians' sessions in the Wainwright's Bar at The Bay Hotel. www.bayfolk.rhbay.co.uk

The **Staithes Festival of Arts and Heritage** celebrates the 'social and industrial history of the generations of families who have lived here, and their traditions, skills, crafts and intertwined relationships'. More than 100 pop-up galleries appear in cottages across the village – a huge community effort – supporting local artists and sculptors. www.staithesfestival.com

Ryedale Folk Museum (YO62 6UA) is a fantastic open-air museum in the beautiful Hutton le Hole. It opens seasonally and has 40,000 objects set within 20 heritage buildings. Exhibits include blacksmith workshops, and a medieval crofter's cottage, thatched longhouse, dairy and schoolroom. It's family-friendly, and you can even feed the farm animals. www.ryedalefolkmuseum.co.uk/visit/

↑ Take the North Yorkshire Moors Railway, pictured here from Skelton Tower.

Land of Iron (TS13 4AP) in Skinningrove looks at ironstone mining and railway construction. www.landofiron.org.uk

Let the train take the strain

The **North Yorkshire Moors Railway** is a cracking way to get around some of the National Park and enjoy the great scenery. Stations include Whitby, Pickering, Goathland, Grosmont, Newtondale Halt and Levisham, and several have tea rooms. www.nymr.co.uk

On your bike

The **North York Moors Cycleway** (www.northyorkmoors.org.uk/northyorkmoorscycleway) passes through the National Park's heather landscape, around hidden valleys, deep forests and coastline. It's a designated 276km (171 mile) figure-of-eight loop that links with the Esk Valley Railway (www.eskvalleyrailway.co.uk). The National Park also has **free e-bike charging points** at six locations, including Sutton Bank (YO7 2EH) and Danby Lodge (YO21 2NB) National Park Centres.

Time to relax

September is mindful month, and each year, local businesses link with the National Park to create a month-long mindfulness-themed events programme to help you de-stress and reconnect. This includes yoga, cheese-making, foraging, social walks and bike rides. It's a brilliant concept and exactly what the National Parks were set up for. www.northyorkmoors.org.uk/mindfulmonth

Eat

The North York Moors has been the self-proclaimed **Capital of Cake** since 2015, and you're invited to dutifully test this claim! A map of the 'capital' and its best bakes can be found on the North York Moors website. The same map features some of the great food across the National Park, written and chosen by professional food writers. www.northyorkmoors.org.uk/capitalofcake

Like cheese? There's a goat's cheese honesty box just outside Rosedale Abbey at **Abbey Farm Cottage** (YO18 8SD) (www.abbeyfarmcottagerosedale.com/cheese), while if you want a beer to go with it, **The New Inn at Cropton** (YO18 8HH) has a delicious brewery (www.newinncropton.co.uk/the-brewery/). For the more adventurous, professional chef and forager Katy Doman, 'the Lazy T', offers wild suppers at her off-grid venue (www.thelazyt.co.uk).

Go for a glide

Sutton Bank has amazing views, so why not see them from the air? **The Yorkshire Gliding Club** offers unique experiences to see the North York Moors from a different perspective. www.ygc.co.uk

Wildlife watching by sea

You can discover **fossils and dinosaur footprints** at Runswick Bay, Ravenscar and Saltwick Bay, and see whales on special tours from Staithes. www.yorkshirecoastnature.co.uk and www.threesister-boatcharter.co.uk

Go gliding with the Yorkshire Gliding Club.

CAR-FREE TRAVEL

➜ Public transport information for most of the places and experiences in the North York Moors can be found at **www.northyorkmoors.org.uk**. Simply search your desired location, and you can find the best way to get there. It is a superb tool.

➜ Visit North Yorkshire release a 'Sit Back and Ride' leaflet annually, which gives details of days out on public transport. www.issuu.com/visitnorthyorkshire/docs/sit_back_and_enjoy_the_ride_guide_2025 The National Park is well linked by bus services. Travel on the Coastliner (#840), it's Britain's most scenic route! www.transdevbus.co.uk/coastliner/

➜ Moorsbus services the National Park in summer. www.moorsbus.org

➜ Bus Service #128 runs all year round from Scarborough to Pickering, Thornton le Dale and Helmsley. www.eastyorkshirebuses.co.uk/services/EY/128

➜ The North Yorkshire Moors Railway is a great way to visit some of the sights. Stations include Whitby, Pickering, Goathland, Grosmont, Newtondale Halt and Levisham. www.nymr.co.uk

➜ The Esk Valley Railway runs from Middlesbrough to Whitby and serves 17 stations along the route. www.eskvalleyrailway.co.uk

PEAK DISTRICT

DESIGNATED: **17 April 1951**
SIZE: **1,438 sq km (555 sq miles)**, HIGHEST PEAK: **Kinder Scout at 636m (2,087ft)**
ANNUAL VISITOR NUMBERS: **13.25 million (2018)**, POPULATION: **36,000**
OFFICIAL WEBSITE: **www.peakdistrict.gov.uk**

Meandering from the Nag's Head pub in Edale is a trail that crosses the Peak District, Yorkshire Dales and Northumberland before landing at the Border Hotel in Kirk Yetholm some 431km (268 miles) later. It was the country's first 'official' long-distance route, inspired by Tom Stephenson, a journalist and champion of walkers' rights. He spoke not only of the need for a 'Long Green Trail' akin to America's Appalachian and John Muir Trails but also to 'allow the public access to wild, open moors'. His *Daily Herald* article of June 1935 suggested such a route would rise 'out of the moor-rimmed bowl of Edale' and head 'northwards to the distant border, through miles of lonely entrancing country'. It took just shy of 30 years for his dream to be realised, but on 24 April 1965, the Pennine Way was officially opened.

It's no surprise that the route originated from the Peak District – the country's first National Park. The area's beauty had long been championed as a destination for curious walkers, urban dwellers and lamenting scribblers. In the 14th century, Benedictine monk Ranulphi Higden wrote of Britain as 'a land of many wonders' and named the High Peak as its first. William Camden's *Britannia* (1586) refers to 'Nine things that please us at the Peak we see; a Cave, a Den, a Hole, the Wonder be'. Poet Michael Drayton had similar ideas, noting his wonders as Peak Cavern, Poole's Hole, Eldon Hole, St Anne's Well in Buxton, The Ebbing and Flowing Well at Tideswell, Sandy Hill and Peak Forest. Philosopher Thomas Hobbes' poem *De Mirabilibus Pecci* (1636) said: 'Of the

➔ Looking back at the packhorse bridge as you climb Jacob's Ladder.

High Peak are seven wonders writ. Two fonts, two caves, one Pallace, Mount and Pit.' He agreed with Drayton but replaced Peak Forest with Chatsworth House. These writers were attempting to emulate the Seven Wonders of the World, with this remote area of England the focus.

Then, in the 20th century, came the Mass Trespass of 1932, which would eventually nudge the needle towards the National Parks and Access to the Countryside Act (1949). Around 15,000 people from Manchester went walking every Sunday, but less than 1 per cent of the Peak District was open for walkers – unless you were part of an official and elite group, who could apply for permission. Kinder, the highest peak in the National Park, was itself closed, albeit for 12 days a year.

With the Ramblers getting nowhere and walkers being turned away on Bleaklow by local gamekeepers, the Lancashire branch of the British Workers' Sport Federation organised a mass trespass on Kinder Scout. Around 400 walkers set off from Bowden Bridge on 24 April 1932 and, after reaching the plateau, scuffled with the Duke of Devonshire's gamekeepers before continuing their walk. After a short distance, they met with a group of trespassers from Sheffield, exchanged pleasantries and then returned from where they came. It was nearly a triumphant moment but later five ramblers – Julius (Jud) Clyne (23), Arthur Walter (Tona) Gillett (19), Harry Mendel (22), David Nussbaum (19) and Bernard (Benny) Rothman (20) – were arrested in Hayfield and joined John Anderson (21), who was taken into custody at the scuffle itself. Five of the six were found guilty and jailed for between two and six months. Benny was seen as the leader and received a three-month sentence for 'riot and inciting riot and assault'. A few weeks later, more than 10,000 ramblers held an access rally at Winnats Pass. It took another 17 years, but it's no surprise that when the National Parks and Access to the Countryside Act was passed, the Peak District became the first National Park, and access to Kinder and Bleaklow was

⬇ The Pennine Way, Edale.

→ A pretty waterfall halfway down Grindsbrook Clough from Kinder.

one of the first things to be negotiated.

The Peak District is a land of fable and legend. It's the epicentre for the eternal class struggle and the right to enjoy open space after long hours of toil. It's a place of togetherness, fighting for what is right and endearing community support. In 1665, the tiny village of Eyam was devastated by the bubonic plague. It is thought to have arrived in a flea-infested cloth from London, which was destined for a local tailor. After it had been hung out to air, George Vicars died, and the rest of his household soon followed. It then spread, wiping out generations of families. Understandably panicked, the village was placed in quarantine thanks to the actions of Reverend William Mompesson and Puritan Minister Thomas Stanley. They agreed that no one should enter or leave the village, and religious services had to be held outdoors. Food and medicine would also enter the quarantined area through a 'Boundary Stone' that marked the line between the infected village and the parishes surrounding it. These had holes drilled into them and were filled with vinegar – an effective disinfectant that allowed villagers to exchange money with the outside world for goods. Other plague stones were a warning to those who may have wanted to enter. By 1666, more than 270 people had died, but that act of self-quarantine certainly halted the infection from spreading to other villages in the region. Their unselfishness, alongside the tragedy, is commemorated every Plague Sunday at Cucklett Delf in the village.

The National Park shares its varied landscape with many. It reaches into five counties: Derbyshire, Cheshire, Staffordshire, Yorkshire and Greater Manchester, and therefore right on its doorstep are the urban centres of Manchester, Sheffield, Derby and Nottingham. Its peaks, while not the highest – 'peak' deriving from the Pecsaetan, an Anglo-Saxon tribe who settled the area – are must-sees. Shutlingsloe, towards the east of the National Park, is a little gem. Beautiful reservoirs are dotted across its landscape, and you can climb at Stanage, visit secret hiding places for worshippers and explore the cheekily named Devil's Arse in Castleton. The Peak District broods, enriches and epitomises exactly what the National Park movement was set up for.

Daniel Defoe criticised the area as a 'howling wilderness', and it probably was when he was touring the country. That is something we now must cherish. The Peak District and its people have been through a lot.

THE CHAMPIONS

John & Pauline Dower

John Dower is seen as the father of the National Park movement following his 1945 White Paper report *National Parks in England and Wales*, which led to the creation of the Peak District National Park (PDNP) and the protection of these special places.

Every movement begins somewhere. The drive for something special, a sea change, is often sparked by a single individual before it's carried forward by many. John Dower was committed to the protection of fine landscapes. Born in 1900, he studied architecture at Cambridge University, became an architect and town planner, and joined the campaign for National Parks. In 1937, he designed YHA Malham Hostel and those at Eskdale and Bellingham. During the Second World War he served as a Royal Engineer, but after contracting tuberculosis, he moved into civil service. In 1942, he was asked to prepare a report on National Parks in England and Wales for post-war Britain.

↑ Unveiling a plaque to celebrate the life of John Dower at YHA Malham Hostel are Robin Dower, Baroness Sue Hayman (Defra Minister), Margaret Hart (Chair, YHA), James Blake (Chief Executive, YHA) and David Butterworth (Chief Executive Officer, YDNPA).

> 'He wrote that National Parks are not for any privileged or otherwise restricted section of the population, but for all who come to refresh their minds and spirit and exercise their bodies in a peaceful setting of natural beauty,' John's son Robin says.

John defined a National Park (peculiar to Britain) as: 'An extensive area of beautiful and relatively wild country in which, for the nation's benefit and by appropriate national decision and action, (a) the characteristic landscape beauty is strictly preserved, (b) access and facilities for public open-air enjoyment are amply provided, (c) wildlife and buildings and places of architectural and historical interest are suitably protected, while (d) established farming use is effectively maintained.'

After the war, his approach, proposing 12 National Parks, was accepted and laid the foundations for the National Parks and Access to the Countryside Act 1949, and the Parks we see today. Sadly, he died in October 1947 from the effects of tuberculosis.

John and his wife, Pauline, had three children: Susan, Michael and Robin. Pauline, the daughter of Sir Charles Trevelyan MP, campaigner for access to mountains, accompanied John on his field visits around the country. She was appointed to the National Parks Commission, created in 1949, and served for 16 years as a member and later as Deputy Chair. She also had a central role in the survey, negotiations and consultations that led to the designation of the PDNP in 1951, as well as being a member of Northumberland National Park Committee for ten years and YHA President from 1981 to 1982, the first woman in that role. She died in 1988.

Robin continues: 'As my father died when I was eight, I cannot remember much about his work on the National Parks Report, except through the lens of my mother's work to fulfil his vision. The friends and colleagues with whom my father had campaigned before the war for the creation of National Parks and the establishment of wider access to the countryside remained a huge and loyal circle of friends for my mother, greatly encouraging her and offering her hospitality both in London, where the Commission's office was her base, and out in or near the National Parks on her frequent field visits to determine boundaries or the impact of proposed quarrying, road development or forestry planting.

We moved to Kirkby Malham at the onset of war, and my father would complete his report there before moving on to Northumberland in 1945. His real recreational pleasure was in the Yorkshire Dales; aesthetically, this probably reflected the historic relationship between geology, topography and human activity, as well as the right of access. The Peak District, which my mother championed, had the same issues, but the pressure on that landscape was from all around. The Peak probably illustrates the pressures more significantly than any other National Park.'

Robin says that his father had great powers of persuasion and networking. When he died, my mother used those networks and her calm persuasion to champion his vision. The struggle to create public access to the countryside remains just as lively today as in those early years.'

He continues: 'In 1985, my brother Michael was appointed Chief Executive of the PDNP. At the time, several National Parks were unpopular with their resident communities, who felt they were hostile to local needs. Indeed, when Michael arrived in Bakewell to take up his post, there were signs saying 'Abolish the Peak'. He listened to the detractors and found solutions to the vacuum of confidence. Within two years, the National Park was pioneering a scheme to pay farmers to carry out environmental management, supporting businesses to make goods reflecting the area's distinctive character, setting up a trust to restore and manage historic buildings, and championing affordable housing. Like my father and mother, he was a negotiator, bringing people together.

I think the National Park system we have now is close to my father's vision. They are concerned with conservation for public benefit, and particularly for access, which fits very well with John's balanced view of what National Parks are about. My view is that this balance is attainable, provided everyone who has a side to take accepts that there could be a balance. I have always been aware of the very limited government funding for National Park Authorities, but I admire the enthusiasm and purpose [of them]. We have a common purpose, and if we hang on to that vision and persuade governments to fund these special places, they will continue to be a huge public benefit at a modest cost.'

> **Robin's favourite thing to do in the National Parks:** 'There is something special about the road over from Settle into Malhamdale. The last time I came over that route, it was absolutely stunning because there was snow on the tops, it was frosty and clear. It was extraordinary to look down on the Dale where I had been privileged to live for six years as a child.'

FACTS AND QUIRKS

Traditions

Castleton Garland Day, which coincides with Oak Apple Day, is said to be in honour of the restoration of King Charles II in 1660. It's a colourful ceremony held every year around the end of May. It sees the Garland King leading a procession through Castleton on horseback. The 'king' is covered to the waist in a bell-shaped floral garland, which is said to represent the oak tree in which King Charles hid after the Battle of Worcester.

Water is important in the Peak District – Buxton Water is especially famous – and this precious resource is celebrated with **well dressing**. More than 70 villages take part in the annual festival, which involves decorating wells with mosaics made from petals and other items. The world's earliest recorded example of this was in Tissington in 1349.

Caves, planes and flashy cash

Caving is king! The **Peak Speedwell System** is more than 18km (11.2 miles) long, with discoveries being found all the time. Within it is the stunning Titan Shaft at 142m (466ft).

In 1943, the **RAF's 617 Squadron** trained over Derwent and Howden reservoirs as they prepared to drop **Barnes Wallis's bouncing bomb** on Germany's Ruhr Valley dams. In 1954, the bombers returned in the classic film *The Dam Busters*.

Flash, the highest village in England, had a reputation for illegal activities such as counterfeiting - commonly known as 'flashy' money!

Legendary tales

Near Kinder Downfall is **Mermaid's Pool**, where an immortal mermaid rises on the eve of Easter to 'reward visitors with the gift of long life … or to lure down her admirers to their doom.' It is also said that you can see her if you look into the water at sunrise on Easter Sunday.

Lud's Church, an open natural chasm, was a hiding place for worshippers in the 14th century. Robin Hood and Bonny Prince Charlie allegedly concealed themselves within its protective walls.

Winnats Pass was the scene of a very grisly murder in 1758 involving a couple called Alan and Clara. They had intended to elope to Peak Forest Chapel after Alan was threatened by Clara's family because he was from a poorer class. They stopped at Castleton on their way, but never made it after coming across some drunken miners. The lead workers thought the couple were rich and plotted to steal from them. They pulled Alan and Clara from their horses as they rode through the Pass, stole their money and then murdered them. Their bodies were thrown down a mine shaft and only discovered a decade later. They are buried in Castleton, and the red leather saddle on display at Speedwell Cavern is said to have belonged to Clara.

Eldon Hole - one of the 'Wonders of the Peak' – is the largest open pothole in Derbyshire at 33.5 x 6.1m (110 x 20ft) at the surface. It descends some 75m (245ft) under the slopes of Eldon Hill. Local legend says that a goose fell down the hole and made its way out to Peak Cavern in Castleton.

WALK 1

Mam Tor, Hollins Cross, Back Tor & Lose Hill

◇◇◇

The Great Ridge in all its glory on a classic circular from Castleton.

Dominating the skyline to the west of Castleton is the Mam Tor. It stands at 517m (1,696ft) and is part of the Great Ridge, which takes in Hollins Cross, Back Tor and Lose Hill – one of the finest walks in the Peak District.

Mam Tor is also known as the 'mother hill' because of the landslips on its eastern side. Its geology causes it to shiver and created several mini hills. Its unstable nature is further enhanced by the fact that the original A625, which connected Chapel-en-le-Frith to Sheffield, was permanently closed because the 'Shivering Mountain' lived up to its name.

This walk takes you from the centre of Castleton and towards the Peak Cavern – also known as the Devil's Arse! – then through to Speedwell Cavern with Long Cliff on the left-hand side. Winnats Pass is tantalisingly close – a collapsed cave system or ravine, depending on who you believe. Cross and head past Treak Cliff and towards the Blue John Cavern before climbing to Mam Tor itself. It's a busy place: there's a car park just below that could save you much of the walk, and no doubt most of the fun, but that would be a shame. The

START/END: Castleton Car Park, Cross Street, Castleton, S33 8WH
DISTANCE: 12km (7.45 miles)
GRADE: Moderate

↑ Wonderful views from Mam Tor.

ridge, like the spine of a crocodile, stretches out before you, and in autumn the sunrises and -sets rival any other. Hope Valley is also in front of you, as are distant hazy views.

The ridge is followed to Hollins Cross and Lose Hill – views for days – before you take the path back down to Castleton.

➜ Some of the magnificent landscape just a couple of kilometres or so from the start of the Pennine Way.

WALK 2

Kinder Scout

◓◓◓

A fine welcome to the Pennine Way and Kinder Scout.

This is a classic adventure along the Pennine Way to Kinder Downfall and Kinder Scout, with the added benefit of some easy scrambling. It may seem simple at 16.5km (10 miles), but this is a navigational challenge; Kinder isn't forgiving in the mist, and deviating off the path following Kinder Downfall may see you buried in the peat … from experience!

Starting at Edale Station, it's a gentle meander to The Old Nags Head before you turn left and take the Pennine Way. Follow the well-used track to Jacob's Ladder and decide whether to use the switchback or the steep path in front. The original Pennine Way would have seen walkers trek north from Edale, straight across Kinder Scout's plateau and then onwards to Bleaklow and beyond. But such was its popularity, it was re-routed towards Upper Booth and Lee House before arriving at Jacob's Ladder and the River Noe and returning north. The new trail effectively followed an old packhorse route that had been used to carry goods across the high Pennine Moors. Here, in the 18th century, Jacob Marshall, a local farmer, created a stepped path to make the journey a little easier. Horses couldn't negotiate the steep ascent, so at the head of the packhorse bridge, they would go left and then

START/END:
Edale Station, Station Road, Edale, S33 7ZN
DISTANCE: **16.5km (10 miles)**
GRADE: **Challenging**

> # Why not try these great walks...
>
> **LUD'S CHURCH AND THE ROACHES:** Visit the mysterious Lud's Church from Gradbach before taking in The Roaches, a climber's paradise, on this 14km (8.7 mile) circular.
>
> **MONSAL TRAIL:** Follow a section of the former Midland Railway through tunnels and along viaducts. The 13.7km (8.5 mile) trail is flat and fully accessible. It runs between Blackwell Mill in Chee Dale and Coombs Road at Bakewell. Accessible entry points can be found at Bakewell, Hassop Station, Monsal Head and Millers Dale.
>
> **PADLEY GORGE:** Walk 6.1km (3.8 miles) from Longshaw Estate or Grindleford to see this deep, narrow valley that will immerse you in nature.

turn a sharp right to arrive at the top of this part of the trail. Marshall then cut a rough route up the hill to the top of the zigzag for the tradesmen to arrive before the horses.

From here, the landscape feels more remote – a 'howling wilderness', as Defoe would have said – and you arrive at Edale Cross, an interesting medieval wayside and boundary cross. The route turns towards Kinder Low and the Edale Rocks, as well as the summit cairn at 633m (2,077ft), just 3m (9.8ft) shy of the official highest point of the 'Scout' plateau, which is at 636m (2,087ft). The varying landscape continues as you approach Kinder Downfall, the close to 30m (98ft) waterfall that freezes solid in winter and blows back on itself in a gale. Make sure you get on to the other side of the waterfall for the return journey and see the expanse of peat that is being restored thanks to various partners. Years ago, this part of the plateau would be grim if you got stuck in massive groughs, the peat eroded beyond what you see now.

Next are the Wool Packs – eroded stones of all shapes and sizes – Crowden Tower and Grindsbrook Clough. The way down is a tricky scramble in places, but it's well worth it, and there's a lovely waterfall midway down. The track then takes you back to Edale.

➜ Some of the unusual rock features that greet you on the way to Grindsbrook Clough.

Key places

The rider...
The Peak District is well served by B&Bs, pubs, guesthouses, hotels and campsites, all varying in price depending on the season. There are several official youth hostels in the National Park offering shared bunks and affordable private rooms alongside camping and cabins. Several independent hostels exist, but most only take larger group bookings.
www.visitpeakdistrict.com/business-directory/category/where-to-stay

Places to visit

Bakewell The home of wonderful puddings on the A6 from Buxton to Matlock and Derby. The National Park's only town is packed with places to eat and drink, including the famous Bakewell pudding. The Grade I listed church here was founded in 920.

Castleton A vital hub of exploration in the White Peak with four caverns to explore, plus Winnats Pass, Mam Tor and Peveril Castle, which was completed in 1086. The Carlton Emporium, a curiosity shop, is worth a visit for the welcoming owner alone.

Eyam Steeped in history and selflessness due to its determination to stop the spread of the bubonic plague, which killed 270 people in the village by 1666. Plaques adorn buildings to mark who died there, and to the east of the village are the Riley Graves, where seven people are interred. Elizabeth Hancock remarkably survived, burying her husband and six children over eight days. Eyam Museum tells the story.

Hathersage On the A6187, not far from Castleton and Bamford. Has become popular in recent times for people exploring Higger Tor and Carl Wark as well as other historic sites. It was the inspiration for Charlotte Brontë's novels and featured in *Jane Eyre* (1847), and she is believed to have stayed in North Lees Hall, below Stanage Edge. St Michael's Church contains the grave of Little John while Robin Hood's Cave on Stanage Edge is nearby. In the village is a small factory – David Mellor Cutlery – which makes cutlery in a strange but inviting-looking round building.

↑ The medieval packhorse bridge at Ashford-in-the-Water.

← Castleton is a popular base for adventure.

↑ Winnats Pass near Castleton, the scene of a very grisly murder in 1758.

Ashford-in-the-Water One of the prettiest 'chocolate box' villages in the country, with idyllic houses and buildings alongside a medieval packhorse bridge. Church of the Holy Trinity is of Norman origin, with the stump of a Grade II listed cross in the churchyard and preserved maidens' garlands. These were carried at the funerals of unmarried girls.

Why not try...

Tideswell The Church of St John the Baptist dominates and is referred to as the 'Cathedral of the Peak'. The ghost of Old Sarah, a Victorian server, has been seen at the George Hotel!

Tissington Home of Tissington Hall, built in 1609, and the 21km (23 mile) Tissington Trail, which follows the former railway connecting Ashbourne to Buxton. The trail also joins on to the High Peak Trail at Parsley Hay.

Matlock Bath Just outside the National Park boundary and like no other place in the area. It looks like a Swiss resort but with arcades, seaside-like attractions and fish and chip shops! It first became popular in the 19th century when it was developed as a spa town. The Heights of Abraham is an award-winning hilltop attraction, with cavern and mine tours is nearby.

→ Church of the Holy Trinity in Ashford-in-the-Water.

VISIT

Must Sees

Chee Dale ① is best approached from the River Wye. Starting at Millers Dale (SK17 8SN), enjoy a stunning walk along a river surrounded by woodland and the Chee Dale Nature Reserve. Signage warns that it isn't passable in wet conditions; that's because the path goes into the river via stepping stones further along the route.

Lud's Church ② (SJ 987 656) is a chasm above Gradbach, formed by a landslip in millstone grit. It is around 107m (350ft) long and 18m (60ft) deep in places, and is thought to have protected persecuted worshippers in the early 14th century. The Lollards were followers of early church reformist John Wycliffe, and they found this a safe spot.

Bleaklow Head, **Bleaklow Stones** and **Higher Shelf Stones** (SK 093 960) offer incredible views across Lancashire, Cheshire, the Hope Valley and Yorkshire, as well as having the benefit of being crowd-free. Visit the wreckage of the USAF Boeing RB-29A Superfortress, which crashed on the way to Burtonwood in Cheshire on 3 November 1948 at Higher Shelf Stones. At 633m (2,077ft), Bleaklow is the second-highest point in Derbyshire and remains a remote, exposed location, with good navigation skills required to explore safely.

There's no finer entrance to Castleton and the Hope Valley than **Winnats Pass** (S33 8WA). Its name means Windy Gates, and it is either a collapsed cave system or a ravine. There are caves and mineshafts all over the limestone and grassy cliffs. The mining of lead here found the rare, semi-precious Blue John, which is used in ornaments and jewellery. This continues on a smaller scale at Blue John Cavern and also at Treak Cliff Cavern.

Upper Derwent Valley reservoirs and dams (S33 0AQ) – Ladybower reservoir was built between 1935 and 1943. The project saw the loss of Ashopton and Derwent villages – but the latter reappears from the water in dry summers. The packhorse bridge near Derwent Hall was also moved piece by piece to Howden Reservoir, and graves at the local church were exhumed and reburied at Bamford.

Alport Castles (SK 142 914) is a strange landscape that looks like castle towers from a distance. The features were created by landslips.

Chatsworth House (DE45 1PN) is a vast stately home and estate with lots to do for all the family. It appeared in *Pride and Prejudice*, as well as many films and period dramas. It's better value for money to go out of season. www.chatsworth.org

Dovedale ③ (DE6 2AY) has the most amazing stepping stones across the River Dove. Beyond are Lover's Leap, the Twelve Apostles, Reynard's Cave – thought to have been inhabited in prehistoric times – and Reynard's Kitchen. Further on are Dove Holes, Ilam Rock and Nags Spring.

Three Shire Heads ④ (SK 009 685) is an oasis of calm, best approached on foot from Knotbury. It is the point on Axe Edge Moor where Cheshire, Derbyshire and Staffordshire meet, and the River Dane joins a tributary to make its way south. Above each body of water are old packhorse bridges, while you can often spot wild swimmers at Panniers Pool.

Must Dos

Have dessert (before your main)

Try a sumptuous **Bakewell pudding**. This moist almond and jam-filled treat was made by mistake because of a misunderstanding between Mrs Greaves, mistress of the White Horse Inn, and her cook. Instead of stirring eggs and almond paste into the pastry, she inadvertently spread it on top of the jam. There are two wonderful places to sample the pud in Bakewell, each laying claim to the recipe. Bloomers (www.bloomersofbakewell.co.uk) on Water Lane is housed in a building dating back to the 1600s and says theirs is the 'first and only original Bakewell pudding' in a recipe from 1889 handed down over the generations. The Old Original Bakewell Pudding shop (www.bakewellpuddingshop.co.uk) claims the resultant pudding was so tasty that Mrs Wilson, wife of a tallow chandler, saw the possibility of producing the puddings to sell, and acquired the original recipe in order to commence a business of her own.

Raise your glasses

The New Inn (SK17 0SW) in Flash has the honour of being the highest village pub in England, while, just outside the Park boundary, in Buxton, you can refresh yourself with natural mineral water at **St Ann's Well**. The town is well known for its spa waters, and in medieval times, pilgrims would seek out its healing waters. **The Crescent** (SK17 6BH), built between 1779 and 1789, is an iconic Grade I listed Georgian building, and one of the most architecturally significant buildings in the country.

Go underground

Showcaves and caverns at **Poole's Cavern** (Buxton, SK17 9DH) (www.poolescavern.co.uk), **Treak Cliff Cavern**

⬇ Solomon's Temple is a short walk from Poole's Cavern.

↑ Poole's Cavern in Buxton is a special place.

→ Some of the stunning features that await in Treak Cliff Cavern.

(Castleton, S33 8WP) (www.bluejohnstone.com), **Blue John Cavern** (Castleton, S33 8WA) (www.bluejohn-cavern.co.uk) and **Speedwell Cavern** (Castleton, S33 8WA) (www.speedwellcavern.co.uk) are open for tours – the latter by boat – but the real highlight is **Peak Cavern** (Castleton, S33 8WS) (www.peakcavern.co.uk) – known as the Devil's Arse. At 18m (60ft) high, 31m (102ft) wide and 104m (340ft) long, its entrance is the largest in Britain. Rope was made there, and at Christmas, it is the site of an acoustically brilliant concert. Beyond the showcave lies one of the most extensive cave systems in the country. The cave was known as the Devil's Arse until around 1880, but changed to 'Peak Cavern' in order not to offend the visiting Queen Victoria. The cave came by that name because of the strange gurgling sounds found within as flood water drained away.

For cavers, the National Park has several interesting subterranean adventures, including **Eldon Hole** (SK 116 808) and **Giants Hole** (SK 119 826), although the latter is very popular with novices and groups. There is a trespass fee of £3.

Go for a long hike ...

The Peak District has 2,575km (1,600 miles) of footpaths, bridleways and tracks, including 103km (64 miles) that are fully accessible to all.

↑ Buxton can be busy, so the lake at the Pavilion Gardens is perfect to relax by.

The **Pennine Way** starts at Edale and is 431km (268 miles) long. Several sections cross the Park and are crowd-free.

... or get on your bike ...

There are 105km (65 miles) of traffic-free cycling and walking trails across the Peak District, with cycle-hire centres at **Ashbourne**, **Blackwell Mill**, **Hassop (Bakewell)**, **Middleton Top**, **Parsley Hay** and **Upper Derwent Valley** (www.visitpeakdistrict.com/business-directory/category/biking-cycle-hire). There are four multi-user trails: **High Peak**, **Tissington**, **Monsal and Thornhill Trails** ranging from 3.2km (2 miles) to 21km (13 miles). Each of these allows for walkers, cyclists, wheelers, horse riders and are traffic free. www.peakdistrict.gov.uk/visiting/places-to-visit/trails

... then glide

The **Gliding Club** at Great Hucklow offers once-in-a-lifetime Glider Flight Experiences. www.glidingclub.org.uk

Climb on

Stanage Edge (SK 243 837) is one of the most popular climbing venues in the UK and stretches close to 5km (3 miles) from Cowper Stone to Stanage End. Some of the toughest graded routes can be found here – baffling to non-climbers, as the cliffs are probably no more than 25 or so metres (82ft) tall. The difficulty comes from the specialist traversing routes, which can progress into thousands of metres. **Robin Hood's Cave** (SK 243 837) is nearby, a series of wind-eroded holes.

Bamford Edge (SK 207 849) offers great views of Ladybower Reservoir and has more than 140 climbing routes.

The Roaches is an impressive ridge not far from Upper Hulme on the A53. They steeply rise some 505m (1,657ft) above sea level. At one time, wallabies could be found here after being released from a private zoo at Swythamley during the Second World War. They survived until the late 1990s, and people still claim to see the odd one now and again.

Nearby is **Doxey Pool** (SK 003 628), a small pond with bottomless waters and a mermaid. It was named after the daughter of Bowyers of the Rocks – the legendary highwayman. Her name was Hannah, but she received the rather unflattering term of 'Doxey'. We'll leave it to you to find out what that means.

Learn about the plague

Discover more about Eyam and the plague at **Eyam Museum** (www.eyam-museum.org.uk). **Mompesson's Well** is located at around SK 221 772 while the **Boundary Stone** is best seen on the path from Stoney Middleton to Eyam at SK 226 758. There are three other Plague Stones noted on the Ordnance Survey map that act as a marker of the village's 'infection' boundary.

Create

Well dressing is a colourful tradition across the Peak from May to September. Volunteers create detailed murals to adorn local wells. The practice began in Pagan times to celebrate pure and clean water and was likely resurrected in the mid-17th century by those villages that didn't suffer from the plague. Flower petals and leaves, among other bits of foliage, grasses and mosses, are pressed into a thin layer of clay that is set into a wooden frame to create a large image. Eyam and Tissington well dressings are personal highlights.

Visit a castle

At **Peveril Castle** (S33 8WQ), you can enjoy great views across Hope and beyond. It's one of England's earliest Norman fortresses and was built by William Peveril before 1086.
www.english-heritage.org.uk/visit/places/peveril-castle/

CAR-FREE TRAVEL

➜ The Hope Valley Line between Manchester and Sheffield gives direct access to the Peak District, with stations at Grindleford, Hathersage, Bamford, Hope and Edale, while the Manchester to Glossop line means you can begin the Longdendale Trail at Padfield Station. The Manchester to Buxton line gives access to Buxton. www.northernrailway.co.uk

➜ The Derwent Valley Line runs from Derby to Matlock (www.eastmidlandsrailway.co.uk) and the Manchester to Huddersfield line stops at Greenfield and Marsden for access to Dove Stones and the Wessenden Moors. www.tpexpress.co.uk

➜ Bus services are frequent across the Park, depending on the location. From Buxton, you can catch the TransPeak bus service, which stops at Rowsley, Haddon Hall, Bakewell, Ashford in the Water, Taddington and Chelmorton.
www.peakdistrict.gov.uk/visiting/planning-your-visit/publictransport/peak-district-bus-routes

➜ You can also visit Castleton, Chatsworth, Bakewell, Bamford, Padley Gorge, Hathersage and the Monsal Trail on Stagecoach's PeakSightseer open-top bus, which is available from March until October.
www.derbysbus.info/times/tt_A_Z.htm

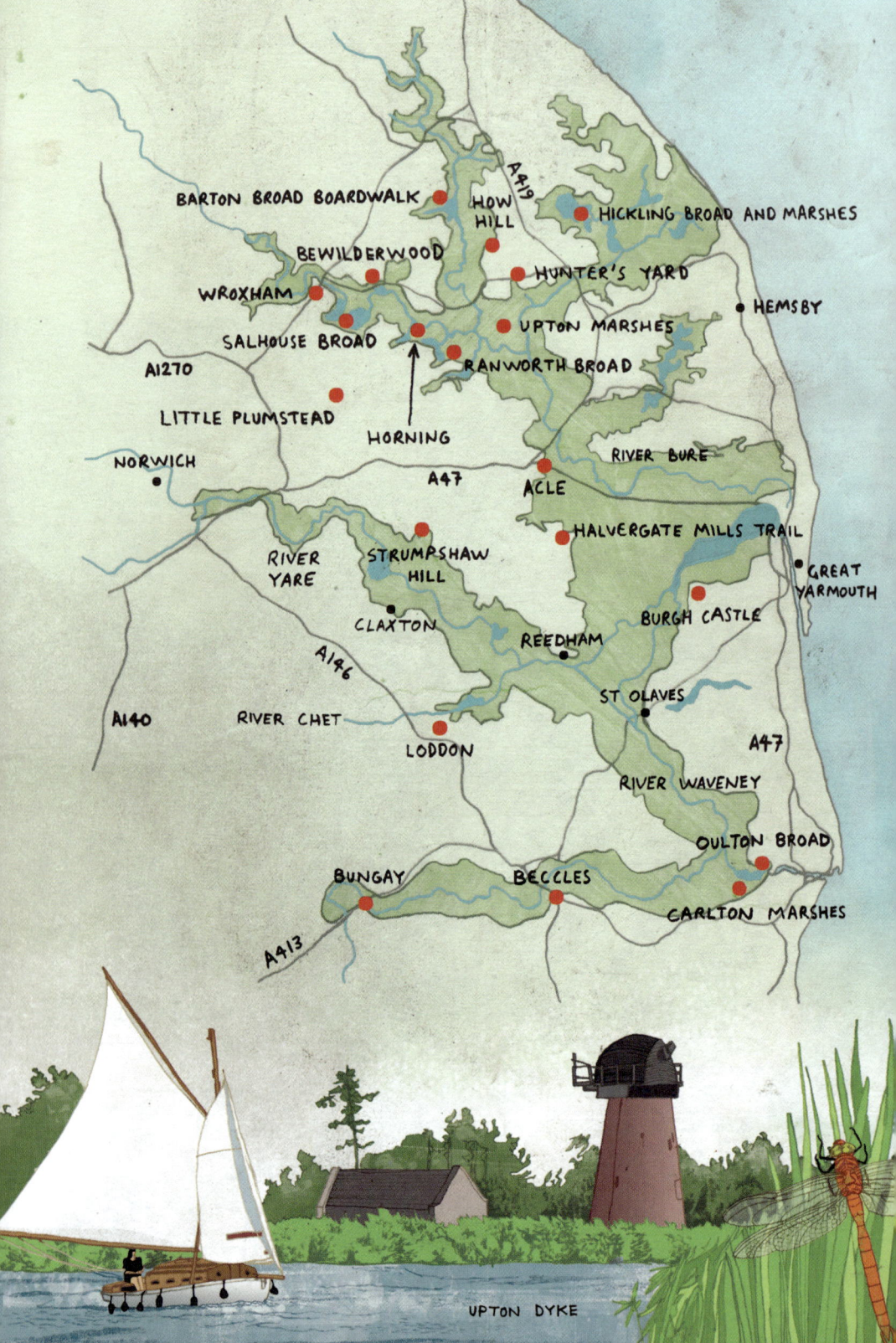

THE BROADS

DESIGNATED: **1 April 1989**
SIZE: **303 sq km (117 sq miles)**
HIGHEST PEAK: **Strumpshaw Hill at approximately 41m (134.5ft)**
ANNUAL VISITOR NUMBERS: **7.971 million (2023)**, POPULATION: **6,300**
OFFICIAL WEBSITE: **www.broads-authority.gov.uk**

The Broads National Park is a unique interleaving of human and natural history; a landscape of waterlines that pen their own story. The origins of the broads (shallow lakes), date back over a thousand years, when they were dug out for peat and later filled with water as levels rose and connected to nearby rivers. Entrepreneurial locals then drained the land between those waters for agriculture and grazing.

Walking or sailing around the Broads National Park, it's hard not to marvel at the ingenuity of that worked landscape. Several mills remain as markers to that bygone age, now cared for by organisations and enthusiastic volunteers who want to protect their heritage. These drainage mills have a romantic quality, sitting on the side of rivers and waterways, sometimes shrouded in mist to create an almost picture-perfect scene. They tell a story of entrepreneurial spirit and human connection.

Across the National Park, some of those drained areas are now being allowed to re-wet as the landscape

↓ The Broads National Park has nine National Nature Reserves.

changes. Thanks to various Wildlife Trusts, volunteers, farmers and the National Park, these rewilded, re-wetted and reworked parts of the Broads are a haven for wildlife. The bittern, one of our rarest breeding birds, has found a home there.

And it's not alone. Carlton Marshes is a prime habitat for the fen raft spider, one of the UK's most threatened species. There are water voles, the European eel, crayfish, Norfolk hawker dragonflies and black longhorn beetles. In fact, 25 per cent of the country's rarest wildlife is in this National Park. The Broads has a multitude of habitats that aren't repeated anywhere else, with nine National Nature Reserves and 28 Sites of Special Scientific Interest.

Connection here is vitally important. The waterways intermingle, navigating 303 sq km (117 sq miles) of varied terrain that is far easier to sail around, for obvious reasons, than drive. It is superbly accessible: the National Park has 63 broads, 13 of which are fully navigable, and a further five that are partially navigable, depending on the season.

⬆ The gatehouse at St Benet's Abbey.

➡ A swallowtail butterfly on marsh thistle.

These can be visited by boat, canoe, paddleboard or kayak. Anyone can turn up and hire a boat for a reasonable cost and then, after some suitable introductory training, get out on the water and discover the National Park for themselves. The Broads

The waterway near St Benet's Abbey.

also has boat trips that are accessible for visitors with disabilities, proving it really is a place for everyone, the true notion of a National Park.

However, what hits home is just how peaceful it is, all of it, even after just one day by the water. The Broads breathes as you do. Along the waterways are reeds that hush and wave in the breeze, filled with a cacophony of insects. It's nature's tinnitus, a constant relaxing white noise minus the irritation, making you ease through the day in relative and simple stasis.

All this means it is an utter privilege to cross timelines with the Broads National Park for just a few brief hours, and you should do so too.

⬥ Relics of the Broads' worked past are dotted around the Park.

THE CHAMPIONS

John Packman & Nick Sanderson

ooo

John Packman retired in 2026 having served 25 years as Chief Executive of the Broads Authority, looking after the Broads National Park. This interview was conducted when he was still in post. Nick Sanderson is the Education Officer for the Authority and is also nearing 25 years of service to the National Park.

Connecting the public to National Parks and helping them understand the special role they play in nature, climate and well-being is vital. The Broads is at the forefront of this – a landscape affected and created by humans, and now containing more than a quarter of the UK's rarest wildlife.

↑ John Packman.

↑ Nick Sanderson.

'I probably have the best job in Britain,' John says. 'The most important thing for me is the people I work with. We have about 100 full-time equivalent staff and about 90 different job descriptions. We are doing a task that is unbelievably complex and fascinating. The Broads is on the frontline of climate change. We're mostly at sea level, and any rise will make a real difference. We also have 25 per cent of Britain's rarest species, and alongside that is a valuable tourism and recreation sector.

It is special and unique. When you're out in the middle of the marshes, you see an amazing sky with birds flying across. We do a lot of dredging to maintain the navigation, and our colleagues have to take direct action to protect nature, such as ensuring water voles are unaffected by our work. Water voles are so rare that you have all sorts of interesting programmes moving and releasing them. We've got hundreds.

The whole idea of taking a holiday on inland waterways was invented in the Broads, and Nelson is rumoured to have learned to sail here. We have a unique culture around our sailing fraternity, with particular designs of boats that are only found in the Broads. The National Park is a magical combination of all those things, and we're here to protect and educate people about it.'

Nick's role is to provide engagement, learning opportunities and outreach to connect people to this special landscape. He says: 'This place is a phenomenal example of the interaction between people, landscape and nature, and there are so many stories that bring it together. You can delve back 2,000 years and look at the Broads through the eyes of a Roman and see the fort that was adjacent to an enormous estuary. Around 1,000 years ago, people were digging peat, we then drained the Broads for agriculture, and now we're facing issues with climate change. The Broads is an economic and post-industrial landscape.

We can take peat cores and pull out bits of intact wood from the ground that date back more than 2,000 years. Schoolchildren can hold those little bits of history and be the first people to do so for millennia. We can say that the last person who saw that tree was probably a Roman. The story we bring to people is the humanity, economy and architecture of this place – and we make it relevant so they understand the pressures we face.'

John adds: 'We have such a good opportunity to tell people about a very fragile place which reflects worldwide threats. The Broads is the place to tell the story about climate change because you can see it happening. You can see the coastlines eroding, you can see the flooding, and it's real. Then you have the fragility, the importance of biodiversity and the sheer variety of what's here. This all depends on a fine balance. Whether we will still have swallowtail butterflies in the future is doubtful because of the way the climate is changing, but we have to tell that story and encourage people to make a change.'

'We know the horrific statistics of the amount of nature deprivation that a lot of children, even local ones, are suffering,' Nick explains. 'We know some schools don't get out into the countryside or build in time in their curriculum for any form of outdoor education or nature engagement. It's understandable because they are under so many other pressures, but we know that when we take children out and show them how special these places are, it resonates and brings benefits in health and well-being. You have to be able to show off these special places to illustrate the best things about the environment, which hopefully will then be translated into them looking after their own nature close to where they live.'

Behavioural change on any scale is difficult, but if we are to fight climate change and save nature, it has to be embraced.

'I remember that one of our previous chairmen was a professor at the School of Environmental Sciences at the University of East Anglia,' John says. 'He said the role of the Broads Authority was to manage an ever-increasing rate of change. This is an environment that's been changing for the last 2,000 years and is going to see further substantial change over the next 100 years. We can either just sit around and wait for nature to do its thing, or we can do our best to work with nature and try and manage that rate of change. We're going to be getting 20 per cent less rainfall in the summer and 20 per cent more rainfall in the winter. That means we're going to get more floods in the winter and more droughts in the summer. It will become more extreme, and we have to be able to manage that, working with local communities and partners. That is why a connection to this landscape and National Park is vital.'

John's favourite thing to do in the Broads National Park: 'I try and have one day out a month with the team here, and those are always my best days. Whether it's helping visitors moor up, going out with Nick and a school group, or visiting a site with our ecologists and seeing them survey water voles, just being out is a real privilege. Being out with my colleagues and the chance to talk to them is all I need.'

Nick's: 'I love canoeing on a quiet stretch of the River Waveney, hearing the bird song of the reedbeds and seeing fish in the clear water below. If I'm lucky, I might catch a glimpse of an otter or spot a marsh harrier. It's such a peaceful and restorative thing to do.'

FACTS AND QUIRKS

Local legends

All areas have their **particular dialect** and terminology, don't they? *Visit the Broads* tells us that the natives call a mole hill an 'umpty-tump', a ladybird a 'bishey-barney-bee', a tadpole a 'polly-wiggle', a woodlouse a 'charlie-pig', and a bittern a 'butterbump'.

Lord Nelson is rumoured to have learned how to sail on the Broads. It's thought by some that this could have taken place at Barton Broad, the second largest broad in the National Park.

In Ludham, legend says that **a dragon**, which was tormenting the village, dug a burrow between the churchyard at St Catherine's and the high street. Villagers would rush to block the tunnel exits that the beast would make when it emerged from its lair.

Ghostly noises

At Hickling Broad, a **phantom drummer** has been seen and heard. *Literary Norfolk* says: 'In the winter before the battle of Waterloo, the boy came home on leave from the army and fell in love with a girl from the village. Unfortunately, the girl's father refused to accept a soldier as a son-in-law, and so the couple were forced to meet in secret at Swim Coots on Hickling Broad. Every February the drummer boy would skate across the broad to meet his love – but one evening the ice gave way and he was drowned.'

St Benet's Abbey is also said to be haunted, by a shrieking monk who was killed by Viking raiders.

A big, angry dog

Bungay's football and running clubs are known as the Black Dogs after **the Black Shuck** terrorised villagers. The vicious hound entered the town's St Mary's Church in August 1577 and then reappeared at Blythburgh Church, where it caused mayhem and was trapped. The **Black Shuck Festival** has been running annually since 2022.

◆ An eerie sunrise at Hickling Broad.

WALK 1

Irstead Staithe & Barton Broad Boardwalk

A simple and accessible wander to Barton Broad and Irstead.

This walk takes you to Barton Broad via an accessible boardwalk and then to the hamlet of Irstead. Some road walking is involved, but this is a peaceful place, and the route aims to keep you away from any potential traffic. There is an accessible car park just down the road from the starting point, and that will take you straight onto the boardwalk.

The boardwalk is a straightforward 610m (2,001ft) loop, with places to ponder and see the varieties of habitat. It has a viewing platform over Barton Broad, too.

⬇ *Irstead Staithe is a peaceful spot on this short walk.*

START/END: Barton Broad, NR12 8XP
DISTANCE: 4.16km (2.28 miles)
GRADE: Easy

Barton Broad, the second-largest broad in the National Park, used to have a rich diversity of plant life, but that declined in the second half of the 20th century due to an increase in algae. The Clear Water 2000 project began to reverse that trend by encouraging daphnia, a common water flea that eats algae, to help keep the water clear. The Broads Authority also introduced a dredging machine to remove silt, and the result is a now-thriving broad home to kingfishers, herons, otters and common terns. On the boardwalk, you will see carr woods – woodlands that thrive in wet conditions – and a great deal of grey willow, downy birch and honeysuckle.

Leaving the boardwalk and turning left, you eventually arrive at Irstead Staithe, a place traditionally used for unloading and loading goods. St Michael's Church, just opposite the River Ant, has one of the oldest rood screens in Norfolk.

➜ St Michael's Church at Irstead.

WALK 2

Upton Marshes
◌◌◌

Enjoy a flat circular walk along the water at Upton Broad and Marshes.

Walk around the Upton Marshes and River Bure to witness the Norfolk and Suffolk Broads in its most serene state. You're at sea level all the way, with peaceful marsh on your left throughout and, towards the end of the walk, the Upton Broad and Marshes Nature Reserve and wild woodland.

Keep Palmer's Drainage Mill on your left as you walk up Upton Dyke, until you arrive at Upton Drainage Mill. Thurne Mouth is ahead – stick to the left and then turn left at the next junction, where you can see St Benet's Abbey across the water.

This now takes you south, with South Walsham Marshes on your right, until woodland appears. This area, the Doles, feels wilder and is a contrast to the scene on your left. It's peaceful and winding, reeds blowing in the breeze before you return to the start.

Why not try these great walks...

THE ROCKLAND RAMBLE: An 8.9km (5.5 mile) walk from The New Inn in Rockland along the River Yare, visiting varied meadow and farmland habitats.

THE WHERRYMAN'S WAY: Starting outside the National Park, at Norwich Train Station, this 59km (37 mile) long-distance walk takes you across the Broads to Great Yarmouth. It follows the route of trading wherries.

HERRINGFLEET HILLS: A simple 2.8km (1.75 mile) walk from Somerleyton moorings to Herringfleet Marshes, Smock Mill and Hills.

Upton Broad and Marshes may be a nature reserve, but it is still as actively managed as it was when it was drained. It was once part of a large river estuary that extended to the sea at Great Yarmouth. The marshes were drained in the 17th century for grazing, with mills built to pump water into the river. Thankfully, Norfolk Wildlife Trust has been restoring the special habitat, reconstructing dykes and raising water levels to encourage wildlife.

START/END:
Upton Yacht Station,
NR13 6BL
DISTANCE: 8km
(5 miles)
GRADE: Easy

→ Upton Drainage Mill.

← Upton Marshes – chewing gum for the soul!

The Broads | 109

Key Places

The rider...
The Broads has a range of places to stay, from hotels and campsites to B&Bs, guesthouses and pubs. You can also stay on a boat and hire one longer term to stay at various moorings around the National Park. www.visitthebroads.co.uk/where-to-stay

Places to visit

Wroxham Known as the 'Capital of the Broads'. A key hub, with shops, cafés and The Kings Head pub, which overlooks the River Bure. Great for rail transport, including the heritage narrow gauge Bure Valley Railway, which follows a picturesque route to Aylsham. Many dayboats are for hire, and there are mooring spots in the centre and at Wroxham Broad. Boat trips available include on the solar-powered boat *Ra*, accessible to wheelchair users. Roys of Wroxham dominates the shopping experience, and is the self-proclaimed largest village store in the world. Wroxham Miniature Worlds is the largest indoor modelling attraction in the UK.

Stalham On the A149, a small town with The Museum of the Broads on Stalham Staithe. It tells the story of Broads life and offers a 50-minute trip on a wheelchair-accessible boat. It also has a Victorian steamboat. www.museumofthebroads.org.uk.

Bungay *Moribus antiquis pareamus* ('let us ever hold fast to the old virtues') is the town's motto, and it celebrates its heritage and traditions with passion. Bungay is a market town, mixing the old with the new, and in the centre is a 17th-century Butter Cross topped by a statue of Justice. It was built after the great fire of 1688, so trade could continue quickly. Wooden steps helped traders show off their butter, eggs and cheeses. The statue was added because criminals awaiting trial were imprisoned in a dungeon beneath the Cross, or in a cage above it. The town has a great heritage trail.

Beccles This 'Gateway to the Broads' is 9.6km (6 miles) to the east of Bungay. There's a heated lido, which is open all year, places to hire boats (the River Waveney connects the town to Bungay) and a vibrant market on a Friday. A Food and Drink Festival takes place each May.

The marina at Wroxham, Capital of the Broads.

↑ The two-tone tower of St Michael's.

→ Moorings at Beccles.

St Michael's Church is in the centre of town, and it has a separate tower. The south entrance is oddly two-toned because it is made from two types of stone: dolomite and limestone. It used to be decorated with colourful pigments, including ultramarine, which was stolen by two men who wanted to fund a trip to London. The porch also housed the town's fire engine at one point.

Loddon Small market town on the River Chet, just off the A146. The 15th-century Holy Trinity Church is at the centre, and there are several special shops. It also hosts a country market each week and has a community cinema.

Why not try...

Horning Beautiful small settlement near Hoveton Little Broad, Decoy Broad and the Woodbastwick Fens and Marshes. The Ferry Inn is down at the marina, while the *Southern Comfort* is a Mississippi-style steamer that runs from near the Swan Hotel. Horning means 'the folk who live on the high ground between the rivers'.

Acle Pretty village where the A47 and A1064 meet. Has the part-thatched, round-towered St Edmund Church, built in the 13th century.

Oulton Broad A large town next to Lowestoft. Busy place, popular for watersports, and has the UK's only working two-chamber sea lock.

← The Butter Cross in Bungay.

VISIT

Must Sees

The Borough Well ❶ (TM 337 898) is a great little hiding spot in Bungay. Now gated for safety, it is fed by a natural spring and was once the main water supply for the town. In 1975, the Town Trust, together with the Bungay Society, raised funds to have it restored, and they found shards of pottery from the 2nd or 3rd century AD. It is known as the Roman Well and can be visited by pre-booked parties.

It is thought that **St Benet's Abbey** ❷ (TG 383 157) was settled by a 'small group of religious hermits' in the 9th century, and was granted abbey status by King Cnut in the 1020s. It survived the Dissolution of the Monasteries, but not the destruction of its gatehouse, which had a windmill built inside it during the 18th century. Designed to crush oilseed, the mill was later used to drain the marshes and is the oldest tower mill in the Broads National Park. The Bishop of Norwich conducts an annual service in the remains of the abbey on the last Sunday of July. The site also has a listening bench that allows visitors to hear prayers and its history, and the Norfolk Archaeological Trust runs guided tours. Please note, the track to the site isn't great for small cars, and the best way to visit is by boat. www.norfarchtrust.org.uk/project/st-benets-abbey/

Not got a boat? St Benet's can be reached on foot from **How Hill** ❸ (TG 372 189). This is an eclectic Nature Reserve, with beautiful reed and sedge fen, marsh and carr woodland, which is accessible on a circular walk. Other activities include the *Electric Eel* boat trip, visiting **Toad Hole Cottage museum** ❹, and including windmill spotting. It's also a haven for wildlife, such as the marsh harrier and bittern. Toad Hole Cottage is open from April to October, while the *Electric Eel* takes you through the marshes. You can also visit the impressive Wherry *Hathor*, which is moored there during the main visitor season. Trading wherries transported goods years ago. *Hathor* was built as a pleasure wherry and sails at various times of the year too.

Burgh Castle ❺ (TG 474 045), also known as Gariannonum, surprises you with its size and completeness. It is one of the best-preserved Roman monuments in the country, with large parts of the remains still standing to their full height. Built in about AD 300, experts also believe it was the site of a Norman castle and perhaps an early Christian monastery.

The views from beside the castle to the Burgh flats and **Berney Marshes** (TG 464 048) are second to none.

Berney Marshes and **Breydon Water** (TG 495 074) can only be visited on foot, by train or by boat, and that makes the trip more than special. You'll find wet grassland, intertidal mud and saltmarsh – ideal for wading birds and wildfowl. www.rspb.org.uk/days-out/reserves/berney-marshes-and-breydon-water

Carlton Marshes ❶ (TM 508 919) is a beautiful Nature Reserve that is home to the fen raft spider, one of the UK's rarest and most threatened species. It has nine viewpoints or hides, four waymarked trails and a foot ferry to Waveney River Centre that runs in peak season. www.suffolkwildlifetrust.org/carlton

Hickling Broad and Marshes ❷ (TG 422 212) is another fine Nature Reserve – the best place to spot bitterns and cranes in the Broads National Park. It's a complex of open water, fen, reedbed, grazing marsh and woodland, and includes a raptor roost where, during November and February, you can see marsh harrier, hen harrier, merlin and owls. Hickling Broad is the National Park's largest. www.norfolkwildlifetrust.org.uk/HicklingBroad

Ranworth Broad ❸ (TG 353 153) is Norfolk Wildlife Trust's flagship Nature Reserve, and it's easy to see why. A 450m (1,476ft) nature trail winds its way through the reserve, emerging at the NWT Broads Wildlife Centre.

Salhouse Broad ❹ (TG 319 157) is an absolute gem, with ancient oaks lining the path to the broad and a joyful mindfulness trail thanks to the Sibling Support charity. It is a dark skies centre, has a campsite and you can grab a bite at the seasonal Hungry Otter café. Across Salhouse is **Hoveton Great Broad Nature Trail** (TG 317 161), only accessible by boat. You can hire a canoe from Salhouse to get there. www.hovetongreatbroad.org.uk

↑↓ Sailing on the Broads – a must-do!

Must Dos

Sail a boat

Probably the most obvious... There are 63 broads in the Broads National Park, 13 of which are fully navigable, with a further five that are partially navigable, depending on the season. Boats can be hired for the day or longer, and you don't need a licence or any special training. Operators give introductions and advice when you collect your vessel, and all have the required safety equipment on board. Most of the Broads has clear navigation points and plenty of places to moor, and the rule is to keep to the right.

Wroxham is a good place to start for dayboat hiring, with boatyards offering a range of craft. www.visitthebroads.co.uk/things-to-do/boating/boathire

Be a 'shipmate'

If manning a boat isn't your thing, then you can get on board a wherry and discover how goods were historically transported around the Broads. A wherry is a traditional type of sailing boat with high-peaked sails and forward-stepped

masts, and was used as early as the 17th century. Only a few now survive, but there are three organisations where you can learn more about them and even enjoy a trip: **Wherry Yacht Charter** (www.wherryyachtcharter.org), **Wherry Albion** (www.wherryalbion.com) and **Wherry Maud Trust** (www.wherrymaudtrust.org).

The immaculate **Wherry *Hathor*** can be seen at **How Hill** (NR29 5PG) (www.visitthebroads.co.uk/the-blog/discovering-the-wherry-hathor), where you can also take a trip on the *Electric Eel*. This eco-friendly boat can take up to six people on a tour that lasts 50 minutes. To book, email toadholetic@broads-authority.gov.uk. Other boat trips are available, such as the wheelchair-accessible *Ra* at Wroxham. www.broads-authority.gov.uk/boating/hiring-a-boat/boat-trips

For more heritage sailing experiences, **Hunter's Yard** (NR29 5QG) near Ludham is a charity dedicated to traditional craft, boatsheds and heritage craft skills. You can learn more about sailing in the Broads National Park and take a trip. www.huntersyard.co.uk

Next to the yard is **Ludham and Potter Heigham Marshes** (NR29 5PT), which have 'one of the best dyke systems in Broadland, with a great range of water plants and animals, including the rare Norfolk hawker dragonfly'. **Womack Water** (NR29 5QZ) is also a special place to visit.

The Big Dog Ferry (NR34 9PL) runs between Beccles Lido and The Locks Inn at **Geldeston** – a 4.8km (3 mile) trip along the River Waveney. www.bigdogferry.co.uk

The *Southern Comfort* is a double-deck paddle boat that runs from **Horning** (NR12 8AA). www.southern-comfort.co.uk

Self-powered travel

There are other ways of getting around! **Canoeing, kayaking and paddleboarding** are popular, and again, several providers are there to help. www.visitthebroads.co.uk/things-to-do/boating/canoekayakpadboard and www.paddlerscode.info

Please note, to use your own canoes, kayaks and stand-up paddleboards (SUPs) you must pay either an annual or short visit toll, depending on how long you plan on staying (www.broads-authority.gov.uk/boating/owning-a-boat/tolls/). The National Park also has an interactive map of where you can launch: www.broads-authority.gov.uk/boating/facilities/slipways-and-launching-points.

Prefer dry land?

You could go **angling** or enjoy the waterways from the comfort of the shore. www.visitthebroads.co.uk/things-to-do/wildlife/angling

Named after the once-important weaving industry, which flourished in the Middle Ages around North Walsham, the

⬇ Paddleboarding is another way to get around.

← Accessible boardwalk below Burgh Castle on the Angles Way.

Weavers' Way runs for 98km (61 miles) between Cromer and Great Yarmouth. www.norfolk.gov.uk/article/42898/Weavers-Way-Cromer-to-Great-Yarmouth

The **Angles Way** is an even more serious ask – a 150km (93 mile) trail following the county boundary of Norfolk and Suffolk from Great Yarmouth to Thetford. It follows the Waveney Valley, and travels through Beccles, Bungay and below Burgh Castle. www.norfolk.gov.uk/42891

There are circular walks linked to both these trails, and also to the Wherryman's Way.

Go windmill spotting

There are more than 60 drainage mills in the Broads National Park, and it's fun to tick them off. You can see two at How Hill: **Boardman's Mill** (TG 369 192) was built in 1897 to drain the adjacent marshes, while the nearby **Clayrack Mill** is a rare survivor of a late 19th-century 'hollow-post' drainage mill. It was originally on Ranworth Marshes. The **Turf Fen Mill** (NR29 5PH) is on Reedham Water.

You can see six mills on the **Halvergate Mills Trail**, a 12.1km (7.5 mile) circular walk that starts on Stones Road (NR13 3GX). watermillsandmarshes.org.uk/trails/halvergate-mills-walk

Climb a church tower

At Ranworth's **St Helen's Church** (NR13 6HT), you can climb its 29m (96ft) tower to see magnificent views. There are 89 uneven steps, two ladders past the church's bells and a heavy trap door to negotiate! www.ranworthchurch.com

↓ Drainage mill spotting.

CAR-FREE TRAVEL

→ The Norfolk and Suffolk Broads has plenty of bus services that connect the main villages and towns, as well as Norwich and Great Yarmouth:
  → First Buses travel from Norwich to Hoveton and Wroxham, and then on to Stalham. They also visit Loddon, Beccles and Lowestoft for connections to Oulton Broad. www.firstbus.co.uk
  → The book-in-advance Acle Area Flexibus connects to several places, including Filby, Fleggburgh, Reedham, Cantley, Freethorpe and Wroxham. For details, call 01493 752223.
  → The X1 and #7 run to Norwich and Great Yarmouth, while the #730 is the Reedham Circular to Yarmouth via Filby.
  → Sanders Coaches run services #6, #6A and X6 from Cromer to Great Yarmouth. www.sanderscoaches.com
  → The Broads Bus (#5B) runs through Wroxham, Horning and Ludham. www.konectbus.co.uk/services/KCTB/5B
→ The Bittern Rail Line runs from Norwich to Sheringham, passing through the northern Broads including Hoveton and Wroxham. www.bitternline.com
→ The Wherry Lines go east and south to Oulton Broad, Lingwood, Acle, Cantley and Reedham. www.wherrylines.com
→ The East Suffolk Line runs to Beccles and Oulton Broad. www.eastsuffolklines.co.uk and www.thetrainline.com
→ Of course, the most obvious way around the Broads National Park is by boat, with many providers available across the Park. St Benet's Abbey is far more accessible by boat or on foot than by public transport or car.

For the kids?

BeWILDerwood (NR12 8JW) is an incredible adventure park made from sustainable wood. Based on the Tom Blofeld books, it has slides, swings, zip wires and more. www.bewilderwood.co.uk

North of Wroxham, **Hoveton Hall Gardens** (NR12 8RJ) has lakeside and woodland walks (www.hovetonhallestate.co.uk), while **Somerleyton Hall Gardens** (NR32 5QQ) also has huge gardens to explore.

And finally...

Woodforde's (NR13 6SW) is an award-winning brewery founded in 1981. You can also dine at the **Fur & Feather** on site, which does amazing Sunday roasts but is really busy. Don't say you haven't been warned! www.woodfordes.com

For a real belly-buster of a meal, while retaining quality, visit the **Brick Kilns in Little Plumstead** (NR13 5JH). Booking is advised, as is not eating for days beforehand!

EXMOOR

DESIGNATED: **19 October 1954**
SIZE: **693 sq km (267 sq miles)**, HIGHEST PEAK: **Dunkery Beacon at 519m (1,703ft)**
ANNUAL VISITOR NUMBERS: **1.64 million (2023)**, POPULATION: **10,284**
OFFICIAL WEBSITE: **www.exmoor-nationalpark.gov.uk**

For one of our smallest National Parks, Exmoor packs a lot in.

In the north are nearly 60km (37 miles) of coastline, consisting of wide shingle beaches to tall, erratic and jagged cliffs shaped by erosion and the weather. The National Park has wild, windswept, open moorland – it's one of only three upland areas in southern Britain – a landscape that has been worked by people and is now revealing enlightening archaeology.

Like the richness of Dartmoor's register (see page 139), there are more than 10,000 records on Exmoor's Historic Environment Record, representing human activity stretching back some 8,000 years. Consequently, Exmoor feels old, earthy and medieval, and none more so than at Dunster near Minehead. This place exudes heritage, from the 11th-century castle and 16th-century Old Yarn Market to the medieval packhorse bridge over the River Avill. The village feels like something from a bygone era.

This is also a National Park that is lived, loved, cherished and preserved. Throughout Exmoor are ancient woodlands, some of the densest and

➤ The beautifully scenic Dunster Forest.

most spectacular in the whole of the country. It has the longest stretch of coastal woodland in England and Wales, featuring perilously rare *Aria vexans* trees, commonly known as the bloody whitebeam, while sessile oak woodlands nestle within valleys to create a world-renowned habitat. The tallest tree in England is here too; a giant Douglas fir, standing at 63m (207ft) tall, at Nutcombe Bottom.

Coupled with extensive moorlands, these woodlands and temperate rainforests are internationally designated for the habitats and biodiversity they support. Exmoor is home to almost 250 species of birds and more than 1,000 different flowering plants and grasses. The National Park is also one of our last bastions for the heath fritillary and high brown fritillary butterflies. Its rivers support otters while the coast, with its inlets, marshes and tidal bays, is home to Red-listed curlew and other waders.

Amazing things are happening to protect these precious landscapes. The Heddon Valley, for example, is undergoing three significant projects

↑ A thatched cottage in historic Dunster.

↓ Tarr Steps, the longest clapper bridge of its kind in Britain at 54m (177ft).

designed to restore its vital habitats. At Tattiscombe, the National Trust is rewetting more than 50ha (124 acres) of land. Rangers are using longhorn cattle

↑ Exmoor has nearly 60km (37 miles) of coastline.

→ The tallest tree in England is at Nutcombe Bottom.

and Mangalitsa pigs to break up the ground for new plants to grow. At West Challacombe Farm in Combe Martin, thousands of trees have been planted, while at Countisbury they are utilising the West Exmoor herd of longhorn cattle and Exmoor ponies to mob graze. Small community groups and charities are also creating new habitats for butterflies and insects. Exmoor is a place of innovation born out of a love for the landscape.

Like most National Parks, Exmoor's communities are welcoming too. There are plenty of quirky settlements; Lynmouth and Lynton are places you'd expect to find in the Alps, and outside the boundary is Minehead, a once-great trading port and now burgeoning town with independent shops and great places to eat. Further inland are smaller communities, historic settlements and people unequivocally passionate about what Exmoor stands for.

It may be small, but Exmoor is mighty and is everything you need from a National Park.

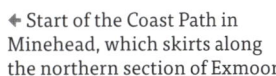

← Start of the Coast Path in Minehead, which skirts along the northern section of Exmoor.

Exmoor | 123

THE CHAMPION

Dr Lucy Shipley

○○○

Dr Lucy Shipley is the Historic Environment Record Officer at Exmoor National Park.

In England, the Levelling-up and Regeneration Act 2022 made keeping and maintaining a Historic Environment Record (HER) (www.exmoorher.co.uk) a statutory duty. With more than 200 Scheduled Monuments in Exmoor and 10,000 records of archaeological sites and historic buildings within its boundary, keeping up that record is a huge task.

> Lucy says: 'My role is to make sure we have a direct record of everything of historical interest within the Park and to provide that information with as much detail as we can. As a country, we have been really good at detailing historical sites but perhaps forgetting the human side of them. As soon as you start scratching the surface of almost anything in our HER, lots of human stories come out. I enjoy finding these stories and interpreting them to enhance the record. Effectively, we have a record of human activity that goes back to the Mesolithic through to the 20th century.

We also have one of the best records of conflict archaeology in the UK and an amazing oral history. A colleague spoke to someone who remembered seeing tanks drive up from Minehead Station. They were unloaded off the train and had to go up to North Hill. She said they took the railings off by the church because they were so big! On that site, there is a defence radar station too, so on one hand, you have a quite dry HER that says there was a tank training range there, and on the other, you have an amazing story.

At All Saints in Monksilver, there are some incredible tombstones but one of the records reads like something out of a true crime podcast. We know that a woman and her two daughters were stabbed while they were having their breakfast, as they were found by the bread boy. The record seems to show that the bakery boy was in the house with the assailant, hiding somewhere, because the bodies were fresh. Again, it's a fascinating bit of detail that adds so many questions but without that depth, it is a dry record in an intimidating repository of information. So, while my role is not only to make sure that those records are good and solid for all the commercial enquiries about land use changes and those who want to put up a fence for instance, it's also about pulling those stories out and saying, people are people, and they've always been people.'

Our National Parks are landscapes where balancing the multi-dimensional needs of people and nature is a delicate act. A connection to the past is vital in managing these places, to avoid damaging them and to plan for the future.

'I don't think it can be overstated how such a connection to the past is important,' Lucy adds. 'You can feel it whenever you talk to somebody, be it farmers or residents in the small towns. People are so knowledgeable about their area. Back in the summer, a nine-year-old boy found a new standing stone over on Ilkerton Ridge. His father had grown up there, and he was raising his son next door to the cottage where he had grown up. The boy had been exploring the moors and knew their local pony herd. He had named them individually after characters from the *Fellowship of the Ring*. He had that deep-seated root in the landscape, and in the younger generation that's quite rare. After finding the stone he was talking about being an archaeologist! Who knows, maybe he'll be doing my job one day.'

Lucy was brought up in Hertfordshire and says she ended up in the South West by accident. She went to the University of Southampton, met her husband who is from Cornwall, and now lives in the Blackdown Hills. She says being an archaeologist is akin to solving complex puzzles.

'After looking at all the evidence, you have to make interpretations of what is in front of you,' she adds. 'They can never be the exact reason why something is there, but an interpretation based on your best judgement. Those interpretations are important, though, as they can have an impact on how an area is managed going forward. The HER is vital in this. When you look at tree planting, for instance, is the idea of a climax woodland that has been gone since the Bronze Age a good thing? Something like that could potentially affect the archaeology. But if you also look at the HER, it is filled with examples of how this land was managed in the past. I'd like to think that with a better understanding of our historic features, we would be able to find ways forward to ensure that the right thing is done in the right places.'

Lucy is hoping the HER will continue to develop over the years and become more of a usable and interactive asset. She is planning to take it to an app and make it much more visual.

'I want to launch an Exmoor thousand words project, because a picture paints a thousand words and so many of our records don't have images. We're very lucky to have our own website, which has an interactive map, but when people are looking to engage with Exmoor's historic environment, it's quite hard with just a wall of text. That said, going out and getting 10,000 pictures is also going to be a bit of an undertaking. The plan is to recruit volunteers, who could take pictures of particular sites when they go out into the Park. In that way, we can bring this landscape to people who cannot physically come here, and enrich the experience of those who can.'

Lucy's favourite thing to do in Exmoor National Park: 'I would pick an area on the HER website's interactive map with sites and monuments I haven't visited, and go out and explore! I always let someone know where I'm going and what time I'll be back and bring a camera with me to take photos for the HER. You'll always see something different, and not just the archaeology – I have been lucky enough to see a common lizard and to hear the larks singing above a roaring east wind that made the sunshine feel cold. The expanse of the Park, the wildness – it's easy to forget that sitting in an office. But in five minutes on the moor, you can feel the enormity of what we are trying to protect, and the responsibility to get it right for the future.'

FACTS AND QUIRKS

Devils and beasts

Would you be surprised to hear that **Tarr Steps** were built by the Devil? He put the bridge across the River Barle and promised to kill anyone who crossed. A cat was sent over to test the theory and, to no one's surprise, was duly dispatched. Worried locals sent their parson to meet the Devil in the middle. The brave man of God stood firm and eventually forced the evil one to concede. But the Devil had one final clause, that if he chose to sunbathe there, it would be closed to people.

Historically, there have been several sightings of big cats across the country, particularly on moorland. Sometimes they are escaped animals while others just can't be explained. **The Beast of Exmoor** was first seen in the 1970s, and 13 years later a farmer called Eric Ley claimed to have lost more than 100 sheep, all to horrifying injuries. *The Daily Express* jumped on board and offered a reward for video footage, while the Royal Marines were employed to hunt it down. Of course, nothing was found, but the beast in various iterations is still claimed to be seen now and again.

In Minehead, it's said that marauding Vikings were sent back out to the sea by a brightly decorated 'horse' that they thought was charging towards them. This may have led to the custom of the **Minehead Hobby Horse** or 'Obby Oss', which tours the streets of the town each May bank holiday.

A monastery at Carhampton was founded by King Arthur after St Carantoc helped him defeat a **dragon**. In English Heritage's *Dragons and their Origins*, Carolyne Larrington writes:

'Carantoc was the son of the king of Cardigan and had left Wales to lead a life as a holy man. Crossing the Severn estuary, his portable marble altar had fallen overboard. King Arthur had been trying in vain to deal with the dragon, and he enlisted Carantoc's help after he found the altar miraculously floating on the river. Carantoc draped his priestly stole around the dragon's neck and led him away where he could do no harm. Arthur rewarded him by building him a church at Carhampton where the marble altar was installed'.

X marks the spot

There's a mound near Challacombe called **Broken Barrow** where a man hoped to find treasure. Starting to dig, he suddenly went deaf, dumb and blind, apparently due to the excruciating din of horses. He died three months later.

At **Wood Barrow**, another man tried to do the same but was driven away by severe thunderstorms. British Folklore (www.britishfolklore.com) also says that in a later version of the tale, 'the diggers are overcome with faintness but their leader, a "conjurer", can catch a glimpse of the treasure for a moment as the lightning flashes. When they recover their senses, all that is left is an empty bronze pan that is all corroded and green – but with a bright shiny spot in the middle to prove that there was indeed treasure there.'

Another tale cites **a raven** protecting buried treasure in Chaw Gulley. If someone descends to try and dig it up, it squawks and a phantom will cut rope.

WALK 1

Simonsbath to Wheal Eliza

◆◆◆

A gentle introduction to the varied habitats of Exmoor.

This easy-going, family-friendly walk is one of the National Park's Exmoor Explorer routes, which follows the Two Moors Way and the River Barle to the disused Wheal Eliza mines.

You pass through the highest beech woodland in the country before reaching Kings Wood, which was planted in 2024 with 6,000 trees. The habitat then changes to open moorland and the River Barle, which is a stronghold of trout, salmon and otter.

The route meanders around Flexbarrow, a natural mound within the valley, before reaching the mines. They were sunk in the mid-1800s to extract copper, and later iron, from shafts up to 91m (300ft) deep. There are remains of these works alongside the ruins of a former mine cottage.

Our walk returns to Simonsbath – with cafés and a Victorian water-powered sawmill – but if you continue along the path around 1.6km (1 mile), you come to Cow Castle, a splendid univallate hillfort, with rampart and ditch. Legend says fairies built it to protect themselves.

A superb summer's day meander.

START/END:
Ashcombe, TA24 7SH
DISTANCE: 3.8km (2.4 miles)
GRADE: Easy

↑ The walk follows the River Barle to Wheal Eliza.

The harbour at Porlock Weir.

WALK 2

Tarr Steps

○○○

Enjoy a historic footbridge and dense woodland with this walk along a peaceful river.

Tarr Steps is a 17-span clapper bridge constructed entirely from large stone slabs and boulders, and the longest of its kind in Britain, at 54m (177ft).

This walk crosses the historic feature and follows the Exe Valley Way to Withypool. It then joins the Two Moors Way to Great Bradley, where an impressive new 28m (92ft) long bridge over the River Barle has been constructed to protect the delicate habitat on the opposite side of the river, before returning to the start through a stunning woodland and National Nature Reserve.

The Tarr Steps were recorded in Tudor times but are likely to be much older. The bridge has been rebuilt several times because of flood damage and, after one particular event, stones of up to 2 tonnes were washed 50m (164ft) downstream. From some angles, the steps look a little unsafe, but they've been crossed for hundreds of years! On your first crossing, pause in the middle (it is 1.5m (5ft) wide in places), look up the River Barle and enjoy the peace.

START/END:
Tarr Steps, TA22 9PY
DISTANCE: 13km
(8.1 miles)
GRADE: Moderate

➨ Tarr Steps.

Why not try these great walks...

THE KING CHARLES III ENGLAND COAST PATH – EXMOOR EDITION: The 60km (36 mile) route from Minehead to Combe Martin has recently been improved to bring walkers safer and closer to the coast. It is the start of the iconic South West Coast Path.

HURLSTONE POINT: A challenging 24.5km (15.2 mile) circular from Selworthy that takes in Allerford, the view from Hurlstone Point, the Coast Path, Minehead and Alcombe before returning through Periton Hill along Macmillan Way West.

PORLOCK MARSH: A 5.8km (3.6 mile) circular from Porlock to the marsh, along an accessible boardwalk, before visiting the village of Bossington and heading back through farmland.

↑ Lynmouth is a delightful small seaside village.

Key Places

The rider...
Exmoor has various camping and caravan sites, hotels, self-catering and B&B options. On the boundary are several other settlements, such as Minehead, a busy market town with places to stay. Keep an eye out for CareMoor for Exmoor business champions, businesses who actively raise funds to help conserve and protect the National Park. www.exmoor-nationalpark.gov.uk/exmoor-for-everyone/plan-your-visit/Where-to-Stay

Places to visit

Lynton and Lynmouth Just off the A39 near Lynmouth, these pretty villages are ideal for exploring the Valley of Rocks and its dramatic cliff-lined coastline (this area is affectionately known as 'Little Switzerland'). They have restaurants, cafés, shops and the Lynton & Lynmouth Cliff Railway. The Exmoor National Park Centre at the Lynmouth Pavilion is the largest in the Park.

Dunster Medieval village with an ancient high street, Old Yam Market, 11th-century castle, Tithe Barn, dovecote and a working water mill. Has independent shops, cafés and pubs as well as the Gallox Bridge, a medieval packhorse bridge over the River Avill. It linked the town to the wool-producing pasture in the south, while its name relates to the execution gallows on Gallox Hill, which in times past were a public place of justice for the lords of Dunster Castle. Dunster is a hub for easy trails to Dunster Park, Grabbist Hill and Butter Cross. There's a National Park Visitor Centre in the town.

Porlock A quiet base on the A39 for exploring Selworthy Beacon, Hurlstone Point and Porlock Weir. The Ship Inn dates back to the 15th century, although the building itself is from 1290. St Dubricius Church stands on the site of an earlier one from c.1120, while the yew tree in the churchyard is believed to be more than 1,000 years old. The village also has a museum, while a forge is in nearby Allerford.

Dulverton On the southern edge of the National Park, near the River Barle's

→ The vast expanse of Exmoor National Park.

↓ The Gallox Bridge in Dunster.

wooded valley. The woods are great for seeing pied flycatchers and redstart, as well as butterflies, including the high brown fritillary. Has many cafés and shops, three pubs, a heritage centre, National Park headquarters and a National Park Centre.

Horner Woods Home to a large ancient oak woodland, a National Nature Reserve managed by the National Trust.

Why not try...

Combe Martin Features some of the most delightful coastlines in the country. Found on the western edge of the National Park, its cove is packed with boats and golden sand. The village, which was a hive of silver and lead mining between the 13th and 19th centuries, claims to have the longest main street of any village in the country.

Simonsbath A small village in the centre of the National Park, on the Two Moors Way. The large Simonsbath House was the original residence of John Knight (who pioneered reclamation of the high moorland at the centre of the National Park) and his family, who purchased the old Royal Forest of Exmoor and tried to convert the moor to farmland in the 1800s.

Minehead Just outside the Park's northern boundary, this busy town – a major port historically – is a good starting point for exploring the Coast Path. Has great views of the Bristol Channel and Wales, a packed high street with boutique shops and places to eat, and The Quay Inn, which was a winning establishment in Channel 4's *Four in a Bed*!

VISIT

Must Sees

Exmoor has some amazing woodland including the longest stretch of continuous coastal woodland – around 12.8km (8 miles) – in England and Wales, which has rare whitebeams. **Burridge Woods** (SS 912 285) is a beautiful oak-lined 22ha (54 acre) woodland on a steep hillside above Dulverton, while **Hawkcombe Woods** (SS 865 454) is a National Nature Reserve near Porlock. They provide an important habitat for heath fritillary butterflies and redwood ant colonies. www.woodlandtrust.org.uk/visiting-woods/woods/hawkcombe-woods/

Dunkery Beacon ❶ (SS 891 416) is the highest point on Exmoor at 519m (1,703ft), with fantastic views across the coast. Bronze Age remains such as cairns, barrows and Iron Age hillforts dot its slopes. The cairn ❷ at the summit commemorates its donation to the National Trust.

Porlock Weir (TA24 8PB) is an ancient seaside port and coastal village. It has a fine pebble beach overlooking Porlock Bay. **Porlock Marsh** (TA24 8NU) is nearby, with an accessible boardwalk connecting it to Porlock.

Great Hangman (SS 601 481), near Combe Martin, is the highest cliff on mainland Britain. The coastal hill is 318m (1,043ft) with a cliff face of 250m (800ft).

The tallest tree in England is at **Nutcombe Bottom** (SS 979 422), near Dunster. The 150-year-old Douglas fir ❸ stands at 63m (207ft), and can be seen on the Tall Trees Trail. Surrounding it are also Britain's tallest dawn redwood and England's tallest magnolia, the latter of which was planted in 1884. www.forestryengland.uk/nutcombe-bottom/tall-trees-trail-nutcombe-bottom

The Yarn Market ❹ in the centre of Dunster is an isolated and welcoming shelter from the village's busy thoroughfare. It was reportedly built in 1609 by George Luttrell, of Dunster Castle, for the sale of local cloth and kerseymere, but may have been there in the 16th century.

Nearby is the impressive **Conygar Tower** (SS 991 441), a folly commissioned by Henry Luttrell in 1775. It is 18m (59ft) tall and has three storeys, though seemingly never had floors or a roof. Its name comes from the medieval *coney* (rabbit) and *garth* (garden), indicating that rabbits could have been bred for food in the area.

Pinkworthy Pond (SS 723 422) is an artificial lake, formed when the River Barle was dammed. It is thought the pond was possibly constructed to provide irrigation water, but there are also several other theories. Whatever the origins, it's a lovely spot for safe wild swimming and exploring Chains Barrow.

The beach at **Dunster** ❺ (ST 003 447), just outside the National Park, is a little gem. It sits on the Steam Coast Trail, a community project aimed at connecting pathways around the region. The beach, shingle ridge and dunes were created by erosion of the cliffs near Minehead. They support a rich diversity of coastal plants as well as wigeon, shelduck, curlew, oystercatchers, little egret and turnstones.

Must Dos

Pub first...

The wonderfully old **Blue Ball Inn** (EX35 6NE) near Lynmouth dates back to the 13th century and offers great food and beer in picturesque surroundings. It's located in Countisbury, on the old coaching road from Porlock to Lynmouth. A plaque inside the pub says that 'Countisbury is thought to mean "camp on the headland" and comes from the impressive Iron Age fort on Wind Hill, about half a mile west. It's believed this is where Odda's Saxon army defeated Danish invaders led by Hubba in 898.'
www.blueballinn.com

Then walk...

There are more than 1,300km (807 miles) of paths and bridleways, and around 17,600ha (43,491 acres) of open access land to enjoy in the Park. One of the finest walks around is the **Valley of Rocks** (EX35 6JH) near Lynton and Lynmouth, with part of it accessible to wheelchairs. This phenomenal landscape of geology – a huge, dry valley wedged between steep valley slopes and towering cliffs – is right on the coast, with dramatic rock features that will keep little ones entertained as they look for the named features. It's thought the Valley could have been formed by the River Lyn, while other theories point towards it being a glacial feature. Archaeological evidence suggests that people were living and farming in the Valley around 3,500 years ago, but one thing is for sure: the wild goats perched on the sheer cliff edges look more than happy with their surroundings! www.exmoor-nationalpark.gov.uk/exmoor-for-everyone/things-to-do/the-valley-of-rocks

↑ Wild goats on the sheer cliffs.

↖→ The Valley of Rocks is simply stunning.

Near Dunster are the **Brendon Hills**. The highest is Lype Hill, at 423m (1,388ft), which can be climbed from Cutcombe on the Coleridge Way. This long-distance walk (80km/50 miles long and often split into six stages) travels from Coleridge Cottage at Nether Stowey (TA5 1NQ) to Lynmouth through the Quantock Hand Brendon Hills: a landscape that inspired the writer. www.visit-exmoor.co.uk/coleridge-way

Look up

Exmoor was Europe's very first **International Dark Sky Reserve**, designated in 2011. It hosts a Dark Sky Festival every autumn and you can also hire a telescope, at a very reasonable price, from the three National Park Centres at Dulverton, Dunster and Lynmouth. www.exmoor-nationalpark.gov.uk/darkskiesfestival

Look down

Dr Lucy Shipley noted 70 historic sites in her 'Exmoor Stories' blog that celebrated the 70th anniversary of Exmoor being designated.

There are plenty of historical features throughout the National Park, but one of our favourites is the deserted medieval settlement at **Badgworthy Water** (SS 793 444). It's believed to be the inspiration for the home of the Doone clan in the RD Blackmore novel of 1869, and one house on the site was inhabited until 1814. It has a fascinating history, with the HER suggesting: 'this may be the site of the Lacoma (Lank Combe) of Domesday Book, which mentions a quarter hide of arable for use as a hermitage attached to Brendon Church. In the 12th century, this area at Badgworthy passed into the hands of the Brethren of the Hospital of St John of Jerusalem. Then in the 13th century, tenancy passed to the family of Badgworthy when it became a considerable village, and the final mention historically is around 1430 when the village was fast falling into decay.' There were at least 12 buildings in this settlement.

See wild ponies

As well as the feral goats at the Valley of Rocks, there are plenty of roaming native **Exmoor ponies** in the Park. They're doing a cracking job in conservation grazing and, if you're lucky, you may see them. The Moorland Mousie Trust, which runs the **Exmoor Pony Centre** (TA22 9QE), was founded to 'ensure that no more foals would leave their mothers on the moor to go to the meat market'. Since 2000, it has taken in more than 500 ponies from moorland herds and trained 100-plus whose owners needed extra support to ensure they could survive. The Centre is open to the public throughout the week except Mondays and Tuesdays.

Your carriage awaits

The **Arlington Court and the National Trust Carriage Museum** (EX31 4LP) has an impressive collection of horse-drawn carriages. It's a curious place, featuring all sorts of collections from model ships

---

CAR-FREE TRAVEL

→ Getting on a bus is the ideal way to get around Exmoor (www.exmoor-national park.gov.uk/exmoor-for-everyone/plan-your-visit).

→ The Exmoor Explorer travels from Blue Anchor to Ilfracombe, calling at Dunster, Minehead, Allerford, Porlock, Culbone, County Gate, Countisbury, Lynmouth, Woody Bay Station, Blackmoor Gate and Combe Martin. Some of these stops operate in the summer only, so check before travelling:

- → #10 travels from Minehead to Selworthy, Porlock and Porlock Weir (all year, Mon–Sat)
- → #25 travels from Taunton Rail Station to Wiveliscombe, while the #26 connects to Wiveliscombe and Dulverton (all year, Mon–Sat)
- → #28 travels from Taunton Rail Station to Bishops Lydeard, Williton, Watchet, Washford, Dunster and Minehead (all year, 7 days a week)
- → #198 travels from Dulverton to Bridgetown, Wheddon Cross, Exford, Timberscombe, Dunster and Minehead (all year, Mon–Sat)
- → #301 travels from Barnstaple to Milltown, Ilfracombe, Watermouth, Berrynarbour and Combe Martin (all year, Mon–Sat)
- → #309/310 travels from Barnstaple to Blackmoor Gate, Parracombe, Woody Bay Station, Barbrook, Lynton and Lynmouth (all year, Mon–Sat)
- → #398 travels from Tiverton to Bolham, Cove, Bampton, Exebridge, Brushford and Dulverton (all year, Mon–Sat)
- → #467 travels from Dulverton to Bridgetown, Winsford, Exford, Wheddon Cross, Timberscombe and Minehead (term time, Mon–Fri)
- → #678 from Dulverton to Brushford, Exebridge, Bury, Upton, Brompton Regis, Timberscombe and Minehead (all year, Thu).

→ There are no mainline rail services in Exmoor.

- → The West Somerset Railway (www.west-somerset-railway.co.uk) is a heritage line on the east of the Park and travels from Bishops Lydeard to Minehead. There is also a heritage service from Woody Bay and Killington Lane (www.lynton-rail.co.uk).
- → The water-powered funicular, run by Lynton and Lynmouth Cliff Railway, connects Lynton and Lynmouth. Open from mid-February to November. www.cliffrailwaylynton.co.uk

Exmoor ponies near Tattiscombe.

to shells. The Carriage Museum in the stables features vehicles for every occasion! www.nationaltrust.org.uk/visit/devon/arlington-court-and-the-national-trust-carriage-museum

Be inspired

As we've said, RD Blackmore wrote *Lorna Doone*, a romance set in Exmoor. **Lorna Doone Valley** (EX35 6NU), near Lynton, is a breathtaking part of the Park that he made famous. It has a tea room and lots of waymarked paths that take in sites linked to the book. www.nationaltrust.org.uk/visit/devon/lorna-doone-valley

Go wild

Heddon Valley (EX31 4PY) is the site of a large landscape-scale conservation project that will restore and revitalise several important habitats. Part of it has seen tree planting and ponds created at a 50ha (124 acre) site in Tattiscombe. Longhorn cattle and Mangalitsa pigs have been brought in to break up the ground. The pigs have wiry hair that picks up seeds as they walk and root. You can follow the **River Heddon** as it heads through a densely wooded valley to the coast. You may even see otters and the rare high brown fritillary butterfly at this SSSI.

The **Hunters Inn** (EX31 4PY) is owned by the National Trust and has been an inn since 1823. www.nationaltrust.org.uk/visit/devon/heddon-valley

↓ The beautiful Exmoor coastline.

DARTMOOR

OKEHAMPTON
A30 EXETER
THE HIGHWAYMAN INN
CASTLE DROGO
A386
MORETONHAMPSTEAD
HIGH WILLHAYS
CANONTEIGN FELLS
LYDFORD GORGE
BENNETT'S CROSS
GRIMSPOUND
A382
POSTBRIDGE
BELLEVER TOR
HAYTOR ROCKS
TAVISTOCK
WIDECOMBE IN THE MOOR
PRINCETOWN
HIGHER UPPACOTT
NEWTON ABBOT
SOUTH HESSARY TOR
ASHBURTON
HOLNE
BUCKFASTLEIGH
DARTINGTON
A38
PLYMOUTH
IVYBRIDGE

CULLEVER STEPS

DARTMOOR

DESIGNATED: 30 October 1951
SIZE: 953 sq km (368 sq miles), HIGHEST PEAK: High Willhays at 621m (2,037ft)
ANNUAL VISITOR NUMBERS: 2.8 million (2024)
POPULATION: 34,500, OFFICIAL WEBSITE: www.dartmoor.gov.uk

In terms of evocative phrases, *Forged by nature, shaped by time and human spirit* is the perfect mantra for this National Park.

The Dartmoor Historic Environment Record contains more than 24,000 records about archaeological sites, historic buildings and landscapes, artefacts and other heritage features. Included in this are 2,750 listed buildings, 1,082 Scheduled Ancient Monuments and 25 Special Conservation Areas recognised for their architectural and historic interest, as well as the remains of more than 5,000 Bronze Age roundhouses and hut circles, five stone rows and 18 stone circles – all within the National Park's 953 sq km (368 sq mile) boundary.

The archaeology in Dartmoor is remarkable. The open moorland has been shaped by human interaction and its movement for millennia, and those lives are documented in amazingly well-preserved remains. This is, in part, thanks to the unique geology and environment of the National Park. Granite, the very foundation of those roundhouses and circles, is durable and withstands the

⬇ The clapper bridge at Postbridge.

← Dartmoor is covered in archaeology. ↓ Grimspound dates from the Late Bronze Age.

harsh, windswept moors, meaning we now have a rich archaeology that allows us to see into the past with great clarity.

The Merrivale Bronze Age ceremonial complex has two double stone rows alongside a stone circle burial cairn. It was constructed between the Late Neolithic and Early Bronze Age. Grimspound is a settlement dating to the Middle Bronze Age, with a boundary wall of around 150m (492ft) in diameter and the remains of 24 stone roundhouses. On Holne Moor are stone banks called reaves, which denote ancient field boundaries. Then, there are the more 'modern' historical remains in terms of what has gone before. Hound Tor is a small, long-abandoned hamlet of four longhouses, while the impressive Higher Uppacott longhouse demonstrates multi-generational living in one place.

Present-day land managers have to work within these historical confines, balancing them with modern-day techniques that must protect this special heritage and nature, while maximising food production. It's not an easy task.

Yet, while Dartmoor is a landscape oozing history, it is a place of adventure and exploration. This National Park has a vast landscape suitable for all manner of activities, from tor bagging and letterboxing to learning important outdoor and life skills. It's no surprise that it's a long-standing place for military training, where endurance and navigation skills can be honed on the moorland. A multitude of Duke of Edinburgh awardees have also gained experience here on the way to Gold Award status, with the Ten Tors Challenge attempted by 2,400 teenagers each year.

Tramping the moors is life-affirming, as is canoeing down the River Dart, seeing the stars and topping out at High Willhays. In winter, the moor becomes a wilderness, with big skies illuminated by the sun amid a carpet of fresh snow.

Dartmoor is a wonderful place, swarming with butterflies and birds, gnarled old-growth woodlands, mysterious moorlands, and welcoming villages packed with people who love its vastness and history. I'm hooked.

Wild ponies on Dartmoor.

THE CHAMPION

Richard Gray
○○○

Richard Gray farms at Priddons Farm, which sits below Holne Common.

Finding a way to work and live sustainably in a National Park, particularly as a farmer, is a challenge. Agriculture is changing, and making ends meet often involves making a few sacrifices. None more so than in the uplands and on the moors.

'I'm a first-generation farmer but probably more of a tenth-generation one,' Richard says. 'My mother's family have farmed in Holne for hundreds of years, whereas my father came down from Scotland. I got the farming bug from him, but he had to stop through ill health. He then sold the animals, and the farm was rented out, so I had to start again. We farm on the land he originally had, and we have South Devon cattle and sheep. It's about 26–28ha (65–70 acres), with a small farmhouse and a couple of barns, and I help manage other people's land with my animals in a low-impact way.

We also have two shepherd's huts, which we let out, mostly to help with the finances, and I also work as a part-time postman. I took that on in 2007, as the farm was struggling. I thought I'd only do it for a couple of years, but it's been really enjoyable. It lets me see the other world, and I get six weeks paid holiday, so that's very different from farming. You could say I have a bit of a mixed life, but it's really interesting!'

Richard says planning is key to balancing his life and making the farm work.

He says: 'It can be frustrating, and you have to plan really well. If it's planned, it works, and the moment it's not, then the wheels fall off ... and nothing wants to be a problem at the right time. I enjoy having a mission to produce a brilliant landscape for the community and good, affordable food for people.'

Dartmoor has been shaped by human interaction. The remnants of previous generations scatter this Park, and the moorland and commons in particular have a significant farming footprint.

'What makes Dartmoor special is this landscape,' Richard continues. 'It's the history; it's all intertangled. If I look at the natural landscape, it's the windswept tops. Where I have some of my cows, you could be in the middle of Montana, on the plains, as the grass swishes for miles in the wind, and you cannot see a soul. It's a big landscape and I cannot imagine anywhere in southern England like it. Farming here is special, and my cows and sheep are vitally important to me.

But what really ticks the box is the archaeology. Half of my home common, which is Holne Common, is covered by archaeology that runs right out the back of my gate. I'm looking at probably 4,000 years of farming. I'll go into the hut circles, stand in the doorways and think of the people who lived, gave birth and died there. It gives me a little bit of a buzz. That's what drives me: the history, the open air, the big landscape and other people coming in and enjoying it.'

Farming common land means Richard's workplace is shared by many people and, therefore, many interests. He says land management in the National Park has become polarised in recent times, but if people realise they need to come together to protect it, then everyone's interests can be met.

'The debate has been polarised between extreme environmentalism and extreme agriculturalism. I have sat with people who want to completely cover Dartmoor with trees and get rid of virtually every animal, and others who want to re-seed the whole of Dartmoor with Italian ryegrass so we can feed the world. I guess I'm in the middle, fighting for upland farmers. You could have 40 per cent of farmers managing meadows and 60 per cent producing good grass. Sadly, it's turned into a battle, and once you get one extreme side, you almost have to weaponise the other.

The critical thing is to look someone in the eye and say this is a shared landscape, a shared world. You have to understand that you have to give as well as take. I think you need to look at the other person's view and come up with a common solution. If each side does that, then those jigsaw pieces can be turned and moved until they fit together. If they don't quite fit together, then you rely on the government to be the referee, and that knocks the corners off the piece that doesn't quite fit.'

The future of farms like Richard's depends on getting a decent price for what they produce and making sure the Environmental Land Management schemes work for land managers.

'There's a debate about carbon and biodiversity net gain and selling it to companies, but I do think that is missing the point. I think if we're doing lots of good work for the vast area that is a National Park, then the very least we should expect is for the government to pay us more. I get frustrated when I hear people saying there isn't enough money because when you work out what National Parks and farmers could deliver if they were paid properly, then it makes sense to fund them. We could do more, so I do get frustrated when people say how valuable we are. Some surveys say that this work cannot be done without public support – but on the flip side, we're told there's no money.

If the government makes up its mind and does value us, then there is a bright future for farming and this landscape, and I could recommend it as a career for my children. If you need to work three jobs to stay farming where you are, could I recommend it to my daughter? At the end of the day, we have to work in partnership to ensure these places have a good future.'

> **Richard's favourite thing to do in Dartmoor National Park:** 'I don't like to sit on my farm, I like to get around Dartmoor and see what's happening. I would go to the highest point on Dartmoor, look in a different direction and see the work someone else has done. I'd take a deep breath, enjoy their hard work, walk back home and go to the pub for a nice drink.'

FACTS AND QUIRKS

The inspiration

Sir Arthur Conan Doyle wrote *The Hound of the Baskervilles* after staying in the Duchy Hotel in Princetown. He is said to have been inspired by the story of Squire Richard Cabell, who died in 1677, but such was his reputation that a pack of hounds took his soul to Hell. Worried about a return, locals entombed his coffin beneath a stone and enclosed it behind iron bars. The tomb is in Buckfastleigh.

John Galsworthy wrote 'The Apple Tree' based on the tale of Kitty Jay, who is buried at a crossroads near Widecombe-in-the-Moor. Kitty was a pregnant farm worker who killed herself when she was scorned by her lover. Suicides were buried at crossroads to confuse the spirits.

Spine-chilling stories

You'd better keep your wits about you on the B3212. Legend says that between Postbridge and Two Bridges, **a pair of hairy hands** may appear on your steering wheel – or handlebars – and try to force you off the road! These hands are said to have offed a medical officer at Dartmoor Prison, while, in 1924, a woman who was camping nearby saw a hairy hand creeping up her caravan window!

Scorhill Stone Circle was said to be home to **a giant ogre** who would devour sheep should they cross into the circle – something they refuse to do to this day. Wise things.

Longaford Tor is said to have **ghost foxes**. A shepherd went missing on the moor, and soon after, human remains were found outside a fox's den. Having got a taste for it, their cries at the Tor can still be heard.

In the heart of Dartmoor lies **Childe's Tomb**. He was the Lord of the Manor of Plymstock, but sadly died in a blizzard. He even killed his horse and climbed into the remains to keep warm. He wrote his last will on a stone in blood, and it said whoever found him would inherit his fortune. Tavistock Abbey monks recovered his body.

At Buckland Abbey is **Drake's Drum**, a snare that accompanied Sir Francis Drake when he circumnavigated the world. Upon his death, he asked for it to be taken to the Abbey under the proviso that if England was under attack, someone should hit the drum, and he would return. Buckland Abbey is also said to be haunted, with undiscovered tunnels connecting it to the local village.

⬥ Scorhill Stone Circle.

WALK 1

Bellever Tor

◆◆◆

Enjoy 360 views with this woodland, moorland and tor circular.

Bellever is one of the most accessible tors in the National Park. This walk from Postbridge takes you to its base via a Miles Without Stiles route, through dense woodland, and gives you the chance to break off the main path to discover Bronze Age burial and settlement sites.

Safely cross the road and follow the track on the right into the woodland, then turn towards the Cycle and Tramper Trail. This is easy walking through a working woodland, full of goldcrests, crossbills and cuckoos depending on the season. The track skirts around the base of Lakehead Hill, and it's well worth venturing onto it to discover the remarkably preserved Bronze Age remains. Kraps Ring is a settlement, while all over the atmospheric moor are cairn circles, stone rows and cists. Excavations have uncovered flint knives, shards of pottery and even a bear skin! There are more than 30 hut circles within the forest.

Returning to the walk, you arrive at Five Ways Cross, and the path on the left will return you to the visitor centre. To the right is the route across

> **START/END:** National Park Visitor Centre, Postbridge, PL20 6TH
> **DISTANCE:** 4.5km (2.8 miles), up to 6.25km (3.9 miles) if climbing Bellever Tor
> **GRADE:** Easy to Moderate

↑ The top of Bellever Tor.

Dartmoor | 145

the moorland and climb to Bellever Tor, although it isn't accessible for wheelchair users. The views from the 443m (1,453ft) tor are well worth the frisky scramble up the rock formation at the top.

The route returns to Five Ways Cross and the National Park Visitor Centre, where you can enjoy viewing some of the finds from Whitehorse Hill and an exhibition on Bronze Age life.

Within Postbridge is one of the best-preserved clapper bridges in the National Park – it appeared on Britain's first-known road atlas in 1675 – and a village store. Towards Two Bridges is Powder Mills Pottery, housed in a former gunpowder factory.

➔ Easy and accessible track through the woodland.

WALK 2

Haytor Quarry and Rocks
○○○

A gentle meander through Haytor's industrial heritage and iconic formations.

Enjoy some of the best views in the National Park on this simple wander to Haytor Quarry and Haytor Rocks. Leave the car park, cross the road, and follow the track to the quarry where granite was extracted and also used in Nelson's Column! At the top of the track is the start of the Templer Way, a route that follows the original 1820 tramway, which carried granite from the quarries to Teignmouth docks.

Turn left and follow the track for 0.5km (0.3 miles) before turning left on a rough path that leads to the impressive Haytor Rocks. These are iconic formations with fantastic 360-degree views across the National Park. From the base of the Rocks, head left on the Dartmoor Way and return to Haytor Quarry.

START/END: Haytor Vale, TQ13 9XT
DISTANCE: 1.4km (0.9 miles), up to 3.8km (2.4 miles) if visiting Haytor Rocks
GRADE: Easy to Moderate

➔ Haytor Quarry, accessible on the walk from Haytor Vale.

Why not try these great walks...

DARTMOOR WAY: Revitalised in 2020, this waymarked 173km (108 mile) route starts in Ivybridge. It can be broken into ten sections, with a further two making up the High Moor Link.

PRINCETOWN TO NUN'S CROSS: A linear 8km (5 mile) moorland route from Princetown to Nun's Cross and back via South Hessary Tor.

WISTMAN'S WOOD AND CROCK OF GOLD: An epic 23km (14.2 mile) circular from Bellever to the tranquil woodland and High Moor Link on the Dartmoor Way. Enjoy the cairn and cist, known as the 'Crock of Gold', on Royal Hill. This is a special place; so stick to the paths and admire the impressive landscape from afar. This will ensure the mosses and lichens flourish.

✦ Haytor Rocks are impressive granite outcrops.

↑ Buckfast Abbey.

Key Places

The rider...
Dartmoor has a range of accommodation for a variety of budgets. B&Bs, pubs, guesthouses, cottages and hotels are available, while it has three youth hostels. There are also a few bunkhouses and several official caravan and camping sites. www.dartmoor.gov.uk/enjoy-dartmoor

Places to visit

Princetown On the B3212, a Victorian village that houses the temporarily closed HMP Dartmoor. It has an interesting museum, which is open throughout the week. Has two bustling pubs as well as the superb Fox Tor Café. Princetown was the brainchild of Thomas Tyrwhitt, Lord Warden of the Stannaries and Private Secretary to the Prince of Wales. He established Tor Royal Farm and, by the end of the 18th century, the settlement that would become Princetown. A brewery is also in the town.

Ashburton An ancient town filled with shops, antique curiosities and cafés, just off the A38 in the south-east of the National Park. Was a stannary, a place where tin was bought and sold. There's an annual food and drink festival in September, while the Little Big Town

→ There's fantastic moorland just a short walk away from the centre of Princetown.

Festival in the same month brings together music and art. The town also hosts a carnival in July. The Ashburton Arts Centre and 15th-century St Lawrence Chapel are worth visiting.

Buckfast and Buckfastleigh The home of the still active 11th-century Buckfast Abbey. You can buy some of the famous Buckfast Tonic Wine, too. Buckfastleigh is the base for a trip along the River Dart via the South Devon Steam Railway.

Okehampton A busy hub just outside the National Park's northern boundary. Has the Museum of Dartmoor Life, a varied high street and a castle. The Old Town Park Local Nature Reserve is next to the River Okement and was once part of the castle's deer park. As well as several trails, such as the Dartmoor Way and the start of the Tarka Trail, the Castle Ham Trail is suitable for wheelchairs and takes you away from the busy town.

Moretonhampstead Between Bovey Tracey and Chagford, this town was mentioned in the Domesday Book as being owned by William the Conqueror. It was granted market status in 1207 but is now very much a crafting community. St Andrew's Church has an art gallery, while Moreton has an open-air community swimming pool and is home to Green Hill Arts, one of Dartmoor's leading galleries.

Why not try...

Chagford Near Moretonhampstead and a good base for exploring the eastern part of the National Park. Has the River Teign on its doorstep. The last castle to be built in England, Castle Drogo, now in the care of the National Trust, is also a short drive away.

Bovey Tracey Self-proclaimed 'Gateway to the Moor' on the edge of the National Park near Haytor. It has a renowned contemporary craft centre (MAKE South West), a museum dedicated to marbles (House of Marbles), a beautiful church with dark connections (Parish Church of St Peter, Paul & Thomas (PPT)), and a thriving food and drink scene with lots of cafés and pubs.

Holne Small and quaint village on the Two Moors Way with a community-owned shop and tea room.

↓ The castle at Okehampton.

VISIT

Must Sees

Grimspound ❶ (SX 700 808) is the finest prehistoric settlement on Dartmoor. It dates from the Late Bronze Age and is surrounded by a boundary wall around 150m (492ft) in diameter, averaging 3m (9.8ft) thick and up to 1.5m (4.9ft) high. Within the settlement are the remains of 24 stone roundhouses in the shadow of Hookney Tor and Hameldown. What makes the site special are those roundhouses. Sitting inside the snug circles brings home what life would have been like some 4,500-plus years ago.

You can link a visit to Grimspound with **Bennetts Cross** ❷ (SX 680 816), a curious boundary stone or marker near the B3212.

Dartmoor has several beautiful woodlands. **Wistman's Wood** ❸ (SX 612 773) is a National Nature Reserve with haunting twisted oaks that are covered in lichens and mosses. A corpse road runs to the site, known as the Way of the Dead. **Lady's Wood** (SX 688 589), managed by the Devon Wildlife Trust, is at the southern end of the National Park. The 3ha (7.4 acre) woodland is a peaceful retreat, decorated by a carpet of bluebells in the spring and home to dormice.

Lydford Gorge (SX 508 845) and the historic **Lydford Village** are in the north-west of the National Park. The gorge, the deepest in the South West, contains the stunning 30m (98ft) **White Lady Waterfall** ❹, which cascades into the River Lyd through ancient woodland and temperate rainforest. Devil's Cauldron is a large pothole in the gorge with a nerve-shattering viewing platform over the river. The site also has two bookshops and tea rooms. www.nationaltrust.org.uk/visit/devon/lydford-gorge

Badger's Holt (SX 673 735) is where the east and west tributaries of the River Dart meet at Dartmeet. It is possible to walk up the 416m (1,365ft) Yar Tor from here, affording magnificent views.

Dartmoor is home to some stunning reservoirs. **Burrator** (PL20 6PE), near Yelverton, is surrounded by open moorland, tors and heritage. It is packed with wildlife, walking trails and angling opportunities, and has a Discovery Centre, which is ideal for families. www.swlakestrust.org.uk/burrator

Meldon Reservoir (SX 561 917) near Okehampton is equally impressive. It has great views of the Okement Valley, common land, the Longstone and Homerton Hills, and the chance to walk up to Yes Tor at 619m (2,032ft) and High Willhays, Dartmoor's highest point at 621m (2,037ft) above sea level. You can also fish for brown trout.

St Michael de Rupe (SX 470 804) on Brent Tor, 6.4km (4 miles) north of Tavistock, is said to be England's highest working church, and it has the most breathtaking views. The original church was founded in 1130 by Robert Giffard, but it seems that this was an important site long before then. Excavations found remains of bodies laid north to south, suggesting it was an important burial site. There was also an Iron Age settlement at the foot of Brent Tor. The existing building was constructed in the 13th and 14th centuries. The church hosts regular services, although you will have to climb to a height of 333m (1,093ft) to get there!

Must Dos

Go for a dip

If you like being outside, in nature, and enjoy an adventure, then you won't be bored in Dartmoor. Responsible wild swimming is very popular, with bathing gems all over the National Park. **Drewe's Pool** (near SX 722 896) on the River Teign, **Sharrah Pool** (SX 697 716) and **Cullever Steps Pool** (SX 605 922) near Belstone are tranquil spots, but there are many others, particularly along the River Dart. Being sensible, not swimming in a flood and knowing your limits is essential.

Camp outside

Wild camping is currently allowed in certain parts of the National Park with the proviso that you carry what you need in your backpack, don't stay longer than a couple of nights, tread lightly and **leave no trace**. Check www.dartmoor.gov.uk/about-us/about-us-maps/camping-map for the latest situation.

⬇ Tor bagging is popular! South Hessary Tor is close to Princetown and fairly simple to walk to.

Bag a tor

Depending on who you talk to, there are between **100 and 928 tors** (and significant rocks) on Dartmoor. A tor is where the granite, on which the National Park is geologically based, substantially pokes through the surface. Tors of Dartmoor (www.torsofdartmoor.co.uk/definitive.php) lists them all, while plotting routes around the more popular tors is great fun. Bouldering at these outcrops is also very popular; the British Mountaineering Council's (BMC) RAD database is a good place to start. https://services.thebmc.co.uk/modules/rad/

Go letterboxing!

Yes, you heard it right! Letterboxing (an older version of geocaching) began on Dartmoor when James Perrott of Chagford set up a small cairn at Cranmere Pool in 1853. He encouraged people to leave a visitor's card in a glass jar. Later, hikers would leave a letter or postcard inside a box on the trail, with the next person visiting collecting the cards and posting them. The activity continues today – a good old-fashioned **treasure hunt** (www.letterboxingondartmoor.co.uk). Geocaching (www.geocaching.com/play) is good fun for kids to use their screens in a productive way.

↑ The medieval longhouse at Higher Uppacott.

Go big and, eventually, go home

Some lengthy trails intersect the National Park. The **Two Moors Way** links Dartmoor with Exmoor on a 164km (102 mile) long-distance walk between Ivybridge and Lynmouth. www.twomoorsway.org

The **Dartmoor Way**, a waymarked 173km (108 mile) route, circumnavigates the National Park. www.dartmoorway.co.uk

The **Templer Way** runs between Haytor and Teign Estuary on the south coast. At 29km (18 miles) long, it follows the tramway that once transported granite from Haytor Quarry to Teignmouth. www.exploredevon.info/activities/walk/long-walks/templer-way/

The **West Devon Way** is a 60km (37 mile) route that runs from Okehampton to Plymouth. www.exploredevon.info/activities/walk/long-walks/drakes-trail-2/

On your bike ...

As well as the long-distance routes, there are several cycleways in the National Park. The **Granite Way** goes from Okehampton to Lydford (18km/11 miles), the **Plym Valley** from Plymouth to Princetown (16km/10 miles), and the **Wray Valley** (11km/7 miles) from Bovey Tracey to Moretonhampstead.

... or a boat

The **River Dart** offers some of the best white water canoeing around, but only for experienced paddlers. You can canoe on the River Dart between 1 October and 31 March each year, and below Dartmeet during the winter. Enter the water at Dartmeet, Newbridge, Holne Weir or at the Dartbridge café. www.dartmoor.gov.uk/enjoy-dartmoor/outdoor-activities/canoeing

Visit a medieval farmhouse ...

Higher Uppacott, located around 1km (0.6 miles) from Poundsgate, is a fascinating Grade I medieval building that still has 'the original shippon' (cattle shelter) inside the longhouse.

People lived on one side of the building, with their cattle on the other – and what is impressive is how generations of life are detailed within the fabric of the structure. It moves from medieval to modern times through a series of noticeable and atmospheric changes. Thanks to committed and knowledgeable volunteers, the National Park runs tours of the building throughout the summer. They are evocative and worth booking on to. www.dartmoor.gov.uk/enjoy-dartmoor/places/higher-uppacott

⬆ As well as canoeing, you can get on a boat and tour the River Dart.

... some tombs ...

The remains of a chambered tomb can be found at **Corringdon Ball** (SX 669 613) near Aish, while **Spinster's Rock** (SX 700 907) is a portal dolmen, dating between 4000 BC and 3000 BC.

... and old settlements

Lydford could have been established as a settlement as early as the 5th and 6th centuries. It has two castles, but originally had a burgh: a fortified settlement built by Alfred the Great. You can see the earthwork defences in the village.

⬅ Spinster's Rock is the remains of an ancient Neolithic burial chamber, also known as a portal dolmen.

Speaking of castles

Castle Drogo (EX6 6PB) is a 20th-century castle overlooking the Teign Gorge. Built by Sir Edwin Lutyens, it is a somewhat opulent building, in total contrast to the ancient woodland it sits above. It hosts themed events and has a wonderful garden trail. www.nationaltrust.org.uk/visit/devon/castle-drogo

Warhorse Valley Country Farm Park (EX19 8SN) is about 19km (12 miles) outside of the National Park, but is well worth a visit. It's packed with stuff for families to do, as well as a museum that tells the story of the invaluable part horses played in the First World War, inspiration for Michael Morpurgo's *War Horse* (1982). www.warhorsevalley.co.uk/the-museum

> ### CAR-FREE TRAVEL
>
> ➜ The Dartmoor Line is a great way to access Dartmoor with services between Exeter and Okehampton. **www.dartmoorline.com**
> ➜ The South Devon Railway is a heritage railway that runs from Buckfastleigh and Totnes Riverside. **www.southdevonrailway.co.uk**
> ➜ The Haytor Hoppa (#271) is a seasonal bus service running every Saturday during the summer months. Operated by Country Bus, the circular departs from Newton Abbot railway station, through to Bovey Tracey, Widecombe-in-the-Moor and Manaton.
> ➜ The #118 links Tavistock via Mary Tavy and Lydford to Okehampton Station, while the Country Bus Service #171 & #172 runs from Newton Abbot to Tavistock Station.
> ➜ **www.dartmoor.gov.uk/enjoy-dartmoor/planning-your-visit/travel-information**

↑ The lake at Canonteign Falls.

Canonteign Falls (EX6 7RH) is another family-friendly country park, with a Victorian Fern Garden and the 70m (230ft) high Lady Exmouth Falls, which were created to keep silver and tin miners in a job in the 1880s. The workers redirected a leet from the sawmill to a rocky outcrop. Amazing! www.canonteignfalls.co.uk

Take in a country show

Dartmoor hosts several shows throughout the year. The **Meldon Wildlife Festival** (August) is wildlife themed, while the **Okehampton** (August), **Chagford** (August) and **Widecombe** (September) shows focus on agriculture. **Lustleigh's** local craft and history show is held over the August bank holiday, and the 12th-century **Tavistock Goose Fair** (October) has traditional stalls and, unsurprisingly, lots of geese.

And finally

The quirky **Highwayman Inn** (EX20 4HN) is a fair old place, with curiosities, an odd entrance and striking decor. We'll leave it for you to discover! www.thehighwaymaninn.net

NEW FOREST

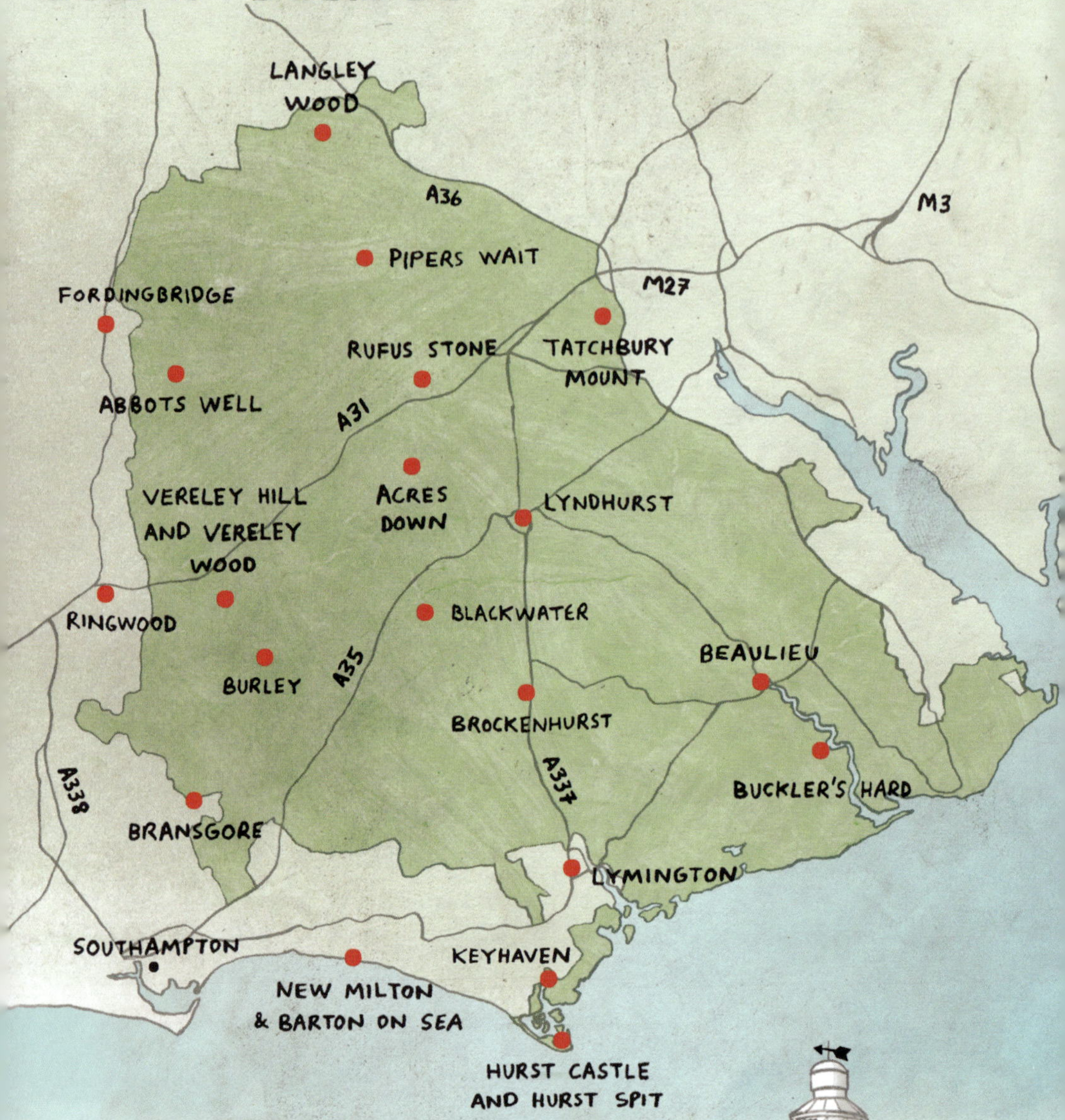

- LANGLEY WOOD
- A36
- PIPERS WAIT
- M3
- M27
- FORDINGBRIDGE
- RUFUS STONE
- TATCHBURY MOUNT
- ABBOTS WELL
- A31
- VERELEY HILL AND VERELEY WOOD
- ACRES DOWN
- LYNDHURST
- RINGWOOD
- BLACKWATER
- BEAULIEU
- A35
- BURLEY
- BROCKENHURST
- BUCKLER'S HARD
- A338
- A337
- BRANSGORE
- LYMINGTON
- SOUTHAMPTON
- KEYHAVEN
- NEW MILTON & BARTON ON SEA
- HURST CASTLE AND HURST SPIT

HURST CASTLE

NEW FOREST

DESIGNATED: 1 March 2005
SIZE: 570 sq km (220 sq miles), **HIGHEST PEAK:** Pipers Wait at 129m (459ft)
ANNUAL VISITOR NUMBERS: 16 million (2023), **POPULATION:** 34,000
OFFICIAL WEBSITE: www.newforestnpa.gov.uk

The New Forest may be the second-youngest of our National Parks, but it has a history stretching back hundreds of years.

Around 1079, William the Conqueror created the Forest as a royal hunting ground for the pursuit of wild deer and boar, and seven hunting lodges would eventually be built to facilitate the pastime. It was once thought that he destroyed 20 villages and hamlets to create the ground, but this claim has been debunked by historians and, more importantly, by a lack of evidence. Yet, it's not beyond the realms of possibility that some of the land was out of bounds to the local population. It's thought the area ran into Dorset, up to Salisbury and even into the South Downs, and it had defined boundaries. It wasn't a forest in the literal sense, of course, but rather a large area containing woodland and open ground.

It would eventually be returned to the people when Henry III confirmed the rights of the commoner in the 1217 Charter of the Forest. A Verderers' Court was set up to enforce the laws and rights, and in doing so, those commoners would eventually create the New Forest landscape we see today.

The New Forest is, and will always be, a working National Park: the very definition of a living and breathing landscape. It has approximately 300 sq km (116 sq miles) of woodland – both broadleaved and planted conifer – and as such, a large amount is still owned by the Crown.

➜ A living landscape with free-roaming deer and ponies.

⬆ The New Forest has a mosaic of habitats.
⬇ The Park also has some amazing coastline.

Commercial forestry and national public spaces, particularly in prospective National Parks, can leave a slightly uneasy taste, but such was the sum of its parts, the positives outweighing the negative connotations, that the New Forest was granted its designation in 2005.

Although the woods are its most obvious attraction, there is much to discover. You can see semi-wild ponies, cattle and deer as they move across the landscape. Head to the coast, and you can enjoy 42km (26 miles) of fresh sea breeze. At Keyhaven, there are views across to the Isle of Wight and huge amounts of birdlife. Inwards, in the heathlands, glades and open spaces, there are rare plants, insects and fungi, as well as goshawks and other raptors.

There's no denying that being so close to major population centres means it is seldom quiet. Over the years, the number of visitors heading to the New Forest has more than doubled. Balancing the needs of the local population and tourism is, like in many other of our national spaces, a real challenge.

Commoning is at the heart of this Park because, without it, the New Forest simply wouldn't look like it does. Its pull: the unique habitat would change if ponies, cattle and other animals were lost. Sadly, this is in real jeopardy, as many farmers and commoners are struggling to make ends meet as we undergo real change in the agricultural sector. A balance will have to be struck, much sooner rather than later, to keep the New Forest as good as it is – the ultimate breathing and learning space, an ark for our wildlife.

At the New Forest Heritage Centre, in Lyndhurst, a video plays on loop. One interviewee says: 'It is a real privilege to be a commoner in the forest because our animals are so intrinsically linked to the landscape, and we know that their grazing contributes massively to the biodiversity of the forest. We're very proud of our commoning culture and heritage, and it feels very important to pass on our skills and knowledge from one generation to another, to ensure that commoning continues into the future and helps to create this fantastic landscape that we live in today.'

People and landscape here are interlinked to create an amazing experience. Explore and enjoy.

↑ Old parts of the forest are home to mosses and lichen.

↓ The Park has around 300 sq km (116 sq miles) of woodland.

THE CHAMPION

Andrew Parry-Norton
○○○

Andrew Parry-Norton is a commoner and Chair of the New Forest Commoners Defence Association.

The New Forest was designated in 2005 for its unique beauty and wildlife, alongside its long-standing cultural heritage. It is a worked National Park, with ponies and cattle free to roam common land, creating a unique landscape that attracts millions of people each year.

← Sarah and Andrew Parry-Norton.

'I'm a commoner and a farmer,' Andrew says. 'I live and work on a family farm. It was my father's, then my grandfather's and my son William will be the fifth generation of commoners here. That history is important, and I found out recently that commoners as a whole in the New Forest have been around longer than the Māori in New Zealand. That's an incredible heritage; families here can trace their histories back hundreds of years and, as a result, we're very proud of our own culture. We even have our own dialect for different parts of the Forest.

The history of commoning in the New Forest stretches back to William the Conqueror, but it wasn't until Henry III that we obtained our officially written down rights. We have the right to pasture and the right to turbary – to dig turf – but we don't do that anymore. We have the right to collect firewood, the right to pannage, which means putting pigs out in the autumn to collect acorns, and finally, the right to marl. This is a mixture of silt and clay, with chalk, which would be spread to neutralise the naturally acidic fields in the area. Commoning is a form of poor man's farming, and I would think most of the holdings in the Forest are quite small compared to others. We use the Forest as an extension to the farm.'

That extra land, and the right to graze it, makes farming in the New Forest more viable. It also allows Andrew and his peers the space and time to make silage and hay.

'The common allows us to turn our animals out in the spring, meaning the grass we have back at home can grow and be available for winter fodder. Without that extra space, we couldn't make this system work. The animals graze all summer out in the Forest, and they live a fantastic, free life. It's the highest welfare you could possibly imagine, as they are free to roam. They browse herbs and grasses, and that is very much reflected in the quality of the produce.

The Forest has been landscaped by our stock. They've been grazing these woodlands and heathlands for 1,000 years, and that is also reflected in the ecology of the landscape. We have plants like the small fleabane that grows here because the cattle poach the ground, and the plant needs that disturbance to germinate. We also have the sundew, the UK's only carnivorous plant. As well as its importance for our farm, and its viability, this grazing plays such an important role in the Forest.'

Sadly, commoning as a practice could be under threat. The public purse is always tight, and changes to land management funding, particularly post-subsidy, could make farming systems like this economically unviable. That would have a massive effect on the culture of the New Forest, but also what attracts people to it in the first place.

'Without this system, the National Park would probably have more high grasses, gorse and scrub,' Andrew explains. 'I know some people will say that eventually, the ecology would adapt, but it has taken 1,000 years of commoning to develop an ecology that is unique to the New Forest. We have species of plant and insect life that aren't found anywhere else in the country. They only thrive here because of commoning and the activities that have taken place over such a long time. Lowland heathland is rarer than the Amazon rainforest, so we have to preserve it.

When people stand here and say, isn't nature wonderful, they need to understand that the scene they are looking at has been made by humans over a long time, and it's developed to be like that because of that activity. We have a £500 million tourist economy that effectively wants the unique landscape of the Forest to stay as it is. Commoners play a vital part in that and need to be supported to do it, but that won't happen if people don't understand the role we play.

This Park provides health, well-being and a tourism economy that supports a lot of people, businesses and communities. We have to share this place, but it has to generate an income for commoners, one way or another. We need to be financially secure to continue what we do and to stop the drain of young people from the sector. I've got a responsibility to hand this farm on to my son, but I've got to hand it over in good condition.

Sadly, at the moment, I think full-time commoners will become a thing of the past. We will have to look at other means of income to try and supplement what we do. However, this will have a dramatic change on this landscape. Around 80 per cent of those animals in the Forest are owned by 20 per cent of the commoners. Any drop in full-time commoning would result in a significant drop in the number of animals that are grazing the Forest. This will have knock-on effects on the landscape and everything this Park is special for. Hopefully, people can see that and support farmers and farming.'

Find out more about the commoners and this ancient tradition at www.realnewforest.org.

Andrew's favourite thing to do in the New Forest: 'It's nice to be able to tack up some of our ponies and just go for a wander. It doesn't matter what the day is; if you do get a couple of hours to be able to put some tack on one of the ponies, jump up and just wander off quietly into the woods; it's superb. It's nice to be able to wind down and not think about things too much.'

You can help care for the New Forest by following the New Forest Code. Like the Countryside Code, it emphasises looking after the landscape, respecting free-roaming animals and wildlife, and keeping people safe. www.newforestnpa.gov.uk/nfcode

FACTS AND QUIRKS

Forests love fungi!

Woodlands are the perfect places for **spotting fungi** as well as lichens, beetles and bats. There have been 2,700 different types of fungi identified within the New Forest National Park, and it has one exclusive that can be found only on pony poo!

In Great Britain, the rare nail fungus (*Poronia punctata*) is found only in the New Forest, linking it with other locations across Europe. It grows on high-fibre, low-nutrition horse poop, and there's plenty of that to go around – there are more than 3,000 ponies in the Park, providing this vital resource!

Look, but don't touch the fungi, and leave it for wildlife and other people to enjoy.

Trees ... lots of them

It's impossible to estimate exactly how many trees there are in the New Forest National Park, but **more than 1,000 ancient trees** have been recorded within the boundary. The Park claims this is the highest concentration of ancient trees in Western Europe. The oaks planted in the New Forest to replace those taken for the Napoleonic wars are now mature enough to be felled ... if they are needed!

Witches, dragons and haunted pubs

Sybil Leek was a **'white witch'** who lived in Burley. She was born in 1923, and in the 1950s, when the Witchcraft Act was repealed, she openly admitted that she practised. She would walk around the village wearing a long black cloak with her pet jackdaw, Mr Hotfoot Jackson, perched on her shoulder. The village was understandably suspicious of Sybil, while others thought it was a wind-up, and eventually, she moved to the USA.

According to an article on the BBC's *Inside Out*, she led an interesting life. 'One of the most incredible claims about her is that she was recruited by the British government during the Second World War,' it reads. 'According to the Second World War author Michael Salazar, her role was to provide phoney horoscopes for the Germans who believed in Astrology. She apparently wrote a chart which convinced the Nazi Rudolf Hess to fly to England, where he was captured'.

At Burley Beacon, just outside the village, Sir Maurice de Berkeley is said to have dispatched **the Bisterne Dragon**, who was upsetting the locals. Tales differ on what landmark it fell at or duly created, but one suggests that its corpse turned into Bolton's Bench in Lyndhurst.

Fleur De Lys in Pilley is said to be haunted by **the Grey Lady** and several other shapeshifting spirits, while locals who visit the 13th-century Angel & Blue Pig in Lymington have seen **a shadowy coach driver, a naval officer and a phantom blonde**!

WALK 1

Tall trees and mighty oaks
○○○

A wander into the heart of Blackwater.

Do you want to see massive trees and an epic oak? This walk charts a circular route through Blackwater, along the Tall Trees Trail, before scouting a route to the Knightwood Oak. It can be started anywhere on Rhinefield Ornamental Drive, but the Blackwater Car Park is a handy spot for basic facilities and a chance to grab a brew. Once replenished, go under the arch across the road and follow the Tall Trees Trail to see the largest trees in the New Forest. Seriously, your neck will hurt from looking skywards!

A few hundred metres in, an obvious track on the left will take you to the colossal giant redwoods. They are staggeringly tall and weigh in at around 105 tonnes. Rejoining the path, the trail continues along quiet woodland to Brock Hill Car Park. The return trail heads right here, and is the extent of the accessible trail on this route. If carrying onwards, go through the car park and turn left on to a forest track. This feels wide open, but you'll need to head right and towards the road before long.

Now, this is the friskiest part of the route, as the road can be busy at peak times, so crossing safely is key. You're heading to the track opposite. Once over, the noise dissipates as you enter the younger forest before heading right to the Knightwood Car Park.

The contrast to the epic redwoods earlier couldn't be more stark. This is

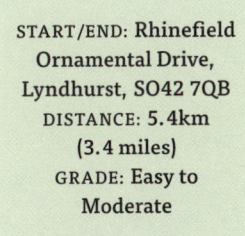

START/END: **Rhinefield Ornamental Drive, Lyndhurst, SO42 7QB**
DISTANCE: **5.4km (3.4 miles)**
GRADE: **Easy to Moderate**

Incredibly tall trees on the trail.

broadleaved woodland and at the forefront is the huge Knightwood Oak, which has stood here for more than 500 years. It's a beast, and has been a tourist destination since Victorian times. The tree was originally pollarded, which not only makes harvesting easier because it doesn't kill the tree but also protects it from browsing. Walk around the tree for a bit before heading back to the car park and turning left on the road. Again, cross the A35 safely and take the first right back into the woodlands, crossing a small but damp ditch, to the Brock Hill Car Park. This time, cross over Rhinefield Ornamental Drive and follow the route back to the start through even more tall trees.

This is a walk best enjoyed early in the morning, perhaps when it is a little frosty, so the woodland feels fresh. Both car parks fill up quickly, especially at the weekend, so exploring the depths of the forest is a welcome relief.

➜ Rhinefield's tall trees will tower over you.

WALK 2

Keyhaven
◇◇◇

Birdwatching along The Solent on the New Forest's coastline.

This is a pleasant wander with views of The Solent and Isle of Wight, alongside the chance to see the birdlife of Keyhaven Marshes.

↓ A haven for wildlife.

START/END:
Keyhaven, SO41 0TP
DISTANCE: **5.2km (3.2 miles)**
GRADE: **Easy**

Start from opposite The Gun Inn, the self-titled best pub in Keyhaven since 1783 (it is a cracker, to be fair), and then follow the road up to the first gate on your right, after another small area of quayside parking. The circular starts here and hugs the coastline, following The Solent Way before cutting left into the heart of Hampshire and Isle of Wight Wildlife Trust's Lymington and Keyhaven Marshes Nature Reserve.

At any time of year, it's possible to see great

164 | The Complete Guide to the UK National Parks

Why not try these great walks...

THE SOLENT WAY: A 97km (60 mile) long-distance walk from Milford on Sea to Emsworth Harbour. The walk takes in the south of the National Park, and visits places like Beaulieu, Hythe and Buckler's Hard on its way to the south-east of Southampton.

FRANKENBURY HILL FORT: A delightful hidden gem of a wander (5.8km/ 3.6 miles) from Godshill to an Iron Age hillfort, with views of the Avon Valley.

BURLEY VILLAGE: Discover this mysterious village on a 6.8km (4.2 mile) circular route around its outskirts. See the ancient hillfort on Castle Hill and the open forest before finishing back in the village and having a pint at the Queen's Head.

Download the National Park's New Forest Walks app for 40 self-guided routes with points of interest included.

birdlife, but winter is when it is best. You'd be hard-pressed not to see wigeon, redshanks and curlews here, as well as pintails, black-tailed godwits, Dartford warblers and reed buntings.

You then head back along a track to the start of your walk – a cracking wildlife-filled wander, and all relatively accessible.

↓ Views from Keyhaven, one of the quieter places in the Park.

Key Places

The rider...
The New Forest has several camping and caravan sites, budget to high-end hotels, self-catering and B&B options. It also has a youth hostel at Burley, where you can book a private room and also camp.
www.thenewforest.co.uk/accommodation/

Places to visit

Lyndhurst The capital of the New Forest and in the centre of the National Park on the A35 and A337. The busy village includes The New Forest Heritage Centre, Waterloo Arms with its thatched roof, and the grave of Mrs Reginald Hargreaves, Alice Liddell, who is thought to be Alice in Lewis Carroll's *Alice in Wonderland*. You can visit it at St Michael & All Angels Church. Bolton's Bench is a fine walk, just minutes away from The Mailmans pub. It has yews, ponies and extensive views into Rushpole Wood.

⬆ Ponies openly grazing near Beaulieu.

Brockenhurst Bustling village south of Lyndhurst and a popular base for cycling into the west of the National Park. Ponies and donkeys roam free, stopping at the ford, or 'Watersplash' as it's affectionately known, at the bottom of the village, while the main strip has a great diversity of shops, cafés, pubs and restaurants. Just outside the village is Black Knowl, an area of low-lying marsh with a walk that connects to more areas of

⬇ Black Knowl at Brockenhurst – just a few minutes away from the village.

↳ Swans on the lake at Beaulieu.

woodland – very different from the heavy conifer elsewhere in the Park.

Burley A curious place with several 'bewitching' shops that celebrate the famous white witch Sybil Leek (see page 162). There are also fudge and gift shops, as well as a cider farm. You can even pick up a horse-drawn carriage ride during the weekends and school holidays (from Easter until October) at Burley Coach Park.

Ringwood Busy town on the A31 with its Market Charter dating back to 1226. It hosts a regular market on Wednesdays as well as a festival in July and carnival in September. Some of Ringwood is slightly outside the Park – and it is worth exploring Poulner Lakes, and the London Tavern, which are nearby.

Fordingbridge Just outside the National Park's boundary in the north on the A338. Known as the northern gateway to the New Forest, with the pretty River Avon running through it. The Fordingbridge Tourist Information Centre operates during the summer and is a vital link to the quieter part of the Park.

Why not try...

Beaulieu Charming and somewhat eclectic village on the Beaulieu River. Dates back to the Cistercian Abbey, which was founded in 1204 on land given by King John, who had a hunting lodge at Beaulieu. The village is now owned by the Montagu family. It is home to the National Motor Museum as well as other attractions, including Britain's oldest monorail.

Bransgore On the south-western edge of the Park. A picturesque small village with three pubs and a vibrant community scene.

Lymington Coastal town that was an ancient seaport. Its status as an important trade hub is celebrated throughout the old town and at the St Barbe Museum and Art Gallery. Boats still sail out of Lymington Harbour, and you can catch a 35-minute ferry to the Isle of Wight.

← Burley was the home of Sybil Leek, and it thrives on that bewitching theme.

New Forest | 167

Must Sees

A visit to **Buckler's Hard** ❶ (SO42 7XB) is a day out in itself. It's a fascinating place to discover where important ships were made in the 18th century alongside its Shipwright's Cottage, St Mary's Chapel, pub and two rows of Georgian cottages descending to the Beaulieu River ❷. Fifty ships for the Royal Navy and many unnamed merchant vessels were built at Buckler's Hard between 1745 and 1814. This is celebrated in the museum (entrance fee applies), where there is also a lock of Nelson's hair! The Beaulieu River forms part of the North Solent National Nature Reserve and is an important feeding ground for birds. www.bucklershard.co.uk

Hurst Castle and **Hurst Spit** ❸ (SO41 0TP) are great places to see seabirds in the Park. The castle was built by Henry VIII and was one of the most advanced artillery fortresses in England. Charles I was imprisoned here in the 17th century. You can visit along the spit on the Solent Way or via a small ferry from Keyhaven. www.english-heritage.org.uk/visit/places/hurst-castle

In 1791, the Reverend William Gilpin wrote: 'The form of the New Forest horse is seldom beautiful, yet as the ornament of a Forest scene, he is very picturesque.' You'd be hard-pressed not to see wild ponies, donkeys and cattle throughout the National Park. They're part of the living landscape, and even though they seem tame enough, they're semi-wild animals and shouldn't be approached, petted or fed. **Bolton's Bench** ❹ (SU 308 079) is a good place to see them – at a distance.

At **Vereley Hill** ❺ and **Vereley Wood** (SU 196 049), deer intermingle with horses, and there have been sightings of a white stag. The view from Smugglers' Road through to Foulford is stunning.

The **Rufus Stone** (SU 271 124) is said to mark the spot where a significant oak stood ... although that's open to interpretation! An arrow shot towards a stag by Sir Walter Tyrrell ricocheted off this tree and struck King William II ('Rufus'), instantly killing him. The slain king was carried to Winchester and buried in the cathedral.

The **Eagle Oak** ❻ (SU 2556 0613) is an absolutely incredible sight in a predominantly conifer plantation. It's called the Eagle Oak as the last sea eagle in the New Forest was shot from its branches in 1810. That said, white-tailed eagles (sometimes known as the 'sea eagle') have recently been reintroduced in the area.

Abbots Well (SU 178 129) is a strange little oddity, looking like a tired, old manhole cover rather than something special. However, it hides a well whose waters were considered sacred, pure and to have healing properties.

A visit to **Hockey's Farm Shop** (SP6 2PW) (www.hockeysfarm.co.uk) is a must-do. Food is sourced from the farm and locally, there's a great café and the kids can meet the animals, too. It was designated as a Sustainability Champion by the National Park Authority and is a member of the New Forest Marque local produce scheme.

The New Forest isn't just trees! **Tatchbury Mount** (SU 330 145) has the remains of an Iron Age hillfort. It's on private land, but on a right of way.

↑ Anderwood is slightly off the beaten track and so a lot quieter.

Must Dos

The obvious start...

It's estimated that there are more than 300 sq km (116 sq miles) of woodland – both broadleaved and plantation – in the New Forest. More than 1,000 ancient trees have also been recorded. Therefore, you have to **explore** the Forest! There is dense and varied woodland all over the Park, intermixed with moor and marsh, which provides differing habitats for lots of wildlife. Please stick to the tracks to help preserve rare wildlife, particularly during ground-nesting bird season (February–August).

Bolderwood (SU 243 086) is a haven for deer and has a viewing platform to make seeing them a little bit easier. It also has an extensive area of ancient and ornamental woodland, which is part of the Ancient Canopy dedicated to the late Queen Elizabeth II in celebration of the Platinum Jubilee in 2022. This is one of the oldest parts of the New Forest, with records dating back to 1325.

Nearby is **Blackwater Arboretum** (SU 265 048), which has a sensory sculpture trail, trees from all over the world and the Tall Trees Trail.

Anderwood (SU 249 058) is quieter than other places nearby but still equally as fun. This is a good place for a walk to the other woodlands in the area without the hassle of battling for parking. Both spruce and broadleaf woodlands are here, making this a superb habitat for woodland birds.

In the north of the Park is **Langley Wood** (SU 231 207), a 217ha (536 acre) National Nature Reserve of international importance due to its variety of wildlife. It is predominantly oak, alder and lime.

At **Acres Down** (SU 267 097), you can see goshawk in early spring and maybe the rare honey buzzard in summer, while at **Whitefield Moor** (SU 249 058) you'll find big views, open forest and heathland.

The **Wilverley Inclosure** (BH25 5TZ) is a lot younger in terms of woodland, but it has a great little trail. In contrast, the **Old Sloden Inclosure** (SU 333 069) has Church Place, the site of a former royal hunting lodge.

Many of these woodlands and enclosures can be visited with experts as part of the annual **New Forest Walking Festival**. The fortnight of events includes talks on fitness and well-being, wildlife, culture and archaeology. Sign up for the National Park Authority's email newsletter on its website to hear about events throughout the year. www.newforestnpa.gov.uk/todo/whats-on

Fancy something wilder?
The **New Forest Wildlife Park** (SO40 4UH) has more than 250 animals, including wolves and bison. www.newforestwildlifepark.co.uk

Something more in keeping with the wildlife you can expect to find in the Park is the **New Forest Reptile Centre** (SO43 7GR). It's a cracking little place with free entry, but donations are welcome. It opens seasonally, and you can see reptiles, amphibians and other species. www.forestryengland.uk/new-forest-reptile-centre

On your bikes and ride
The New Forest has more than 160km (100 miles) of waymarked cycle routes, and you can hire bikes, too. www.forestryengland.uk/new-forest/cycling-the-new-forest

Although it's outside the Park, you'll find more challenging routes as well as single-track cycling at **Moors Valley Country Park and Forest** (BH24 2ET) (www.moors-valley.co.uk/health/cycling/). If you fancy something more competitive, then the **Big Bike Bash at Avon Tyrrell** (BH23 8ED) will certainly test you (www.bigbikebash.org.uk).

If you need support, the Park's inclusive cycling partner **PEDALL** can help the trails become more accessible. www.pedall.org.uk

↓ Peaceful trail at Blackwater.

Go for a dip

New Milton and **Barton on Sea** (BH25 7EG) are ideal spots for a swim, and you can explore the fossil beds, while at **Hythe** (SO45 6AT) you can ride along the world's oldest continuously operating pier train (Hythe Pier is 640m (2,099ft) long)! www.hytheferry.co.uk

Make your marque

Keep an eye out for the New Forest Marque, which is awarded to 'produce which has been grown, reared, caught, brewed, produced or processed within the New Forest'. There is also a New Forest Marque-inspired scheme of arts and crafts. www.newforestmarque.co.uk

Hit the pub

The Three Tuns (BH23 8JH) in Bransgore is an award-winning 17th-century pub with a fantastic menu, while the friendly **London Tavern** (BH24 1TY) in Ringwood has been on Linford Road since the 19th century. The 13th-century **Angel & Blue Pig** (SO41 9AP) in Lymington is haunted, but still delivers great food! Burley's **New Forest Cider Brewery** (BH24 4ED) has a shop and stable gallery.

> ### CAR-FREE TRAVEL
>
> ➜ Public transport information for many of the popular walks in the New Forest can be found at www.newforestnpa.gov.uk/things-to-do/walking/new-forest-walks/.
> ➜ Three open-top New Forest Tour routes run throughout the summer. These are great ways of seeing most of the National Park, and you can take your bike. www.newforesttour.info
> ➜ Bluestar runs connecting services from Southampton into the National Park, with the #6, #8 and #9 collectively stopping at the key hubs of Hythe, Lyndhurst, Brockenhurst and Lymington. www.bluestarbus.co.uk/services
> ➜ For services from Bournemouth and Salisbury, see www.morebus.co.uk.
> ➜ At www.myjourneyhampshire.com you can download a full-size version of the New Forest Travel Map.
> ➜ Rail services from South Western Railway and Cross Country run into Brockenhurst, Ashurst, Beaulieu Road, Sway, New Milton, Lymington Town and Lymington Pier. www.traveline.info

Learn about the Forest

The **New Forest Heritage Centre** (SO43 7NY) is a great place to learn more about the New Forest National Park and how it is managed. Two floors of exhibits include a museum, library, extensive archive, gallery and café with shop. It also hosts regular events and workshops.

One of the best ways to see the Forest is via the **New Forest Tour** open-top bus, which runs throughout the summer. There are three circular routes, with audio commentary, for you to enjoy. The **Red Route** runs from Lyndhurst to Burley, Ringwood, Fordingbridge, Sandy Balls and the New Forest Wildlife Park, the **Green Route** starts at Lyndhurst and visits Brockenhurst, Lymington, Beaulieu, Exbury Gardens and the Hythe Ferry, while the **Blue Route** runs from Lymington to Brockenhurst, Burley, New Milton, Barton on Sea and Milford on Sea. You can take your bikes on each service. www.newforesttour.info

↓ Beach huts at Milford on Sea.

SOUTH DOWNS

DESIGNATED: 31 March 2010
SIZE: 1,624 sq km (627 sq miles), **HIGHEST PEAK:** Black Down at 280m (919ft)
ANNUAL VISITOR NUMBERS: 18 million (2024), **POPULATION:** 113,339
OFFICIAL WEBSITE: www.southdowns.gov.uk

One of the main reasons for the National Park movement was the need to give people from urban areas dedicated access to the countryside. After a long week in factories, a visit to a National Park was a chance to breathe, recuperate and enjoy green space. While those early drivers are now somewhat in the rearview mirror, creating accessible places and a connection to nature in a time of climate crisis is still just as important.

Our youngest National Park, the South Downs, was created in 2010. It is our most densely populated park, close to Brighton and easily accessible by train from London. As a result, it welcomes more than 18 million visitors a year, and it's easy to see why. It has miles of coastline, chalk streams, grasslands and dark skies, and because it is so big at 1,624 sq km (627 sq miles), there are plenty of places to find quiet reflection.

The Downs are historic, too. Kingley Vale near Chichester has thousands of years of human life within its boundary,

⬇ The South Downs have sweeping views ...

and it's still being uncovered. In its Field Museum, it says that flint axe heads are still being discovered across the site ... and this author may have found one and then discarded it, thinking it was just a piece of rock.

Across the Downs, entrepreneurs are taking advantage of the unique climate and soil to create new wines. There are more than 60 vineyards in the Park, and no doubt more will appear over the years as the temperature rises, making it more favourable to grow grapes and continue the burgeoning English sparkling wine sector.

Naturally, the focus is on the Seven Sisters Country Park and Beachy Head, with their glorious views, crisp winds and hushed skies. The National Park is working hard to ensure its precious chalk grassland habitat recovers, while managing an increasing number of visitors and ensuring they can connect to nature. There's safety to consider, too

↓ Wild ponies grazing at Butser Hill.

→ The River Arun near Houghton Bridge.

– the cliffs are prone to erosion, and Park officials and their partners encourage people to not get too close. That seems really obvious, but accidents happen far more frequently than they should.

The South Downs are almost too big to have a single identity and way too big to enjoy in one go. The South Downs Way is a 160km (100 mile) National Trail, from Winchester to Eastbourne, that follows old routes and tracks along the northern escarpment of the chalk Downs, but even that misses some of what makes this part of the country special. The Downs is a place to savour, to walk through slowly, visit medieval villages and chat to locals who are more than happy to talk about their culture and heritage.

As Paul Gorringe, a ranger for Brighton & Hove City Council, says: 'I think people – in Brighton and beyond – cherish their Downs. It feels natural to say it's our Downs because we feel it's ours.'

→ Many of the Downs' towns are historic, like Lewes.

THE CHAMPION

Paul Gorringe
ooo

Paul Gorringe is a ranger for Brighton & Hove City Council.

It's not often the opportunity to create a new piece of habitat presents itself, but when Brighton & Hove City Council officials agreed for the former Waterhall golf course to become a Local Nature Reserve, it was a chance they couldn't afford to miss. Ninety hectares (220 acres) of land are now being rewilded, with a passionate local man leading the project.

> 'I'm a ranger for the Council, and I enjoy showcasing the magic of what we've got on the doorstep, and especially in Brighton,' Paul says. 'The city is such an anomaly because we've got the sea, the city and then the Downs. It's an incredible mix of habitats, landscapes and seascapes, and it's just a pleasure to be able to show it off as much as I can.

I've been working in the city for more than 17 years. I grew up on the Downs before it was a National Park, and I've always been attached to the outdoors. I was a horse rider like my mum and I also got into competitive mountain biking and a lot of running. I worked as a lifeguard and then as a lifeguard trainer, and then travelled around the world as a surfer. When I returned, I wanted to do something different, and knew it had to be in ecology or the environment. It felt natural to me, but I had much more of an international scope in my head, and I wanted to save the orangutans in Borneo. I even started to save up to do it, too. Then, one day, I was on the beach at low tide in Worthing and could see the Downs. It was like an epiphany; I thought, why go to Borneo, because if we all invested in our local areas, imagine what we could achieve. I wanted to become a bit of a champion for that, and here I am.'

Paul's role is to look after the Wilding Waterhall project, which is part of the Changing Chalk landscape-scale partnership, led by the National Trust and funded by the National Lottery Heritage Fund. This 90ha (220 acre) site has a mixture of habitats, from chalk grassland to native scrub and woodland, and a dew pond.

'When the Waterhall Golf Course shut in February 2020, and it only shut because it was failing, a lot of interested parties came and had a look at it but didn't take it on,' Paul adds. 'I think people saw its scale and topography and it just didn't work for them. The Council eventually took over, and I was charged with taking the landscape in a completely new direction; balancing the restoration of our renowned and incredibly species-rich chalk grassland with a more relaxed management approach that encourages natural processes. I'm still technically a ranger, but have been known to romantically call myself a 'rewilding officer' because that's a big part of what we're doing here!

We're working with animals that were native to our Downs, rather than just sheep, which are originally from Asia. We have a herd of 25 Sussex cattle and seven New Forest wild ponies on different parts of the site. We're able to see how nature responds and then make interventions when we need to. We're allowing the ecosystem to reconnect with itself by gradually nurturing the landscape rather than heavily managing it. We also don't worm our cattle or use any chemicals or machinery. It's all about organic animal and people power, as we also work with hundreds of volunteers who can help fill many of the ecological gaps in the system due to missing species such as predators and scavengers.'

It's early days, but Waterhall's landscape is already changing. Habitats are regenerating, people are gradually learning about nature recovery through engagement and education, and the public is increasingly interacting with the site with a sense of shared ownership.

'It's been a great experience, but we do have issues with off-lead dogs on the Nature Reserve during breeding season, and that's something we're working hard to balance. This is a designated Local Nature Reserve with important species and rare habitats, but we understand people also need access to nature more than ever before. Our animals are gradually "wilding", but have become very used to the number of dogs. Yet, this is a calcareous landscape on limestone, which means it has very porous and nutrient-poor topsoils. With an increasing number of dogs comes more faeces and urine, which will enrich the ground and have an impact on the ph. levels, which in turn will damage the unique ecology. The Downs has evolved as this nutrient-impoverished landscape, which has created, ecologically, a lot of wildflower competition. They're all fighting each other for space and nutrients, and that adversarial community is what helps to create these super ecosystems. It's important to protect that, and so we need to educate people about responsible dog walking at Nature Reserves like this, as nature should always come first in a Nature Reserve!

On the plus side, these conversations are becoming, on the whole, easier to have. It's lovely to know as a resident that you've got this massive resource on your doorstep, whether you know about how special the butterflies are or not. At the end of the day, the South Downs is a massive, biomass-rich green lung on compacted chalk that was pushed up to create the Downs millions of years ago, when the T. rex was roaming around.'

Paul's favourite thing to do in the South Downs: 'I take full advantage of the fact that I'm sandwiched between the sea and the Downs. I'm a very passionate water man, so if there are waves, I'm there. If not, I'll be at the skate park or I'll go up to Southwick Hill, with or without our dog, which is where I grew up. I've settled down less than 100m (328ft) from where I was born, so I go there with my wife and take a long walk. We'd talk about the week, the kids and just enjoy being outside in nature.'

FACTS AND QUIRKS

A unique grassland

Chalk grassland is internationally rare and can support as many as 40 plant species per square metre. Harebell, rockrose, dropwort and wild thyme can be found growing within it, and it's a haven for butterflies. It is carefully managed to encourage these plants, and at Seven Sisters, the Park has added selective grazing to allow this precious habitat to regenerate.

Literary connections

Jane Austen spent almost all of her life in the village of Chawton, near Alton in Hampshire, and you can visit her **House Museum** to see where she lived with her mother and sister. From 1809 to 1817, she lived in the house and penned *Pride and Prejudice*, as well as editing *Sense and Sensibility* and *Northanger Abbey*.

Ruth Rendell's debut novel *From Doon with Death* (1964) focuses on a murder in Kingsmarkham, which she admits is based on Midhurst, a market town at the heart of the South Downs National Park, and HG Wells spent time in Uppark, West Sussex, as a young man. Flora Thompson, who wrote *Lark Rise to Candleford* (first published as a single volume in 1945), was inspired by the South Downs, as was the poet Edward Thomas.

Devils, fairies and dragons

The Trundle is an Iron Age hillfort built on St Roche's Hill, north of Chichester. It apparently has a golden calf buried beneath it, but the Devil won't allow it to be uncovered. One man is reported to have tried but was beaten back by thunder and severe weather.

Harrow Hill has evidence of flint mine shafts and an Iron Age enclosure, and is alleged to be the last place in England where fairies were seen. They left when archaeologists came to uncover some of the secrets of the hill. At Bignor Hill, there are folds in the ground that show the remains of a dragon, which used the hill as its lair.

A panting pooch

Moulsecoomb Railway Station is considered one of the most haunted stations in the country. It is said to be patrolled by a dog who died on the tracks. There have been reports of passengers seeing a shadowy animal stalking them, as well as sounds of panting and growling!

Jane Austen's House Museum.

WALK 1

Kingley Vale circular
◇◇◇

Varied habitats and archaeological remains on this gem of a walk.

Kingley Vale is a 160ha (395 acre) Nature Reserve with chalk grassland, scrub, woodland and the oldest tree grove in the country. A multitude of archaeological features are dotted throughout the landscape, from the Bronze Age right up to the Second World War.

There are several interesting trails around Kingley Vale, and therefore many ways of seeing everything it has to offer. This circular gets the relatively simple climb out of the way first, taking in burial mounds and a holloway before finding the prehistoric Goosehill Camp, and back through a haunting yew grove.

Start at the West Stoke Car Park and amble up the track to the Kingley Vale Field Museum – a handy shelter in the rain.

↑ Dew pond with a view near Bow Hill.

START/END: **Kingley Vale National Nature Reserve, PO18 9BE**
DISTANCE: **11.2km (7 miles)**
GRADE: **Moderate**

Retrace your steps to the gate and go left, up the hill. Eventually, as the path opens up, on your right, you will find remains of a Second World War hiding spot for the Home Guard.

Return to the path and keep climbing until you arrive at The Devil's Humps; two burial barrows, which may have been faced with white chalk to signify their importance from a distance. They could also be the burial site of Viking lords defeated by local men in the 9th century.

Just past the trig point, turn left and traverse a cross dyke and long barrow before turning right into an area of woodland. This eventually takes you down to the remains of Goosehill Camp, an Iron Age settlement. Irregular concentric rings mark its spot within the woodland, and it's easy to realise why the camp was here: the

South Downs | 181

views would have been far-reaching. There were three roundhouses here, marked by small groves of yew trees.

The path to and from Goosehill is a quagmire in the wet, particularly at the top, so when you return, turn left and

↑ What a beauty! A gnarly yew.

enjoy a slippery, sloppy wander to Bow Hill Camp, a small hilltop enclosure from the Late Bronze Age, which is located on a holloway path.

Continuing back on the main route, you wander into a yew grove, dark and brooding, before opening up into lush green and hilly pasture. A dew pond is on your right, a habitat for frogs and toads, smooth and palmate newts, and dragonflies. It also includes the UK's only native water lily (*Nymphaea alba*, the white water lily). Marvel at the large landscape – very different from the outward journey – and then chart a route back to the Field Museum. There are some gnarly old yews in this part – likely 500 or more years old.

WALK 2

Seven Sisters to Beachy Head (and bus stop!)

○○○

Seven Sisters, Birling Gap and Beachy Head … the best clifftop walk in Britain?

This is an epic linear wander along the South Downs Way from the Seven Sisters Country Park to Birling Gap and Beachy Head before catching a bus back to the start.

Follow the South Downs Way out of Seven Sisters and Combe Bottom before making the climb to join the path above the chalk cliffs. The route continues along those dramatic cliffs – a series of seven ups and downs, some steeper than others (!) – before arriving at Birling Gap. This is a busy but lovely spot for a cracking view of

START/END: Seven Sisters Country Park, BN25 4AD
DISTANCE: 10.5km (6.5 miles), up to 13.5km (8.4 miles)
GRADE: Moderate

the sea, before you continue past Belle Tout Lighthouse, which is now a B&B. The lighthouse, which was built in 1831, was relocated 16m (52ft) back from the cliff edge in 1999 because it was in danger of falling into the sea. A major engineering feat!

The route here moves inland slightly as the cliffs are unstable, but you can see the smaller red and white lighthouse at the bottom. Continue to climb upwards (another steep one, sorry), and you'll eventually come to Beachy Head. There

Why not try these great walks...

THE SOUTH DOWNS WAY: A 160km (100 mile) trail from Winchester to Eastbourne, which follows old routes and tracks along the northern escarpment of the chalk Downs. It can be split into sections.

CHATTRI MEMORIAL: A Miles Without Stiles circular route (8km/5 miles) to the memorial, which is suitable for off-road class 3 all-terrain mobility scooters. Takes in the Clayton Windmills, known locally as Jack and Jill, and the South Downs Way.

LEWES AND SWANBOROUGH HILL: This 20km (12.4 mile) route follows the Sussex Ouse Valley Way from Lewes, and joins the South Downs Way to Swanborough Hill (191m/627ft) before returning to the town ... and a beer!

are amenities here if you need them and, depending on the season, you can get a bus back to Seven Sisters.

No such luck on our walk, though, as the bus wasn't running! Follow the South Downs Way to a trig point, which has great views to Eastbourne, then walk to the A259, turn left and pick up the bus.

↓ You won't get bored on this walk!

Key Places

The rider...
In the South Downs, you can stay at farms, B&Bs, hotels, bunkhouses and campsites – particularly along the South Downs Way. Check out www.southdowns.gov.uk/directory/ for a list of sustainably minded providers across the Park.
www.southdowns.gov.uk/where-to-stay/

Places to visit...

Arundel On the A27 in the south of the Park, this is a historic market town packed with antique curios and map shops, as well as a cathedral and castle. Arundel Blackfriars Priory was founded in the 13th century, while the castle, open from the end of March to October, contains paintings and furniture from the 16th century. St Nicholas and Fitzalan Chapel dates from 1380. Arundel Park is pretty, while Swanbourne Lake is a calm oasis and only a short walk from the busy town. You can hire boats on the lake and the River Arun. The heated Arundel Lido is open all year round.

Steyning Just outside the Park's boundary in the north. Here you'll find the Norman church of St Andrew's and the ruins of Bramber Castle. The high street is a mixture of old and new and features timber-framed buildings from the Tudor and Stuart eras. It's thought King Charles II lingered in Steyning as he fled Oliver Cromwell on the way to France. There are tea shops, pubs and cafés as well as places to stay, making it a good base to explore the National Park.

Lewes Busy market town that hosts the world-famous Bonfire Night on 5 November. The Ann of Cleves House Museum is a short walk from the town centre, and the Railway Land Local Nature Reserve covers 10ha (25 acres) along former railway sidings. It has wet woodland, reedbeds, meadows and a chalk stream. The town centre has plenty of shops and places to eat, a vibrant eco feel, and a splendid 15th-century

⬇ Swanbourne Lake in Arundel.

↦ The 15th-century bookshop in Lewes.

bookshop on the high street towards Rotten Row.

Amberley Quaint and quiet village on the South Downs Way, around 8km (5 miles) from Arundel. Medieval in layout, it has thatched cottages, a Norman church and a 12th-century castle that is now a hotel and restaurant. The community village store is fantastic for provisions of all kinds, while the Black Horse features great food, beer and bar snacks beyond the usual crisps. The Old Engine Shed is the taproom for Fauna Brewery – an environmentally conscious brewer that supports a different wildlife conservation cause each time they make a new beer.

Petersfield Where the A2 and A272 meet, an ideal base for lots of activities. Visitors can access the Hangers Way, Serpent Trail, Shipwrights Way or the South Downs Way, as well as Butser Hill. The town has held two regular markets since the 12th century. There's a 17th-century-styled physic garden, which houses medicinal plants, a museum and gallery, and the Norman church of St Peter's.

Why not try?

Midhurst Fascinating historical place in the heart of the National Park that has inspired the likes of HG Wells and Ruth Rendell. Cowdray, now a ruin, played host to King Henry VIII and Queen Elizabeth I.

Hassocks Good place to visit after being at the nearby Bronze Age settlement at Wolstonbury Hill. The village, whose name means 'rough tussocks of grass', has several shops and places to eat.

Pulborough On the A284 north of Arundel. Pretty village with joyful views of the Arun Valley and South Downs. The RSPB's Pulborough Brooks is a great place to see lapwing and other waders, set in wildflower meadows, pools and heathland. It is a haven for the rare little whirlpool ramshorn snail.

↤ Amberley retains its medieval charm.

VISIT

Must Sees

The painter John Constable said the view from the top of **Devil's Dyke** ❶ (TQ 258 110) –the longest, deepest and widest dry valley in the UK – was the grandest in the world. It is certainly impressive from all angles. Legend has it that the Devil dug it to drown the Christian parishioners of the Weald, and that he and his wife are buried there. At the bottom of the Dyke you'll find two humps, graves if you wish, and if you run backwards seven times around them, while holding your breath, he will return. Devil's Dyke was the site of an Iron Age hillfort, while the Victorians turned it into a fairground. There is also earthwork of a motte and bailey castle and a medieval settlement. The Devil's Dyke pub is at the top.

The **Jill Windmill** ❷ (TQ 361 405) – Jack is its neighbour – is a fully working 200-year-old mill. It is beautifully presented, maintained by volunteers and open on Sunday afternoons from May to September. www.jillwindmill.org.uk

There has been a church at **St Michael's in Amberley** ❸ (BN18 9NF) since the early 12th century. Inside is a series of intricate wall paintings depicting the Passion Cycle on the south side of the chancel, which could date back to the 14th century.

The views from **Butser Hill** ❹ (SU 716 203), the highest point on the South Downs ridge at 271m (889ft), are superb. It's probably the best place to stargaze, as the Park is a designated International Dark Sky Reserve. There are plenty of routes around the hill, which is part of the Queen Elizabeth Country Park, while in the valley below is East Meon, home to a medieval court house.

The views from **Black Down and the Temple of the Winds** (SU 920 292) inspired Alfred, Lord Tennyson, who said: 'You came and looked and loved the view, long known and loved by me, Green Sussex fading into blue with one grey glimpse of sea.' www.nationaltrust.org.uk/black-down

Cissbury Ring (TQ 138 080) is one of the largest Iron Age hillforts in the Park. Its ditch and ramparts enclose 24ha (60 acres) while the Site of Special Scientific Interest (SSSI) it encompasses is around 84ha (207 acres). It is one of the best places to see butterflies such as the adonis and chalkhill blues, dark green fritillaries and marbled whites.

Like Cissbury, **Ditchling Beacon** (TQ 331 130) offers some of the best views in the Park. At 248m (814ft) high, this was once the site of a beacon used to warn the Queen about the incoming Spanish Armada.

A golf course is being rewilded as part of the unique **Wilding Waterhall** (BN45 7DB) project. It will see chalk grassland restored to improve biodiversity. Brighton & Hove City Council has designated the 90ha (222 acre) site a Local Nature Reserve and is planting native scrub and woodland, and adding new dew ponds. www.brighton-hove.gov.uk/libraries-leisure-and-arts/parks-and-green-spaces/wilding-waterhall

At **Palmers Ball** (SU 785 303), you could be lucky to see four of the country's rarest reptiles. As part of the Woolmer Forest SSSI, it is home to smooth snakes, adders, common lizards and reintroduced sand lizards.

↑ Preparations for paragliding at Devil's Dyke.

Must Dos

Cliffs, beaches, wetland, grassland...

... an all-for-one at **Seven Sisters Country Park** (BN25 4AD), near Seaford. This is the best place to see the dramatic Seven Sisters chalk cliffs and walk part of the South Downs Way to Birling Gap and Beachy Head – and it's all superbly connected by public transport. The National Park Visitor Centre and Just Around the Corner Café are good places to start (and end), and you can hire a bike from Cuckmere Cycle Company (www.cuckmerecycle.co), located just beside the South Downs Way.

Several trails run from the visitor centre, including a 1.6km (1 mile) beach trail suitable for all, a 2.4km (1.5 mile) walk to Seaford Head Nature Reserve, and a must-do 7.7km (4.8 mile) yomp around the whole Country Park. National Park officials took over the 280ha (692 acre) site in 2021 and are managing the chalk grassland on the opposite side of the A259. This type of habitat is said to be more diverse than rainforests and contains round-headed rampion, clustered bellflower, pyramidal orchids and *Spiranthes spiralis*, commonly known as autumn lady tresses. All can be seen on the Country Park Trail.
www.sevensisters.org.uk

Into the woods

The South Downs has more woodland than any other National Park in England or Wales. **Friston Forest** (BN20 0AT) adjoins Seven Sisters, while **Ebernoe Common** (SU 976 270) is an ancient woodland with oak and beech. **The Mens** (RH14 0HR), managed by Sussex Wildlife Trust (www.sussexwildlifetrust.org.uk/visit/the-mens), is a beyond wild, mysterious place.

Have an adventure

At **Cuckmere Meanders** (TV 518 988), Park staff and volunteers are working hard to create a thriving wetland habitat. The meanders are a popular place for canoeing, within set boundaries, and wild swimming. Good kayaking can be found elsewhere in the Park too, particularly through Alfriston and Lewes. The Kayak Coach offers guided trips along the Cuckmere estuary (www.thekayakcoach.com) and, along the coast, there are opportunities for all sorts of watersports.

Paragliding takes place at **Devil's Dyke**, and several operators can help you take your first nervous steps to seeing the Downs from above! www.milehighparagliding.com/where-we-fly/devils-dyke/

Witness nature

Nightingales migrate from West Africa to breed in the UK, and the Downs is one of the best places to hear their magical call. Sussex Wildlife Trust recommends **Ebernoe Common**, **Pulborough Brooks** (RH20 2EL) and **Abbot's Wood** (BN26 6SL) to hear them, usually at dawn or dusk during May.

Sussex Wildlife Trust also looks after 85ha (210 acres) of reserve at **Malling Down** (BN7 2RU), which has a multitude of rare flowers and butterflies. www.sussexwildlifetrust.org.uk/visit/malling-down

The **WWT Arundel Wetland Centre** has eight hides, boardwalks and a guided boat safari! www.wwt.org.uk/wetland-centres/arundel

⬇ You can canoe and swim at Cuckmere Meanders ... or just enjoy the work to make it a sustainable habitat.

Spot chalk figures

The impressive **Long Man of Wilmington** (TQ 542 034) is a 69m (226ft) figure cut into chalk on Windover Hill, while the **Litlington White Horse** (TQ 510 009) is on High and Over. The first white horse on the hill was cut by James Pagden, his brothers and a cousin in 1836, and was replaced in a single night in 1924 thanks to John T Ade, Eric Hobbis and Stephen Bovis.

Experience culture and heritage

Speaking of art, the 17th-century **Petworth House** (GU28 9LR) has a fine art collection (www.nationaltrust.org.uk/visit/sussex/petworth), while there is also a good art gallery and museum in **Petersfield** (GU32 3HX) (www.petersfieldmuseum.co.uk). It's home to the Edward Thomas Centre, which houses the Tim Wilton-Steer Collection, a collection of works that celebrate the poet, who lived locally in the village of Steep.

The **Weald & Downland Living Museum** (PO18 0EU) (www.wealddown.co.uk) is a fascinating place, featuring more than 50 relocated historic houses that depict life through the ages.

The Litlington White Horse.

Ditchling Museum of Art and Craft (BN6 8SP) (www.ditchlingmuseumartcraft.org.uk) showcases the artists and craftspeople who made the village a creative hub, while the seasonal **Amberley Museum** (BN18 9LT) (www.amberleymuseum.co.uk) is an interesting potpourri of a place. It has historic buildings and vintage machinery among other things.

If historic remains are more your thing, the **Bignor Roman Villa** (RH20 1PH) (www.bignorromanvilla.co.uk) is the remains of a Roman home with mosaic floors and opens seasonally, while **Arundel Castle** (BN18 9AB) (www.arundelcastle.org) is the ancestral home of the Dukes of Norfolk and is open from the end of March to the end of October (closed on Mondays, except bank holidays and in August).

Explore a vineyard

There are more than 60 vineyards in the South Downs National Park. **Ridgeview** (BN6 8TP) is one of the most popular and does tours (www.ridgeview.co.uk), as is the **Bolney Wine Estate** (RH17 5NB) (www.bolneywineestate.com), but there are many others. Unsurprisingly, the area is great for breweries too, with **The Cider Tap & Brewhouse** (RH17 5SE)

← Arundel Castle.

(www.wobblegate.co.uk) well worth a visit for the pizza alone.

Picking a pub to visit in the Downs is a hard one, as there are so many great and historic examples. **The Amberley Black Horse** (BN18 9NL) is worth a visit, as is **The Bridge Inn** (BN18 9LT), nearby at Houghton Bridge. For a pub with character and great food, you can't go wrong with **The George & Dragon** (BN18 9LW) up the road, one of the oldest pubs in Sussex, dating back to 1276. It proudly boasts that King Charles II stopped there in 1651 when fleeing the country after his defeat at the Battle of Worcester.

Horse racing

The sport of kings takes place at **Goodwood** (PO18 0PS) with regular horse racing meetings, while the Goodwood Estate also holds the famous Festival of Speed among other events. www.goodwood.com

→ The Cider Tap near Bolney.

CAR-FREE TRAVEL

→ Public transport information for most of the walks and experiences in the South Downs can be found at www.southdowns.gov.uk/walks/

→ There are several bus services that link the National Park's main villages and attractions, and you can purchase a South Downs Discovery Ticket, which gives you unlimited travel across the entire Park for a day. www.southdowns.gov.uk/travelling-around/south-downs-discovery-ticket/

→ The Brighton & Hove Coaster bus route (Coaster 12, Coaster 12A, Coaster 12X, N12) runs from Brighton to Eastbourne, passing through Seven Sisters, Birling Gap and Beachy Head. Some services are dependent on the season. www.buses.co.uk/services/BH/12

→ The Stagecoach 60 runs from Chichester to Midhurst, taking in Cowdray Ruins, the Weald & Downland Living Museum, West Dean Gardens and Chichester Cathedral.

→ Brighton's Breeze bus services connect to Devil's Dyke (#77), Stanmer Park (#78) and Ditchling Beacon (#79). www.buses.co.uk/breeze-downs

→ The South Downs Rambler Bus runs from Winchester and Petersfield every Sunday from mid-July to mid-September, as well as on the August bank holiday Monday. www.southdowns.gov.uk/travelling-around/south-downs-rambler-bus/

→ The South Downs are very accessible by rail. Gateway towns such as Winchester, Petersfield and Lewes are well served, while Amberley, Southease and Liss are ideal starting points for exploration. www.southwesternrailway.com and www.nationalrail.co.uk

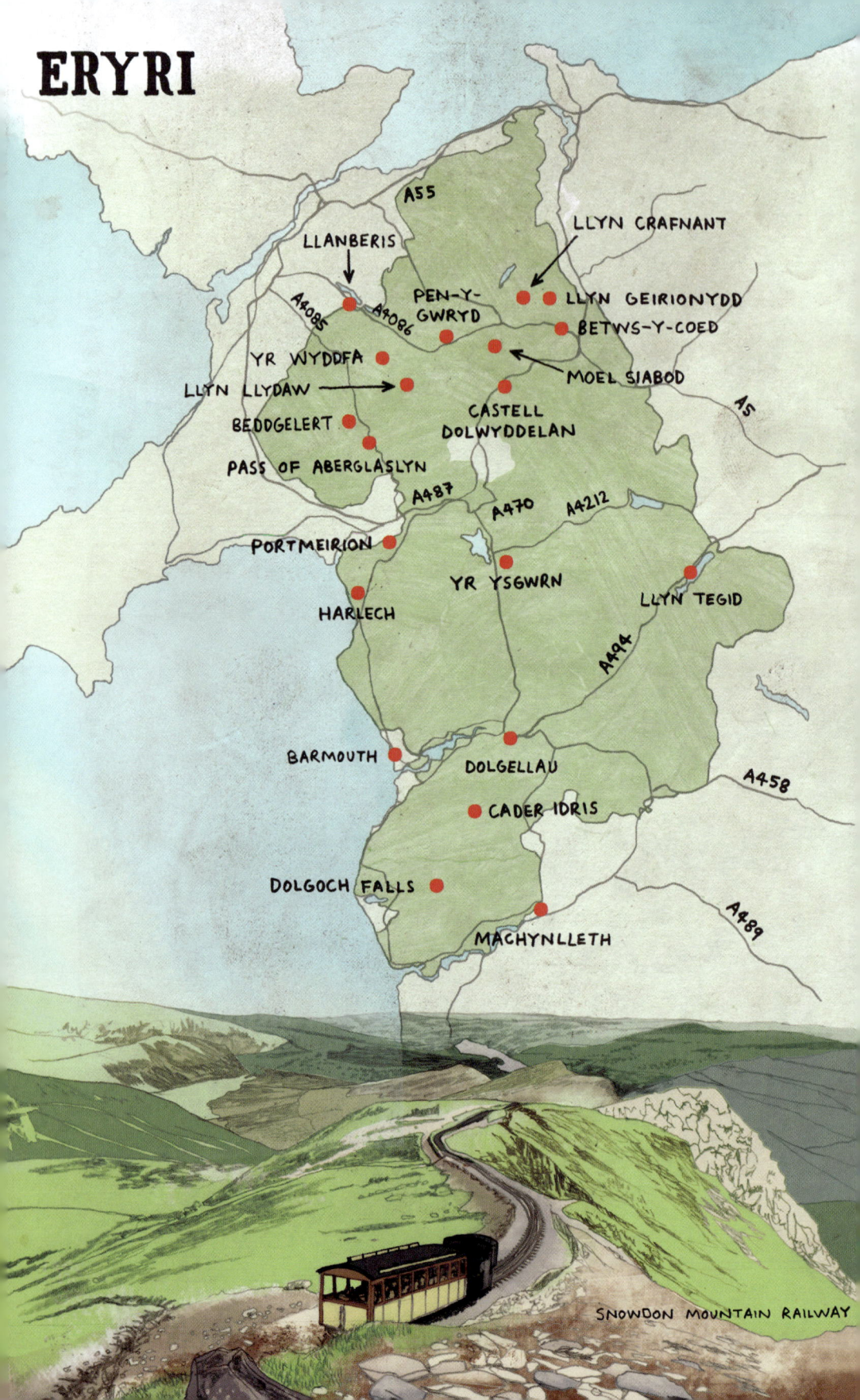

ERYRI

DESIGNATED: **18 October 1951**
SIZE: **2,132 sq km (823 sq miles)**
HIGHEST PEAK: **Yr Wyddfa (Snowdon) at 1,085m (3,560ft)**
ANNUAL VISITOR NUMBERS: **4.27 million (2020)**, POPULATION: **26,000**
OFFICIAL WEBSITE: **www.eryri.gov.wales**

Mae yna air yn yr iaith Gymraeg sy'n golygu perthyn, galwad i gartref, a theimlad mewnol o fod yn un â'ch tirwedd. Mae Hiraeth yn cynrychioli'r cysylltiad â'ch gorffennol, eich hunan fewnol, tyniad tuag at eich gwreiddiau, a chysylltiad â lle. Mae'n dynodi cymuned, cryfder mewn niferoedd, angerdd, a balchder; yn anochel sy'n canolbwyntio ar yr hyn oeddech chi a beth ydych chi nawr.*

Returning to self in Eryri has been an important transition. Wales is a proud country, has its own language and has long promoted its own identity. Welsh is of Celtic origin, proudly spoken and often the first language in schools, but has faced anglicisation. Road signage is in dual language, and place names are often referred to in English, rather than the native tongue.

However, the tide is turning ... or returning. In 2011, the Welsh Language (Wales) Measure emphasised several measures to ensure the Welsh language could flourish and remain a key part of the country's heritage and, most notably, established the office of the Welsh Language Commissioner. Their role was to 'promote and facilitate the use of the Welsh language and ... to work towards

↑ The sprawling landscape of Eryri National Park.

---

* There is a word in the Welsh language that means belonging, a call to home, and an inner feeling of being at one with your landscape. 'Hiraeth' represents the link to your past, your inner self, a pull towards your origins, and a connection to place. It signifies community, strength in numbers, passion, and pride; an inevitable centring on what you were and what you now are.

ensuring that the Welsh language is treated no less favourably than the English language'.

Snowdonia was the name of this National Park since 18 October 1951, but there has always been a strong urge to recognise the fact that it is the heart of Wales. In 2022, the Park committed to prioritising the Welsh names Eryri (Snowdonia) and Yr Wyddfa (Snowdon) in all communications, a decision ratified in late 2024 when they decided to drop the bracketed name completely. Of the move, Eryri National Park Chief Executive Jonathan Cawley said: 'The shift to using only "Eryri" in the Authority's logo reflects our dedication to the cultural heritage of the region and the values of the Welsh language. This updated branding will strengthen the Park's identity and reinforce the Authority's role in celebrating the unique heritage of the area.'

The move wasn't popular with some, as these things rarely are. Some thought the change to Welsh names would suggest these mountains and areas

⬆ The Ffestiniog and Welsh Highland Railway cuts through some of the best landscapes in the country.

were new, effectively counteracting what the move was supposed to achieve. On the flip side, supporters were jubilant at reclaiming their heritage, their home, their Hiraeth, and people would just have to get used to giving things their real

⬇ Much quieter way up Yr Wyddfa – the Rhyd Ddu Path.

name. After all, while Mont Blanc is the name of the mountain in France, it is Monte Bianco in Italy. Changes do not mean a blanket ban on other monikers.

Dolbadarn Castle.

Identity is important in Eryri as so much of the Park offering is centred on heritage. Yr Wyddfa means 'grave' or 'burial mound'. Its lakes are steeped in mythology, and its castles are lasting monuments to when the Welsh were battling their neighbours across the border.

Ultimately, this is a National Park of dramatic landscapes, a rich history and a proud people that are coming together to reclaim it as their own, finding that sense of self we all have deep down. It is crammed with welcoming villages, smiling locals, amazing hospitality and a range of things to enjoy and celebrate.

It has that sense of belonging, summed up perfectly by Val Bethell on *Wales Arts* on BBC Cymru (2003). She wrote: 'I know what it means. Hiraeth is in the mountains where the wind speaks in many tongues and the buzzards fly on silent wings. It's the call of my spiritual home, it's where ancient peoples made their home. We're high on a hill, where saints bathed sore feet in a healing spring and had a cure.'

Eryri is the complete National Park.

Llyn Crafnant.

THE CHAMPION

Alun Gethin Jones
○○○

Alun Gethin Jones is the Area Warden for the Yr Wyddfa region in the Eryri National Park.

Yr Wyddfa is the jewel in the crown in Eryri and, as such, receives an incredible amount of footfall. There are six main routes up the 1,085m (3,560ft) summit, and they transport thousands of people to witness some of the finest views in the world. But with close to 700,000 visitors each year, there is a huge pressure to ensure it remains viable long into the future.

'Since the pandemic, I think people want to see what they have on the doorstep, and that has meant an increased footfall in areas like these,' Alun says. 'People see how beautiful it is on social media, and they want to come to see it – and why not, this is a space for everyone. The Watkin Path has some amazing features, but sadly they can't cope with hundreds of visitors, and that also has a huge effect on the local community. You can't plan for that instant influx of people, but we are working through it.'

As with natural wonders around the world, social media has had a huge impact on our National Parks. It helps them communicate with a larger audience, promoting what is on offer as well as educating visitors on responsible tourism. On the flip side, all it takes is one viral shot that has the unintended consequence of directing a huge influx of people to these protected places. Eryri has always been a busy place, and it keeps getting busier.

'It can be difficult,' Alun continues. 'We have parking issues, and when places get full, people park on verges, and that destroys them. The water should be pristine, but I have noticed that it can be cloudy with sunscreen at busy times. There is only so much you can do. This role is about being on top of things and talking to people in the right manner. We don't have the legal power to fine people or send them off elsewhere. It is a delicate balancing act.'

Alun has been a warden for the Yr Wyddfa area for the last six years and, having been born and raised locally, he admits it was a job he always wanted.

He says: 'I initially wanted to be a teacher, but when this role came up, I couldn't not go for it. It was outside and meant working in an area I love so much. There is always work to be done on the mountain, but mainly, I work with people. One of my main roles is to go around schools promoting conservation and the different projects we undertake as wardens. This could be about the delicate landscape or the microplastics that have been found on the summit. I raise the issues that might happen with higher footfall and reiterate the ethos of respecting the environment and taking things home with you. We also have a Plastic Free Officer, who is working with local communities and local businesses to reduce single-use plastics.

I also work with local businesses and farmers to solve access issues. Twenty-six different landowners are invested in the area, and striking a balance between their needs and our issues is important. We want to work with them closely to look after the land because it is a special place with Sites of Special Scientific Interest (SSSIs), rare plants and animals.

I think people think that wardens just go and walk mountains every day. That would be perfect, as hiking is one of my passions, but obviously, there's a lot more to it, sadly! If local communities in the area have issues, they will come to me, and I will address it to the Welsh government or the organisations that we work with. It's about getting the best for this area, often with limited resources.'

Alun's key time is 'peak season' when the entire Yr Wyddfa area is busy, often around the clock.

'Our peak season starts at Easter and ends around early November,' he continues. 'From then, it is still very busy, as you have to be on top of what needs doing or repairing. During the peak season, we don't get much time to focus on things like project work because we're dealing with the general public a lot. Over the winter, we can deal with things like access work, stiles and paths, and also conservation.

After lockdown, we saw that peak season would be a lot busier and that our infrastructure couldn't sustain the numbers of visitors. We know there's not enough parking, but most parks have a similar issue. Pen-y-Pass has only got 64 spaces, and that is where two of the main paths up the mountain are. I remember coming back here the first day after lockdown was lifted and seeing all the cars double-parked down the road. That made the national news, as people couldn't get through. So, we introduced a booking system for the car park from April until November, and directed people to a new park and ride bus. It did alleviate the pressure and seems to be working.'

In his first year in the role, Alun reckons he climbed Yr Wyddfa around 55 times. He has seen frosty mornings and amazing sunsets but says the most important thing is meeting people at the top.

'It's great to meet so many different people from all over the world. I love seeing teenagers or kids with their parents get to the top for the first time. It brings back that memory of me doing it for the first time. I talk to all manner of people in this area, and it puts a smile on your face when you hear them say that they've come here to make themselves feel better.

It's such a privilege to be able to advocate a National Park that wants to help make people happy. That's what the Park is there for; it's for people to come out, relax and enjoy the environment.'

Alun's favourite thing to do in Eryri:
'It would be an ideal working day. I would start at our base in Pen-y-Pass with a conservation project such as planting trees or something to help red squirrels in the area. Then I'd survey the paths around the lakes. It needs to be done, but it's also a good excuse for a walk! I've done a lot of hiking around the world, but I wouldn't change it for walking here.'

FACTS AND QUIRKS

Land of legends

Ogof Glyndŵr (Glyndŵr's Cave) is said to be the hiding place of Welsh prince Owain Glyndŵr after he was pursued by English soldiers. He'd been chased to Moel Hebog but climbed a 91m (300ft) crevice in the rock to evade capture. He hid in the cave and was secretly fed by his friend Rhys Goch Eryri until the soldiers left. He then rallied his troops and took on the English once more.

In Beddgelert is **Gelert's Grave**, the resting place of a loyal dog. One day, Llywelyn, the Prince of North Wales, went hunting without his dog, but when he returned, he found the pooch stained and smeared with blood. Alarmed, he 'hastened to find his son and saw the infant's cot empty, the bedclothes and floor covered with blood', and duly dispatched the dog with his sword. But as soon as he'd done the deed, he heard a child's cry. Llywelyn eventually found the boy unharmed, but nearby lay the body of a mighty wolf, which Gelert had slain. The prince, filled with remorse, is said to have never smiled again.

According to legend, **Cantre'r Gwaelod** is a mythical city in Cardigan Bay. It was surrounded by gates to protect it from flooding during higher tides, and a young lad called Seithennyn had the duty of making sure they were closed each evening. But one evening, he'd had a few and forgot, so the city was flooded. According to the Park's website, 'many claim that on quiet days, you can hear the bells of Cantre'r Gwaelod ringing underwater'. Clearly, they've been on what Seithennyn had. **Llyn Tegid** is also said to have a town deep beneath its surface.

The Devil's Kitchen is the name given to a black crack that splits Clogwyn y Geifr. Steam often rises from the crack, and when this happens, people say the Devil is cooking.

What's in a name

The name **Yr Wyddfa** means 'grave' or 'burial mound'. Legend says that the giant Rhita Gawr was buried on the mountain after a battle with King Arthur. It was originally thought that **Eryri** meant 'place of eagles', but evidence now suggests it comes from rise or highlands. **Snowdon** comes from the Saxon 'snow hill'.

Llyn Llydaw is supposedly the final resting place of Excalibur, Arthur's sword, after it was thrown in the lake on his death.

Foodies

Welsh cakes, bara brith, Welsh rarebit ... several delicious dishes across the Park tempt visitors! In areas of North Wales, **cawl, also known as lobscows**, is a stew of lamb and veg that will warm up the frostiest of hillwalkers!

Gold fever

Welsh gold is famous throughout the world, but was there a modern day klondike in the Park? Along the Mawddach Valley, near the **Clogau gold mine**, digging took place in several locations while panning also took place in the river itself.

WALK 1

Yr Wyddfa

◆ ◆ ◆

Take the 'easier' Llanberis Path to the summit of Yr Wyddfa and enjoy a route that's more than a ticking-off exercise.

Every year, more than 600,000 people climb Yr Wyddfa using the Llanberis Path, billed as the 'easier' route up the mountain. It's ideal for people wanting to summit for the first time or those who want a lesser gradient than the five other main routes. Yet, Yr Wyddfa is an unforgiving mountain; any route is challenging (this one ascends more than 914m (3,000ft) over its length), and you need to be prepared, even if the path to the top is well marked. In winter, this walk requires winter skills.

Leaving Llanberis at the far end of Victoria Terrace, follow the obvious path that roughly follows the Snowdon Mountain Railway, which opened in 1898. Below is Cwm Brwynog Valley, where you can see the ruins of an old, close-knit community. There were 25 dwellings here, and the remains of Capel Hebron (Hebron Chapel) can still be seen.

Keep climbing, and you will eventually reach Clogwyn, one of three stations along the mountain railway track. This area is known locally as Cwm Hetiau – or 'Valley of the Hats'. The summit isn't too far ahead from here, and there's a welcoming visitor centre – Hafod Eryri – where you can take a pitstop for refreshments before you make the journey back down from where you came.

START/END: Far end of Victoria Terrace, Llanberis, LL55 4TN
DISTANCE: 13.9km (8.64 miles)
GRADE: Challenging

↑ Yr Wyddfa from Llynau Mymbyr.

Eryri | 199

WALK 2

Mawddach Trail

◌ ◌ ◌

A gentle access-for-all trail along the Mawddach Estuary.

This all-access path is suitable for bikes, wheelchairs and walkers. It follows the southern shore of the Mawddach Estuary from Barmouth to Dolgellau but can be taken in sections at several locations, including Pont y Wernddu, Penmaenpool, Arthog and Morfa Mawddach, where there is a train station.

The route from Barmouth takes in a bridge that is 820m (2,690ft) long across the estuary. It is the longest timber viaduct in Wales and has been rebuilt several times because it's difficult to maintain. You're asked to pay a small fee to the troll under the bridge to help with its upkeep ... the bridge, not the troll.

The Mawddach Estuary is an SSSI due to its saltmarsh and lowland peat habitats.

START/END: Barmouth Viaduct, LL42 1EQ
DISTANCE: 15km (9.32 miles) – one way
GRADE: Easy

↑ The walk follows the southern shore of the Mawddach Estuary.

↓ Part of the Mawddach Trail between Barmouth and Dolgellau.

↑ Beddgelert is a place of mystery and myth.

Why not try these great walks...

LLANBERIS HERITAGE WALK: A gem of a 5.5km (3.41 mile) circular route that takes you to Dolbadarn Castle and Padarn Country Park before reaching the remnants of slate quarrying and Anglesey Barracks.

CADAIR IDRIS: Take the shortish but steep Minffordd Path to the top of the 893m (2,930ft) summit from the Dôl Idris Car Park. Navigational care is needed descending from the summit. There and back is 10km (6 miles).

MOEL SIABOD: A 10.8km (6.71-mile) circular from Bryn Glo near Capel Curig to climb the impressive 872m (2,861ft) summit. Has an exciting grade 1 scramble up Daear Ddu Ridge.

Key Places

The rider...
Eryri has a vast range of accommodation available for a variety of budgets. B&Bs, guesthouses and hotels are available, as well as several bunkhouses, caravan parks and campsites.
www.visitsnowdonia.info/accommodation-snowdonia-and-llyn-north-wales

Places to visit

Llanberis The hub for Yr Wyddfa and outdoor adventures. It's a busy base, but that's understandable given its dramatic location. You'll find slate mining remains, grand views all around, the Llanberis Railway, which runs along the north shore of Llyn Padarn, the Snowdon Mountain Railway, and 'the lonely tree' on the edge of Llyn Padarn.

Betws-y-Coed Best approached from Llanrwst so you can see the 15th-century Tu Hwnt I'r Bont tea room over the river. In autumn, the exterior's foliage provides a multicolour show. The town is packed with outdoor shops, places to eat and an alpine-style strip near the railway station. Experiences at Zip World can be booked from here, as well as bike hire. St Mary's Church often has Welsh choir performances.

Barmouth Coastal town on the edge of the Park boundary. Feels distant from the northern parts of Eryri, as there's plenty of shops, an arcade, donkey rides and a large viaduct across the estuary connecting to the southern part of the Park ... as long as you pay your toll to the troll.

Beddgelert On the junction of the A4085 and A498, with the Afon Colwyn running through it. A place of mystery, with ancient woodlands, a magnificent river walk, quaint shops and a heritage railway. In the centre is Ty Isaf, a National Trust shop that was one of only two farmhouses in the village and is thought to date from *c.*1580.

Machynlleth Beautiful market town in the shadow of Caider Idris. It is part of the UNESCO Biosphere Reserve, which designated the Dyfi Estuary and surroundings as an important place for

⬇ The River Conwy runs through the bustling Betsw-y-Coed.

biodiversity – one of only seven such reserves in the UK. It is packed with shops (which have an eco vibe) and galleries – MOMA, Wales (Museum of Modern Art, Wales) is the highlight, as well as the Owain Glyndŵr Centre, which tells the story of the 1404 Parliament. A market is held on a Wednesday, and there's an internationally recognised comedy festival each May bank holiday.

Why not try...

Harlech Just inside the Park boundary, with a beautiful beach, castle and homemade ice cream shop.

Dolgellau Market town beneath Caider Idris. The Sesiwn Fawr folk festival is held on the first weekend of the school summer holidays.

Portmeirion Built by Welsh architect Clough Williams-Ellis, this quirky tourist town is a must-see for fans of *The Prisoner* TV series (which was filmed here). Has Italianate-style architecture, extensive gardens, estuary views and all sorts of places to visit – and you can even get married here.

↑ Llanberis isn't short of great scenery.

↓ ... make sure you pay your toll to the troll at Barmouth!

Eryri | 203

VISIT

Must Sees

Yr Ysgwrn (LL41 4UW) is a historic centre at Cwm Prysor, Trawsfynydd, which was originally the home of poet Hedd Wyn, who was killed in the Battle of Passchendaele in 1917, a couple of weeks before he posthumously won the National Eisteddfod Chair, the most prestigious award for poetry in the Welsh language. Fascinatingly, the family have kept the house to that period, and the National Park has renovated parts so people can visit. www.yrysgwrn.com

At **Gelert's Grave** ❶ (SH 59050 47780), you can discover the sad story of Gelert, the faithful pooch of Llywelyn ❷, the Prince of North Wales, and see if you can spot a visitor nearby. The walk from Beddgelert, along the peaceful Afon Colwyn, is joyful.

Continuing along the route from Gelert's resting place is the **Fisherman's Path** ❸, which takes you along Llwybr Llechi Eryri (the Snowdonia Slate Trail). The Afon Colwyn has carved a route through the Pass of Aberglaslyn, with rapids, birdlife and a sense of adventure. It passes a copper mine and arrives at a fine viewpoint (SH 594 462) before the calm plain of Nantmor. An absolute gem.

Llyn Crafnant ❹ (SH 749 610) is a peaceful reservoir at the end of a winding single-track road. Has four walks, from easy and accessible to moderate, stretching 400m (1,312ft) to 7.2km (4.5 miles).

Surrounding Betws-y-Coed is the huge **Gwydir Forest Park** ❺ (LL24 0AA). It has five waymarked trails, which start from Pont y Pair Car Park in the centre of the town – the walk to Llyn Elsi begins behind St Mary's Church. The red route from SH 76214 57595 climbs through Coed Craig-Forris and up to a viewpoint where you can see breathtaking views of some of Eryri's summits, including Moel Siabod, Glyder Fawr and Pen yr Ole Wen.

Castell Dolwyddelan ❻ (LL25 0JD) sits at the bottom of the **Crimea Pass** ❼. A walk from the layby at SH 72946 52397 picks its way up to the castle, which was built by Llywelyn ab Iorwerth, Prince of Gwynedd, in the 1220s but was conquered by Edward I in 1283. The inner part of the castle is open from April to September on Fridays, Saturdays, Sundays and bank holidays from 10am to 4pm.

Rising out of Llanberis is **Dinorwig Slate Quarry** (SH 592 605), a stark reminder of the toil of thousands of people to mine this important building material and send it all around the world.

Depending on how you reach the quarry, you can visit **Dre Newydd** or **Anglesey Barracks** (SH 589 602) on the way up or down. These bleak structures were built in the 1870s to house quarrymen. They're simple cottages, in two rows of 11, which offered little protection from the elements – a grim existence. The name derives from navvies who would travel from Gwynedd and Anglesey to work at the quarry.

Eryri has some stunning waterfalls. **Aber Falls** (SH 668 701) in Abergwyngregyn is beautiful, as are **Swallow Falls** (SH 765 577) near Betws-y-Coed. Entry to the latter is £2 and can be paid at the machine at the entrance. It's best visited after significant rainfall as the Afon Llugwy flows 42m (138ft) through a narrow chasm, creating a spectacular cascade.

Must Dos

Oh starry night

Eryri National Park is one of 22 International Dark Sky Reserves in the world. Move a mile or two away from the busy towns, and the night sky opens up with a spectacular show. The Park, alongside its partners, runs regular night sky events throughout the year for you to witness the marvels above our heads. The best place to start is at **Llyn y Dywarchen** (SH 560 534), from September to March.

Take to the water

Several of Eryri's mountain lakes are fantastic for watersports and swimming. At **Llyn Geirionydd** (SH 763 604), you can waterski, sail and row, and there is a designated safe swimming spot for those fancying a dip. On land, the walk around the lake is delightful too.

Llyn Tegid (SH 908 334) is another well-known watersports and swimming destination. It is Wales' largest natural lake, measuring 5.63km (3.5 miles) long. Paddleboarding, canoeing, windsurfing and fishing all take place here, and there are several providers in and around the lake to help make the experience special. You'll need a permit to do anything on the lake other than swim, but it's a worthwhile cost to keep the facilities vibrant, and the scenery more than repays. www.eryri.gov.wales/visit/llyn-tegid/

↗ Llyn Geirionydd.

← Eryri is a climber's paradise!

↓ There's plenty of enticing-looking bouldering opportunities, too.

Take an impressive rail journey...

Don't fancy the yomp up Yr Wyddfa? Then take the **Snowdon Mountain Railway** from Llanberis and save your legs. The trip isn't just about letting the train take the strain; the views on the way up are second to none, and the railway is a feat of engineering in itself. It is the only rack-and-pinion mountain railway open to the public in the UK, and the return journey takes two and a half hours. Some of the steam engines that push the carriages up the hill are more than 100 years old and have been in operation since the railway was opened in 1896. The trains run on a seasonal basis and you need to book in advance. Single fares are available on the way up but are on a first come, first served basis for the descent. So if you're climbing Yr Wyddfa, don't expect a lift down! www.snowdonrailway.co.uk

The **Ffestiniog and Welsh Highland Railway** is another seasonal heritage service offering an alternative way to visit iconic places in the Park – in real style. The Ffestiniog Railway is the world's oldest narrow-gauge railway, with almost 200 years of history. You can travel from Porthmadog to the slate-quarrying town of Blaenau Ffestiniog – that's 21.73km (13.5 miles). The Welsh Highland Railway is the UK's longest heritage railway and runs for 40km (25 miles) from Caernarfon, through some of the most varied landscapes in Wales – and on to Porthmadog. www.festrail.co.uk

Get high and rugged

With such a cragged landscape, there are plenty of opportunities to climb, particularly around Yr Wyddfa. **Clogwyn Du'r Arddu** (SH 597 556) is a cliff face visible from the Llanberis Path and is a climbers' paradise. It was called 'the best crag in the world' by internationally acclaimed climber Leo Houlding and has classic routes in almost every grade – most of them full on. Climbers will know the Indian Face and Master's Wall; there's a multitude of long and arduous routes.

Get an edge

Not a climber? Then, walk the knife-edge ridge of **Crib Goch** (SH 624 551). It is one of Britain's best ridge routes, rivalling that of Carn Mor Dearg arête in Scotland. It's exposed throughout and therefore not for the fainthearted, but it takes you away from the trade routes to the summit

↞ Stay at the Pen-y-Gwryd Hotel and hear the gong...

of Yr Wyddfa. The route starts at Pen-y-Pass and follows the Pyg track up onto the ridge. There's some tricky scrambling – nerves of steel are required. Going in good weather with someone who has done it before is vital.

Stay at the 'Everest' hotel

The **Pen-y-Gwryd Hotel** near Pen-y-Pass is an incredible cornucopia of mountain history coupled with unique hospitality and a perfect setting. Glyder Fawr is its backdrop, but inside is where the real scenery lies. It was built in 1810 as a farmhouse before being used as a coaching inn. It then became the HQ of the 1953 Everest climbing expedition, with members of the party plying their craft on the Yr Wyddfa range. The hotel has avoided modern trappings and is elegantly decorated, with comfortable rooms to stay in and several exhibits from the successful Everest climb. We could wax on ... it has a residents' room packed full of mountaineering nostalgia, and a gong announces dinner. Just incredible.
www.pyg.co.uk

CAR-FREE TRAVEL

➜ Peak season in Eryri adds pressure to a National Park that has limited infrastructure. Yr Wyddfa and Ogwen have significant footfall, and planning will help you have a good experience.
➜ The Park has an extensive bus network, with the Traws Cymru T10 stopping at Ogwen. www.traws.cymru/en
➜ The Sherpa'r Wyddfa is a fantastic way of reaching the trailhead of six routes to the summit of Yr Wyddfa. For the Llanberis Path, buses stop at Llanberis (S1 and S2); Pyg and Miners' Track – Pen-y-Pass bus stop (S1, S2, S4, S5); Snowdon Ranger Path – Snowdon Ranger YHA bus stop (S3); Rhyd Ddu Path – Rhyd Ddu bus stop (S3) and Watkin Path – Pont Bethania bus stop (S4). For information on the services and their starting points, visit www.eryri.gov.wales/visit/plan-your-visit/snowdon-sherpa/. Timetables can be found at www.sherparwyddfa.wales/times.shtml.
➜ For rail services, the Cambrian and Conwy Valley lines travel in and around the Park. In addition, the Ffestiniog and Welsh Highland Railway are steam train services that travel around the north-west area. www.traveline.cymru/
➜ The Snowdon Mountain Railway operates seasonally. www.snowdonrailway.co.uk

↑ The haunting Dre Newydd (Anglesey Barracks).

→ The National Slate Museum is set to reopen in 2026.

Try some delicacies

Available across Wales but seemingly more prominent in Eryri is **bara brith** – a tea-infused bread with dried fruit that you must slather with butter. **Welsh rarebit** is hot cheese with either ale or mustard on toast, while **Welsh cakes** – *picau ar y maen* (cakes on the stone) – are a simple sweet bread with dried fruit. The Popty Tandderwen Bakery in Betws-y-Coed is a great place to pick up these treats.

↓ Find yourself some friendly mountain goats!

Find the not-so-shy mountain goats!

There's a herd of wild mountain goats in and around **Coed Dinorwig** (SH 584 607) that hide in the woodlands and on the slate quarry itself. They are cheeky characters that are quite happy to see walkers intruding on their territory as they graze quite peacefully.

Find out more

The **National Slate Museum** in Llanberis is undergoing a £21 million renovation and is expected to reopen in 2026. Established in 1972, it is part of several Grade I listed buildings around the Dinorwig Slate Quarry.
www.museum.wales/slate/

CAREW CASTLE

PEMBROKESHIRE COAST

DESIGNATED: **29 February 1952**
SIZE: **621 sq km (240 sq miles)**, HIGHEST PEAK: **Foel Cwmcerwyn at 536m (1,759ft)**
ANNUAL VISITOR NUMBERS: **7.91 million (2024)**, POPULATION: **21,145 (2022)**
OFFICIAL WEBSITE: **www.pembrokeshirecoast.wales**

Pembrokeshire Coast National Park feels remote, a defining part of its charm. Cardiff, the Welsh capital, is two hours away, a journey of rolling green hills and endless skies that beckon you west. It boasts several islands, thriving with wildlife, and connected only by boat, manned by resolute sailors across blue seas. Its communities are the heartbeat, shaping the landscape over generations through agriculture and tourism, the lifeblood for so many.

Rural areas were the most significantly affected during the pandemic, and those in the UK's only coastal National Park felt it more than most. Gone were the tourists and seasonal bustle, and self-reliance came to the fore. When the Park

⬇ What a view of the coast!

← Pembrokeshire is full of heritage, like 11th-century Carew Castle.

→ It's not just coastline.

reopened, it was almost as if its hidden secrets – the surfing, birdlife, and the wide and long sandy beaches – had been uncovered. If ever there was a National Park that had to deliver its remit on access to nature and well-being, it was this one.

For Park Authority officials, it gave them a glimpse into the future, and of what could also be lost. James Parkin, Director of Nature and Tourism, said it was almost like stepping into a time machine; the lockdowns showed what could happen when nature is allowed breathing space. Then, reopening brought people, a boom to local businesses, and with them a sense of what the Authority had to do to ensure the Park balances the needs of everyone in the long term. It also has to act with the Wales Well-being of Future Generations Act in mind. This requires public bodies to think about the long-term impact of their decisions. As a coastal Park, Pembrokeshire will be directly affected by sea-level rise, and flooding will become more frequent. Decisions taken now will have an impact well into the future.

And that's important, because the Pembrokeshire Coast National Park is brilliantly unique. The Pembrokeshire Coast Path National Trail offers 299km (186 miles) of Coast Path and 100-plus beaches, while nowhere in the Park is more than 16km (10 miles) from the sea, with the Irish Sea to the north and west, and the Bristol Channel to the south. But if you travel a few miles inland, you can visit the wild moorland, grassland and heathland of the Preseli Hills, which

were saved from public closure in 1947 thanks to the diehard spirit of the local community who didn't want it to become a permanent military training ground. Then there are estuaries, confluences, marshland, bogs, woodland and a soon-to-be restored 59ha (146 acre) Celtic rainforest near Fishguard.

The hotspots of Tenby, St Davids and associated beaches will always be busy. Rightly so; they are thriving, bustling communities with enough to keep visitors occupied all day long. If you're looking for an archetypal Pembrokeshire beach holiday, then this is the place to go. But there's also enough room to spread your wings and be relatively alone while still supporting the Park's economy. Whitesands and Newgale get lots of love, yet you can have Broad Haven all to yourself depending on the time you visit, while the rocky nooks and crannies of the north are worth the extra effort along the Coast Path.

As I was told before I visited, 'It's a real effort to get here, it will take you a while, so you might as well enjoy *all* of it'.

Lifting a glass of Pembrokeshire Cider, let's drink to that.

↓ Views for miles from Foel Eryr in the Preseli.

THE CHAMPION

James Parkin
○○○

James Parkin is the Director of Nature and Tourism at Pembrokeshire Coast National Park Authority.

Pembrokeshire may not have the big mountains and lakes of other National Parks, but it packs a real punch. It has 50 publicly accessible beaches, 299km (186 miles) of Coast Path, and some of the best surfing spots in the world. It is also a densely populated National Park, and managing a transient population with local communities is a difficult balancing act.

" 'Ironically, I wasn't particularly looking to work in a National Park, but it was one of those serendipitous sorts of things where a few people told me the role had come up and that I would be suited to it. I'm from Sheffield but have been living in Wales since 1999. I came down here to work across the ex-Coalfield communities and then moved to the Countryside Council for Wales, which was about unlocking the health benefits of access to green spaces. That experience coalesced with the idea of the Park reaching out to new audiences, and I've now been here for more than 15 years.

My role is to look after the ecology of the Park and then try to open up access to that for as many people as possible, but obviously in a sensitive way. That's the love of the job for me; I'm trying to look after this precious thing for Wales and the UK, while also maximising its use. It's a tricky task balancing nature, local communities and tourism, but it's one I enjoy.'

James has lived in Wales for 25 years and says in that time he's noticed a lot of change, particularly with the climate and the number of visitors.

'Changes to those two things are accelerating,' he adds. 'I saw some change in the climate when I first came to Pembrokeshire, especially with the impact of sea-level rise on cliff erosion, but that is now more frequent, and we have more flooding. In terms of tourism, before the pandemic, it felt like Pembrokeshire was a bit of a secret. Now, the word is out and there are more people. It's great because that's why we are here, for people to access this place, but it's put more pressure on the environment and our communities. It takes a lot more balancing than it did historically.

I think the pandemic was like time travel. When everything shut down, it was like looking into the past, when we didn't have as many visitors and there was more space for nature to breathe. When the restrictions were lifted, we had far more visitors than ever – it was like looking into the future. At the time, I was wondering whether that was the future we wanted or could even plan for, but it did give us an idea of how we needed to consistently manage the Park for nature and local communities.'

Sustainable tourism is something all National Parks are focusing on, and

James wants Pembrokeshire to be at the forefront, especially in the face of those two challenges.

'Everybody can imagine what a beach day is like in Pembrokeshire,' he says. 'It's the pinnacle of that sort of experience, I would argue, in the whole of the UK. Sadly, I feel that some visitors only engage with that at a relatively superficial level, and of course, there's nothing wrong with that, but what we want to create is a real sense of connection to the place, as well as the language and culture. This means they will have a better holiday, feel a sense of belonging and leave with a greater sense of wanting to look after it. It also means there'll be a better balance between tourism, and making communities work for local people.

It means we need to focus on regenerative tourism and design experiences that help people leave this Park in a better place than when they arrived. That is such a fundamental shift in thinking, and we're only just starting on that journey, but we're committed to it. Could we get to a point where a visit to Pembrokeshire could at least be carbon neutral, if not carbon positive? Could the environment be enhanced through a visit rather than us just trying to patch up the damage? Such a visit could also see local communities improved, and support more understanding of the real Pembrokeshire and its cultural and natural heritage.

It's hard to find the exact solution or way forward, but we know it has to be the answer. I think we'll know whether we've got that approach right when people understand the full impact and value of their trip and how visiting here is much more than just spending money. It's about how this place is enriched and conserved.'

James' thoughts link directly to the National Park principles of conserving and enhancing the natural beauty, wildlife and cultural heritage, and promoting opportunities for public understanding and enjoyment of the special qualities, of these spaces.

He continues: 'With regenerative tourism, you are triple accounting, so it isn't just about the financial bottom line. You have to monitor the environmental, social and economic impacts. It's almost like we're putting the environmental and social measures back into that equation because, as a society, we've been going away from that. If tourism is just about the finances, then it's a race to the bottom because you're constantly diluting the culture or damaging the environment. I think all of us have become aware of what sustainability really means, and having our health threatened by a pandemic brought that front and centre. I think New Zealand has the best tourism strategy in the world because it starts with the need to look after nature, reduce carbon and support culture. The economic impact is third or fourth in that narrative.

When you look at Wales and our Well-being of Future Generations Act, which requires public bodies here to think about the long-term impact of decisions, then this approach is vital. It probably differentiates us from some of the other nations because we're trying to take that long view and measure those impacts for future generations. National Parks are perfectly placed to do this, and we want Pembrokeshire to be at the forefront.'

James' favourite thing to do in Pembrokeshire: 'There are 50 publicly accessible beaches in the Park, but if you can kayak or get along the coast, then you could visit more than 100. But I got engaged at St Justinian's, so that place will always have a special affinity for me.'

FACTS AND QUIRKS

Legendary landmarks

Near the southernmost tip of the National Park is **Huntsman's Leap**. This natural chasm is a popular spot for climbers, and legend says it is named after a chased huntsman. In a stricken panic, he leapt across the gap on his horse but then died of shock when he looked back and saw what he'd done.

Just a few hundred metres along the coast is **St Govan's Chapel**. This is said to be the hiding place of St Govan, a Celtic missionary who was pursued by pirates. As he ran along the coast a cleft in a rock opened up for him to hide in. Once inside, it closed, protecting him from his chasers, and he stayed there to worship and teach until he died in 586. There are rib-like markings in the rock, too ... the imprints of St Govan's body?

Adam de Rupe built the 12th-century **Roch Castle** after a witch's prophecy. She told him he would die within a year from a snake bite, but if he avoided one, he would live a long and healthy life. He thought a castle would protect him from such a fate – and he lived in the highest room. But, during winter, he needed to stay warm and had some wood brought up to him to make a fire. Sadly, a snake was lurking, and he was duly bitten. Poor man.

Fishguard repels borders

The last foreign invasion of Britain wasn't in 1066, but 700 years later, when French soldiers landed in **Fishguard**. In 1797, Napoleon hatched a plan to send troops to destroy Bristol before heading north. Having duly set sail, the weather beat them back, so they decided to aim for South Wales instead. On 22 February, they entered Fishguard Bay but were met by cannon fire. Assuming they were under attack – it was a warning for the town rather than returned fire – they retreated and eventually landed in Llanwnda, just a few kilometres away.

After unloading supplies and gunpowder, the plan was good to go. However, it seems that the soldiers were more interested in the local food and wine instead. They got drunk, and would eventually surrender to a local militia led by Lord Cawdor three days later. Local woman Jemma Nicolas would go down in history, as when she heard of the landing, she went to Llanwnda and rounded up 12 Frenchmen.

Ancient stones

In the Preseli Hills is the Neolithic circle of standing stones known as **Bedd Arthur ('Arthur's Grave')**, which folklore suggests is the final resting place of King Arthur. The burial chamber of Pentre Ifan is said to have been inhabited by fairies. Those who have seen them say they 'resemble little children in clothes like soldiers' clothes and with red caps'.

The **Devil's Quoit**, also known as Stackpole Warren Stone or Harold's Stone after the last Saxon king of England, Harold Godwinson, is a Scheduled Monument erected around 1400 BC and standing at 1.7m (5.5ft) tall. It is one of the Dancing Stones of Stackpole that are said to meet at Saxon's Ford, where they dance to a tune played by the Devil on his flute.

WALK 1

Strumble Head

◇◇◇

A magnificent wildlife-filled circular.

This circular route takes you along the Pembrokeshire Coast Path National Trail, with views over epic cliff edges and blue seas, to Strumble Head. Starting from the car park, an easy climb will take you to the 213m (699ft) Garn Fawr, an excellent viewpoint and preserved hillfort, before heading west to the Coast Path.

Pembrokeshire is well known for its wildlife, and you may see porpoise and bottlenose dolphins along the route, and you're *almost* guaranteed to see grey seals near the cliffs and at Strumble Head itself. The walk never gets too navigationally tasking, although when you reach Penrhyn Cottage, you need to head east to follow the right path.

Finally, on the return journey, you'll spot Welsh mountain ponies grazing the land before you arrive back at the car park. Here, the Garn Fechan hillfort is on the opposite side, and a short path leads to it – more than worth the extra few minutes on your walk.

For everything Pembrokeshire Coast has to offer, this is a complete introduction: wildlife, dramatic cliffs, lighthouses, farming and history all rolled into one.

START/END:
Garn Fawr, SA64 0LT
DISTANCE: 11km
(6.8 miles)
GRADE: Moderate

⬇ The lighthouse.

WALK 2

Lawrenny

◯◯◯

It's not all coastline in Pembrokeshire!

Finding a walk in Pembrokeshire isn't difficult, but why stick to the coast all the time? The Park has inlets, estuaries and woodland just waiting to be explored.

This walk begins at Lawrenny Quay, near the confluence of the Carew and

START/END: Lawrenny Quay, SA68 0PR
DISTANCE: 4.4km (2.7 miles)
GRADE: Easy

⬆ Lawrenny Quay.

⬅ Former fence line at Garron Pill.

Cresswell rivers and the Daugleddau, and returns via the village and its 12th-century church. Parking sensibly by the quay, follow a permissive path into Lawrenny Woods, a hauntingly beautiful ancient woodland filled with sessile oak and holly. It's a special place, away from the crowds and filled with birds.

Eventually, it opens out to Garron Pill, a peaceful foreshore off the Daugleddau that is packed with birds and, on occasion, the rare western marsh harrier. This route can be affected by high tides and is inaccessible during a 7m (23ft) tide. The walk then follows the road back to the village and the Norman church before arriving back at the Quay. Finish off with a visit to the Quayside Tearoom here; you won't be disappointed!

↑ Garron Pill is pretty special.

Why not try these great walks...

HAROLDSTON WOODS: From the car park in Broad Haven, a 5.12km (3.2 mile) circular takes you to a 19th-century woodland that was planted for hunting and timber.

PEMBROKESHIRE COAST PATH NATIONAL TRAIL: The big one! At 299km (186 miles) long, it can be broken into sections. Highlights include Strumble Head, Newgale and Den's Door.

NEWPORT PARROG: A short 1.1km (0.7-mile) purpose-built wheelchair path along the Afon Nyfer to Iron Bridge.

Key Places

The rider...
Accommodation in Pembrokeshire is varied and ranges from B&Bs, hotels and guesthouses, to bunkhouses and three youth hostels. The main populated areas of Tenby and St Davids are a little more expensive but there are also plenty of caravan and camping sites nearby. Haverfordwest is outside the Park's boundaries but is an excellent base to explore the north and south.
www.visitpembrokeshire.com/holiday-accommodation

Places to visit

Broad Haven A seaside village on the B4341 from Haverfordwest. Has great views over St Brides Bay and, like most of the Park's beaches, is ideal for surfing and other watersports. Local bars and cafés offer traditional food, while, as well as being on the Coast Path, there are walks through Haroldston Woods and around the village. Slash Pond is a community-run wetland area, formed by old opencast workings.

← Lower Fishguard is a bustling harbour.

↓ Broad Haven is a beautiful beach and less busy than others.

→ Solva Harbour.

Fishguard Has a transient feel due to a busy harbour with ferries to Rosslare in Ireland. The first settlement in the area was at the mouth of the River Gwaun, which gave the town its Abergwaun name. It was a shipbuilding hub, with the last ship – the *Gwain Maid* – built in 1846. The Royal Oak still houses the table on which a peace treaty with France was signed in 1797 following the last attempted invasion of Britain by a foreign power.

St Davids A bustling destination that has an impressive 12th-century cathedral, which makes it Britain's smallest city. Oriel y Parc is the National Park Discovery Centre, hosting a world-class art gallery, featuring artefacts from Amgueddfa Cymru (the National Museum of Wales). As well as shops, cafés and restaurants (busy in peak season), you can visit the islands of Ramsey, Skomer and others to see puffins and other wildlife.

Tenby Known as Dinbych-y-Pysgod (Little Fortress of the Fish), this is the archetypal Pembrokeshire coastal town. Has four distinctly different beaches: North, South, Harbour and Castle. A 20-minute boat trip takes you to Caldey Island, which is owned and run by a community of Cistercian monks. There's also a museum and art gallery, a ghost walk and a treasure hunt for kids!

Saundersfoot North of Tenby, this is a beautiful village on the B4316. Quieter than its neighbours with a wide sandy beach.

Why not try...

Pembroke Busy historic town in the south of the county. You'll find a castle, The Pembrokeshire Cider Co. microbrewery, whose bottle shop is in an ironmongers, and fantastic hostelries.

Newgale A large white beach on St Brides Bay. Ideal for swimming, surfing and getting away from more popular beaches.

Solva Off the A487, this small village is split into upper and lower Solva. Can get packed, particularly in the summer, but the walk along the Gribin headland offers expansive views.

Must Sees

St Govan's Chapel ❶ ❷ ❸
(SR 996 929) served as the hiding place for St Govan after he evaded capture by pirates. The chapel dates back to the 13th century, but it's likely been a site of worship since the 6th century. It's a tranquil place overlooking the Bristol Channel and was once thought to contain a healing well that cured eye complaints, skin diseases and rheumatism! There's also a bell-shaped rock outside, which was entombed and returned to St Govan by angels after it was stolen by pirates. When St Govan tapped, he found it made a noise a thousand times stronger than the original silver bell.

Carew Castle and Tidal Mill ❹ (SA70 8SL) is a stunning 11th-century castle set near its own causeway. Usually, castles are a set of ruins ❺ with several interpretation panels, but Carew aims to offer a different experience. It has interactive exhibits, an audio tour and the chance to find out what life was like when it was built. The North West Tower is said to be haunted by the ghost of an ape. Apparently, it killed a 17th-century tenant, Sir Roland Rhys, who kept it as a pet! The café is second to none, while a walk to the Tidal Mill and through the meadow ends a perfect trip. The site is managed by the Park Authority.
www.pembrokeshirecoast.wales/carew-castle/

Cilgerran Castle (SA43 2SF) is another fine example of a well-preserved 13th-century fortress. It overlooks Teifi Gorge and is open all year round. www.nationaltrust.org.uk/visit/wales/cilgerran-castle

Stackpole Walled Gardens (SA71 5DJ) are on the Stackpole Estate near Pembroke. They were created in 1770 by Sir John Campbell and were used to produce plants and food for the estate. The gardens, which are open daily from 11am–3.30pm, still hold that original purpose and are run by local charity, Pembrokeshire Mencap.

Pentre Ifan burial chamber ❻ (SN 099 370) is the remarkable remains of a Neolithic tomb. The chambered burial site would have originally been covered in earth and features a 5m (16.4ft) capstone. Another 4.6km (2.8 miles) away is the **Carreg Coetan Arthur Chambered Tomb** (SN 060 393). King Arthur is supposed to have played quoits with the stone of the tomb. This site is only accessible by foot.

❸

Dyffryn Fernant ❶ (SA65 9SP) is a beautifully curated garden near Fishguard ❷, a 2.43ha (6 acre) festival of colour created from literally nothing. Christina Shand started the project in 1996 with the idea of cultivating a front and kitchen garden. There was hardly any topsoil, lots of rock, marsh, bog and thick blue clay – hardly conducive to the wonderful garden at the site today. You can visit – the entrance fee is reasonable – from 12 noon to 5pm, April to October. There is also a cottage set within the garden ❸, which is available to stay in. www.dyffrynfernant.co.uk

St Davids Cathedral ❹ ❺ (SA62 6RD) sits on a former 6th-century monastery built by St David, the patron saint of Wales. The present cathedral was built between 1180 and 1182, and 'it has survived both the collapse of its tower and an earthquake in the 13th century, although today the floor slopes noticeably, the arcades veer from the vertical, and the east and west ends of the building differ in height by about 4m (13ft)!' It has been extended several times but retains its original charm and purpose. www.stdavidscathedral.org.uk

Strumble Head (SM 894 411) is the perfect spot for wildlife watching. Seals, porpoises and dolphins have been seen here, as well as the odd shark!

Green Bridge of Wales ❻ (SR 924 944) is an awe-inspiring 24m (80ft) natural arch. It's located on the Castlemartin Range, used as a military training area, and therefore access can be restricted. The nearby Elegug Stacks – two pillars of limestone detached from the cliffs – are special.

6

↑ A pair of puffins against the green coastal backdrop of Skomer Island.

Must Dos

Go wildlife spotting

There is no better place in the UK to see seabirds and other wildlife than Pembrokeshire.

The only boat trip to Skomer Island and the famous puffin colony sails from **Martin's Haven** (SA62 3BJ). Tickets must be booked in advance and are run by Pembrokeshire Islands Boat Trips (www.pembrokeshire-islands.co.uk). Skomer is home to Britain's largest undisturbed Iron Age settlement and contains hut circles, cemeteries and field systems. The 'Wildgoose Race', a particularly turbulent tidal whirlpool, forms west of the island.

Puffins, choughs and peregrines can also be seen on **Ramsey Island** via boat from the St Davids peninsula (www.ramseyisland.com/landing-on-ramsey-island), while most of the Park's coastline offers the chance to see grey seals.

Stackpole Quay (SA71 5LS) is the place to snorkel and see spider crabs, while the causeway near **Carew Castle and Tidal Mill** (SA70 8SL) is one of the best spots for crab catching, particularly around high tide.

At **Cenarth Falls** (SA38 9JL), a series of small waterfalls and pools on the River Teifi, you can watch salmon returning to their spawning fields. There are also otters at **Bosherston Lily Ponds** (SA71 5DH) on the Stackpole Estate. The **Welsh Wildlife Centre at Cilgerran** (SA43 2TB)

↓ Wildlife along the Coast Path.

and nearby **Teifi Marshes Nature Reserve** are home to kingfisher, otter and wading birds.

And finally, on the **Preseli Hills**, there are wild ponies!

It's not just coast

Foel Eryr (SN 065 320), at 468m (1,535ft), is in the heart of the Preselau and easily walkable from the layby on the B4329 (SN 075 321). **Foel Cwmcerwyn** (SN 093 311) is taller at 536m (1,759ft), but views at Foel Eryr to the coast win out! You'll also find what is thought to be a Bronze Age burial cairn at the summit. These hills wouldn't be accessible to walkers if it wasn't for the local community. In November 1946, the War Office put forward a proposal to make the Preselau a permanent military training area, a move that would have seen 200 farmers evicted from their homes and the area closed to the public. A campaign led by local ministers and headteachers forced them to drop the plan two years later.

Find geological marvels

As well as the Green Bridge of Wales, the Pembrokeshire Coast is punctuated with caves, rock stacks and natural arches. **Sleek Stone** (SM 859 144) is a cigar-shaped rock near Broadhaven, with **Den's Door** (SM 859 143) – a stack pierced by two arches – nearby. **Witches Cauldron** (SN 102 450) is a collapsed cave that can be accessed along the Pembrokeshire Coast Path National Trail – or even better by sea kayak to witness its full wonder.

Confucius Hole (SR 983 943) is a small cave near Trefalen and is very popular with adventurous sea climbers. There are also small caves and coves at **Aber Bach** (SM 996 386).

↓ The scenic view of Foel Cwmcerwyn.

← Ancient woodland in Lawrenny.

↓ The view from Foel Eryr.

This way to the beach

With 50 accessible public beaches and twice as many if you jump in a kayak, finding a busy one is just sheer bad luck or bad planning! Pembrokeshire is a hub for diving, paddleboarding, coasteering, fishing, sailing, kite surfing and powerboating.

Freshwater West (SM 881 001) is one such premier surfing and windsurfing spot, as is **Broad Haven** (SM 859 137), **Manorbier Bay** (SS 059 974), **Newgale** (SM 848 216), **Whitesands** (SM 731 261) and **Manorbier Bay** (SS 059 974). More cragged cliff-like coastlines can be found in the north, offering dramatic views and rock pools closer to the shore.

The coast is best seen via the **Pembrokeshire Coast Path National Trail**, which starts at St Dogmaels in the north and runs to Amroth in the south. It's 299km (186 miles) long and is usually split up into 15 sections by hikers taking on the whole route.

Wanderlust

Speaking of epic walks, the **Landsker Borderlands Trail** (93.8km/58.3 miles) follows the Landsker Line, which was said to be the boundary of the west-speaking north of the Park and the south.

Canaston Wood (SN 078 138) and **Lawrenny** (SN 010 067) offer ancient woodlands and a chance to avoid the busy beaches, and soon the **Gwaun Valley**, which runs from lower Fishguard to the Preseli Hills, will return to its rainforest origin when it is restored by the Wildlife Trust of South and West Wales.

CAR-FREE TRAVEL

→ Buses operate through the Park, usually seven days a week during the summer months. Coastal Buses run along the Pembrokeshire Coast and are a vital backup for the Pembrokeshire Coast Path National Trail.

→ In the peak season, the Coastal Cruiser (#387/#388) covers the Angle Peninsula, while the #400 Puffin Shuttle runs between St Davids and Marloes. The #403 Celtic Coaster travels along the St Davids Peninsula, the 404 Strumble Shuttle operates between Fishguard and St Davids, and the Tenby Coaster runs between Tenby and Saundersfoot. www.pembrokeshire.gov.uk/bus-routes-and-timetables/bus-routes-list-coastal-buses

→ Fflecsi Pembrokeshire is an on-demand transport service operating in north-west and south-west Pembrokeshire. It runs within a set zone and is available anytime between 7.30am and 6.30pm (Mon–Sat). You can book via the Fflecsi App or by 0300 234 0300 (Mon–Sat: 7am–7pm and Sun: 9am–6pm). www.tfw.wales/fflecsi/locations/pembrokeshire and www.traveline.cymru

→ St Justinian is a departure point for boat trips to Ramsey Island and the more offshore islands, while you can access Skomer through pre-booked tickets only from Martin's Haven.

→ Train services link the towns to the coast, particularly in the south. www.tfw.wales/service-status/timetables

Apples and cheeses

The usually closed **heritage orchard at St Brides** opens each September for an Apples and Ancient Orchards celebration. Events include children's craft activities, apple pressing, a self-guided history tour and an apple trail.

You can also call in at **Pant Mawr Farmhouse Cheeses** (SA66 7QU) in the Preseli Hills, who offer traditional cheese from local milk sources. Samples are available, and the farm shop is fantastic! www.pantmawrcheeses.co.uk

Night skies

Like its siblings in Eryri and Bannau Brycheiniog, Pembrokeshire has its own **Dark Sky Discovery Sites**, the nationally recognised designation for stargazing spots. The best sites can be found at **Broad Haven South** (SR 975 937), **Garn Fawr** (SM 899 388), **Kete** (SM 803 042), **Martin's Haven** (SM 761 089), **Newgale** (SM 850 217), **Poppit Sands** (SN 152 485), **Skrinkle Haven** (SS 083 975) and **Sychpant picnic site.** (SN 045 349). www.pembrokeshirecoast.wales/things-to-do/outdoor-activities/dark-skies/

✦ Sand yachting at Newgale.

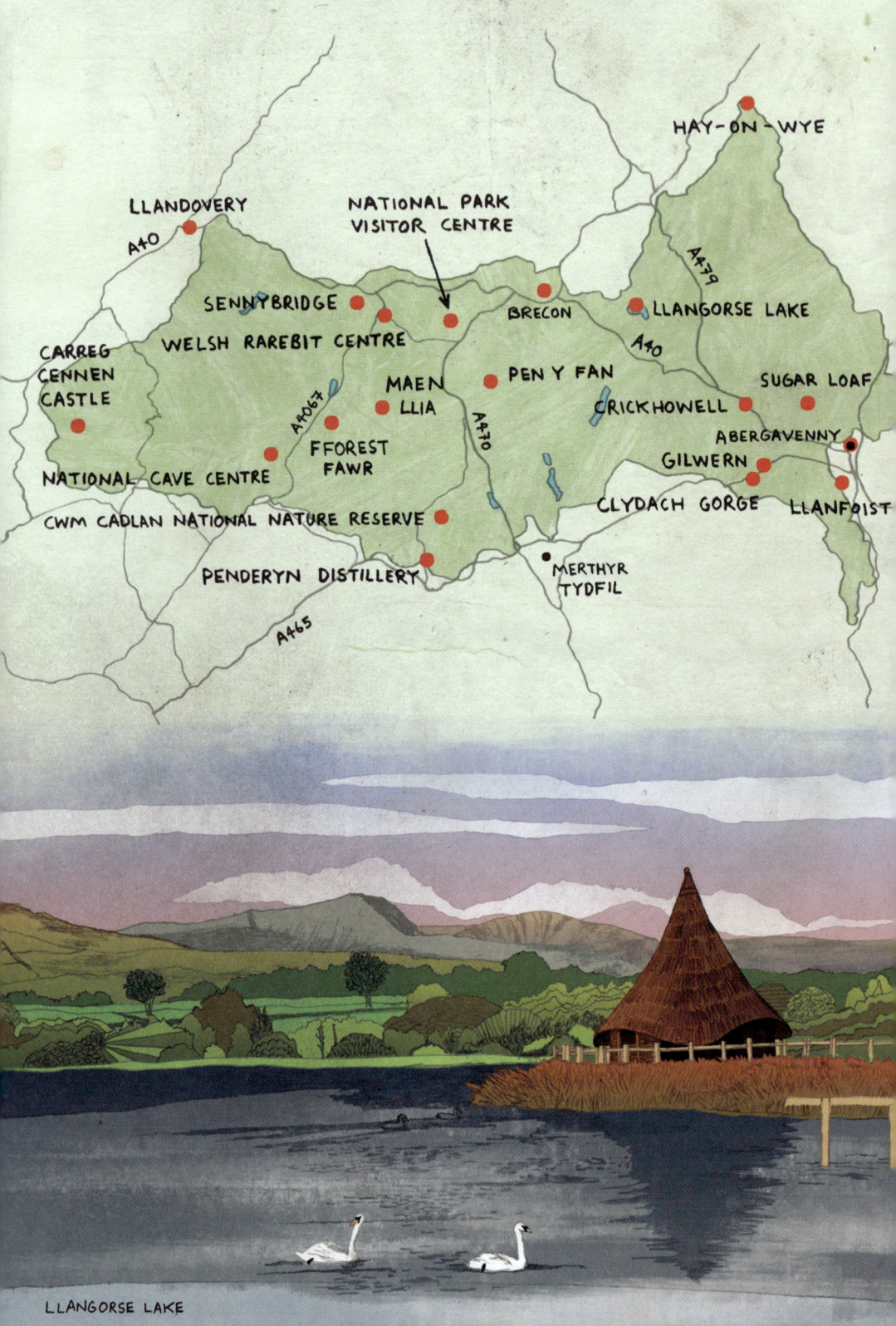

BANNAU BRYCHEINIOG

DESIGNATED: **17 April 1957**
SIZE: **1,344 sq km (519 sq miles)**, HIGHEST PEAK: **Pen y Fan at 886m (2,907ft)**
ANNUAL VISITOR NUMBERS: **4.15 million (2020)**, POPULATION: **33,000**
OFFICIAL WEBSITE: **www.bannaubrycheiniog.org**

The sun was coming up, illuminating the dew on the ground, and I was first serenaded by a wren, its cheerful chirps plucking me from the willowy tiredness before a meadow pipit stopped to say hello. I spent a good hour watching the day awake before begrudgingly deciding to open my map and make my way back to the road. I chose the long way.

Bannau Brycheiniog (Brecon Beacons) National Park brings up all sorts of surprises, and the 629m (2,063ft) climb up Craig Cerrig Gleisiad from YHA Brecon Beacons was one of them. I'd found it by chance: a restless night coupled with a far too active mind forcing me to leave a comfortable bed in search of some

⬇ The mainline railway below Sugar Loaf mountain in the Black Mountains.

solace in the dead of night. Wandering up the side of the A470, I crossed over after noticing a signposted path that led through a small woodland. Donning a head torch and watching my breath mist up in front of me, I half walked, half stumbled into the early morning. The path gradually opened up and came to the relatively steep climb up on to Craig Cerrig Gleisiad. Adrenaline kicked in, and it wasn't long before I was at the top, pausing to see where I had come from.

Many people heading to Bannau Brycheiniog go to Hay-on-Wye for the book festival, tramp up Pen y Fan and gaggle with the crowds in Waterfall Country. These places are honeypots because they are must-visits. No trip to Bannau Brycheiniog could be complete without at least trying a couple of them. But the Park offers so much more, particularly in the west. It has mountains, moorland, woods, meadows, lakes, rivers and a rich industrial heritage. It's also intrinsically a historical place, with castles, archaeological remains, folklore and legend heading back generations.

And it's that sense of ancient togetherness and a connection to the land that saw the Park follow Eryri in reclaiming its Welsh name. In April 2023,

↑ Bannau Brycheiniog has four distinct areas, all of them breathtaking.

↓ Follow the path.

it decided to refer to itself as Bannau Brycheiniog – or informally as 'Y Bannau'. The name is derived from the plural of 'ban', meaning 'peak' while 'Brycheiniog' refers to the old kingdom of King Brychan. Translated, it means 'The Peaks of Brychan's Kingdom'.

A statement said: 'With the central Beacons mountain range covering a small proportion of the Park's geography, and history showing no evidence that burning beacons ever existed on the Park's summits, it was felt the area warranted a title more in keeping with its Welsh heritage.'

Once again, like Eryri, the change caused some consternation among the public, most notably the then prime minister Rishi Sunak saying he would stick with the English name. The leader of the Conservatives in the Senedd, Andrew RT Davies, also said the name change 'undermined an already well-known tourist destination'.

The Eryri name-change arguments probably do not need to be repeated here. We all know change can be a positive thing, as is trying different things, going off that beaten track and turning right on to a path with your head torch when the obvious thing to do would be to turn 180 degrees and head somewhere you know.

So, instead of heading to those well-visited sites across Bannau Brycheiniog, take the plunge and try something new. You won't regret it.

↑ Looking out to Blorenge from Abergavenny.
↓ Dramatic escarpments in Bannau Brycheiniog.

> THE CHAMPION

Alan Bowring
ooo

Alan Bowring is the Geopark officer at Fforest Fawr, a UNESCO Global Geopark.

Anyone visiting Bannau Brycheiniog will notice the array of landscapes it has to offer. In roughly its centre is the Fforest Fawr massif that gives its name to a rather larger UNESCO Global Geopark, which stretches from Llandovery in the north to Merthyr Tydfil in the south and from Llandeilo in the west to Brecon in the east. It's a 763 sq km (300 sq miles) mosaic of different landscapes, each with its own challenges

‘I grew up in Cheshire on the New Red Sandstone,’ Alan says. ‘I always had a real interest in geology and a real love affair both with the Torridonian of north-west Scotland, which is another Geopark, and the limestone and grit of the Pennines. When I was a geology student at Leeds, I was a member of the university caving club and would often be underground enjoying the geology. I've been at Fforest Fawr since 2007, after working as a rights-of-way officer in Cheshire and doing various countryside management roles across Staffordshire and Derbyshire. I wasn't taken on as a geologist, although at heart I am, but as a tourism officer in the tourism section to boost the Geopark, which had been set up a couple of years earlier in 2005. I helped it become a Global Geopark in 2015.’

According to UNESCO, Global Geoparks (UGGps) are ‘single, unified geographical areas where sites and landscapes of international geological significance are managed with a holistic concept of protection, education and sustainable development. At present, there are over 200 UNESCO Global Geoparks in more than 50 countries.’

Fforest Fawr's landscape, and the way people have interacted with it over centuries, make it the ideal Geopark. There are mountains and moorland, woods and meadows, towns and villages, lakes and rivers – alongside the heritage of a land that has been worked and is archaeologically deep.

Alan continues: ‘When I joined, we were "just" a Geopark, but when we became a Global Geopark under UNESCO's wing ten years ago, suddenly we were part of a significant worldwide family of special places. My role was to originally boost tourism numbers – call it sustainable tourism if you like – but it is now more about managing people and the impact they can have. We try to direct people to other places where there are great stories and a fantastic landscape or encourage them to come midweek in November rather than bank holiday weekend in the summer. This means working with all our partners and stakeholders.’

Alan is the go-to when it comes to geology in Bannau Brycheiniog, and he's regularly running guided walks to help better people's understanding. He's also acquainted himself with each square kilometre of the Park, documenting some of it through the popular website Geograph, and that's helped him amass a real depth of knowledge, as well as an understanding of the issues, across the entire Park.

'We have differing pressures here,' he continues. 'Waterfall Country is a huge draw for people as it's spectacular, but the infrastructure doesn't support the numbers that want to visit. It can be tough for the communities there, so for that reason, we don't promote it as a destination. We do, however, try to influence people's behaviour through social media and have had some measure of success. Sadly, it doesn't always get through, and we've had life-changing injuries around the falls and some fatalities, too. It's hard to manage as you don't want to put signs up everywhere, but we do produce literature and have installed numbered posts to show people where they are. That said, we're lucky that we don't have the pressures of other Parks in terms of being on the National Three Peaks circuit, for example.'

A key role of the Geopark, as well as Bannau Brycheiniog as a whole, is to address a variety of important environmental issues identified by the Welsh Government and others. The Geopark ties into the National Park's management plan, with key outcomes around matters of climate change, biodiversity loss, social and economic inequality, and sustainability for future generations. As Alan says, it's a big challenge, but something National Parks were set up to tackle.

'One thing that could help is the expansion of the Geopark,' he says. 'We have regular inspections by our peers to ensure our UNESCO status remains and are given recommendations. One we have been working on is expanding the Geopark beyond the National Park boundaries into the coalfield fringe communities. This would mean that those communities could enjoy some of the benefits of Geopark status, and at the same time, we wouldn't be drawing more people into the National Park.

Some of those communities have infrastructure in place, and we could divert visitors from areas that are overcrowded into these special places within the Coalfield fringe that have fantastic stories to be told. There are great opportunities for adrenaline sports, too, such as zip lines and mountain biking. This brings opportunities to put the visitor pound into the local economy, and we can do that without impinging on the qualities of the National Park and what it was established to do. That's something we're actively exploring in this Park; openly looking at ways to help those communities outside of our boundaries.'

Alan's favourite thing to do in Bannau Brycheiniog: 'The places I like to go are those where the fourth dimension – that of time – strongly asserts its presence. These are typically places with a rich geological history, and so often, the seemingly ongoing presence of our ancestors is evident in archaeological features. I'd suggest that Cribarth is one such extraordinary place. Though of humble stature, this ridge of limestone and gritstone rising above the upper Swansea Valley was thrown into commotion not once but twice; first by tectonic forces 300 million years ago and then again as the Industrial Revolution took hold 250 years ago. What results is a landscape in which natural crags and 19th-century quarries reveal intensely faulted and folded rocks, with miles of tramroad offering easier walking – the past colliding spectacularly with the present. The essence of a Geopark set in the splendour of a National Park.'

FACTS AND QUIRKS

Old trees

The **yew in St Cynog's churchyard**, Defynnog, could be the UK's oldest tree. It's said to be between 2,000 and 3,000 years old, maybe older, and rivals the Fortingall yew in Perthshire. However, some believe that tree could be a staggering 5,000 years old, leaving the Bannau Brycheiniog yew with some catching up to do. Yews only become 'ancient' when they reach 900 years old; in comparison, you'd expect an ash tree to gain that status at 200 and an oak at 400.

Legends, ghosts and goblins

Maen Llia is a huge Bronze Age monolith with a legend surrounding it that whenever a cock crows, the stone moves off to drink in the River Nedd. Other stories say it goes down to the local stream (Afon Llia) to drink at midsummer sunset.

Not connected with the Arthurian legend is the **Lady of Llyn y Fan Fach**. A young farmer was gazing into the clear waters of the lake and saw a beautiful woman, the likes of whom he had never seen before, walking towards him. He instantly fell in love, as is usual for these tales, and she offered him the chance of an amazing future if they married. He agreed, but there were a series of conditions – a prenup of sorts. The first was that he wouldn't strike her three times and that he should never reveal where she came from. All was going swimmingly until, hoisted by his own wealth and good fortune, the man became arrogant and angry. Wealth bred contempt. Eventually, he would strike his wife three times, and she duly returned to the lake, taking all his livestock with her. Another version of this tale involves him tapping her on the shoulder but still falling foul of the rules.

The Skirrid Inn in Llanvihangel Crucorney is more than 900 years old and, as such, it is mandatory for it to be haunted. They host ghost hunts throughout the year!

John o'Kent (also known as Jack) is a mysterious sorcerer from the Welsh borders. His legend dates back to the early 16th century. He tricks the Devil in games, having sold his soul to him as a young boy to gain amazing powers. Like similar tales across the country, he helped to build a bridge over the Monnow with the rule that the Devil could have the first soul that went across it. Of course, this happened to be a dog who Jack threw a bone to.

As well as being an enchanting place, **Clydach Gorge** is said to have inspired William Shakespeare to write *A Midsummer Night's Dream*. Locals talk about it being full of ghostly happenings, while a *Pwca*, a goblin, lived there.

Mynydd Epynt

Just outside the National Park's boundary, a community was evicted from **Mynydd Epynt** in 1940 to create a training area for the military. Around 200 people were relocated, something said to have had a profound effect on the Welsh language because these people were moved into predominantly English-speaking areas.

The Sennybridge Training Area is still the largest military training area in the country.

WALK 1

Pen y Fan
◯◯◯

A simple but enjoyable meander to the highest point in Bannau Brycheiniog.

This busy walk is a must do in Bannau Brycheiniog, particularly when the air is fresh during sunrise or sunset. As such, it is rarely people-free, but there are enough routes off the main drag to the top – and back down – to enjoy everything this hill has to offer. Start early, off-season, and you can have it to yourself.

Completing the walk 'in reverse', up the Cambrian Way from the Storey Arms Centre, is another great way of avoiding the crowds, although it is a little more taxing on the legs straight off.

For this route, the classic anticlockwise way, leave the newly renovated car park at Pont ar Daf (there's currently a £7.50 charge for non-National Trust members) and take the obvious path up the hill, enjoying the views behind you all the way. Several routes converge shy of the 873m (2,864ft) peak of Corn Du, and the spectacular ridges behind you.

From Corn Du, follow the path to Pen y Fan and then retrace your steps to Corn Du, and turn right along the Craig Cwm Llwch to the Obelisk, which marks the spot where the body of five-year-old Tommy Jones was found. He lost his way between Cwm Llwch Farm and the Login on the night of 4 August 1900.

Most people will return the way they came, so this route is relatively calm, if a little painful on the knees, and gives you the chance to see down the valley. You could come back via Y Gyrn if you wanted a different route away from the Cambrian Way.

START/END:
Pont ar Daf, LD3 8NL
DISTANCE: 8km (5 miles)
GRADE: Moderate

⬆ The walk starts at Pont ar Daf and steadily climbs.

Bannau Brycheiniog | 237

When at the bottom, turn left and chart your way through the woods, back to your car, or bus.

While this route is relatively simple in good weather, the route from Corn Du to Pen y Fan is pretty foul in poor conditions, and there are, sadly, several opportunities to lose your way, which isn't favourable when there are ridges all around these summits.

The woods at Pont ar Daf – just a few more steps to go!

WALK 2

Along the Govilon Line

○○○

A pleasant accessible-to-all route between Llanfoist and Govilon.

START: **Llanfoist Crossing Car Park, NP7 9LP**
END: **Former Govilon Station, NP7 9RG**
DISTANCE: **2.4km (1.5 miles)**
GRADE: **Easy**

This accessible walk connects two canalside villages along the Govilon Line, a former railway that runs below The Blorenge's verdant wooded slopes. It starts just south of Abergavenny and can be taken all year round.

The route meanders through cuttings and embankments and has indicators of its heritage past, including mileposts, gradient signs and lineside buildings such as the old Govilon Station. There are also great views of the woodlands around Llanfoist.

➤ Narrowboats on the Monmouthshire and Brecon Canal in Govilon.

Why not try these great walks...

FAN Y BIG: There are several ways up this 719m (2,359ft) hill, which is part of the Beacons Horseshoe Hike. Our favourite is the 12km (7.5 mile) circular from Blaen-y-Glyn, with its waterfalls and stunning ridge views.

SUGAR LOAF: A fine 596m (1,955ft) hill in the Black Mountains, which can be walked there and back on the Cambrian Way from the centre of Abergavenny. It's just over 10km (6.2 miles) long and passes through Deri Fach woods.

PENDERYN MINERAL LINE: A 2.7km (1.68 mile) one-way route, which starts just up the road from the distillery. It follows the old tramway between Penderyn and Hirwaun, and you can download a free Hirwaun Audio Trail to help you on your way!

Key Places

The rider...
Bannau Brycheiniog has a variety of places to stay within its boundaries, such as the towns of Brecon and Abergavenny. Accommodation ranges from hotels and guesthouses, pubs and B&Bs to camping and caravan sites. There are several bunkhouses too, including three YHA hostels. Seek out the Green Tourism Business Scheme standard when booking.
www.bannaubrycheiniog.org/where-to-stay

Places to visit

Brecon A key hub on the A470. Has a busy market on Tuesdays and Fridays, as well as a farmers' market on the second Saturday of the month. The Cathedral Church of St John the Evangelist is worth a visit to the town alone. Has two great museums – the Royal Welsh Regimental Museum and Y Gaer. Brecon plays host to an annual jazz festival held every August. There's also the Theatr Brycheiniog alongside the Monmouthshire & Brecon Canal basin.

Hay-on-Wye At the top-right of the Park, this town is famous for its annual book festival. There's a market every Thursday, lots of hidden gems in the side streets and the lovely 900-plus-year-old Hay Castle too, which was built as a Norman stronghold on the Wales–England border.

Abergavenny On the outskirts of the Park. A historic market town with plenty of shops and cafés, a museum, castle and medieval priory, and opportunities to walk nearby. It was the site of a Roman fort – Gobannium – which was built in AD 54. Sadly, no remains are visible, but there are

↑ Head to the Canal Basin to catch a boat, or visit the Theatr Brycheiniog.

↓ Abergavenny Castle – the remains are quite impressive, and they host regular events.

artefacts in the museum. Just outside the town is Ysgyryd Fach and you can get a good view from Twyn-yr-allt.

Llandovery In the west of the Park and an ideal place to explore Y Mynydd Du (the Black Mountain, not to be confused with the Black Mountains, in the east of the Park). It's a quaint market town, which made its wealth during the 19th-century Welsh wool trade. Has a thriving events list including a carnival, sheep festival and motorbike festival weekend.

Crickhowell Just a few miles east along the A40 from Abergavenny. Has become a thriving town in the Usk Valley with independent shops, great pubs and Crug Hywel, a well-preserved Iron Age fort.

Why not try...

Llandeilo Small, picturesque market town on the River Towy by the A483. A real jewel in the Park – has the fine St Teilo's Church and Castell Dinefwr.

↑ Crickhowell is a thriving town in the Usk Valley.

→ The Cathedral Church of St John the Evangelist is a place of calm in busy Brecon.

The woods are covered in bluebells in May.

Gilwern A large village to the west of Abergavenny. You can hire boats to cruise on the Monmouthshire and Brecon Canal while the wooded Clydach Gorge is nearby.

Merthyr Tydfil A significant town on the A465 and just outside the Park. It's a busy place with plenty of options for staying. The Grade I listed Cyfarthfa Castle was built in 1824 by the Crawshay family.

Must Sees

Llangorse Lake ① (SO 128 272) is the second largest natural lake in Wales, at around 1.6km (1 mile), set within hills, fields and meadows. An ideal spot for sailing and watersports – and birdwatching – it has what is considered to be an ancient royal retreat: a humanmade island of oak, willow and hazel wood on the north-west shore.

Bannau Brycheiniog's main visitor centre at **Libanus** ② (LD3 8ER) is packed full of information, with a superb café. It's the starting point of several walks, including one to the Iron Age hill fort of Twyn y Gaer, which is found at the northern edge of Mynydd Illtyd. A Roman road that linked North and South Wales can also be traced. Mynydd Illtyd is a living landscape with red kites and skylarks. www.bannaubrycheiniog.org/visitor-centres

The Bronze Age standing stone **Maen Llia** ③ (SN 924 191) is 3.7m (12ft) tall and a Scheduled Ancient Monument. It dominates the moorland near Ystradfellte.

Cwm Cadlan National Nature Reserve (CF44 0YJ) is a marshy grassland that is home to several rare plants such as the globeflower, tawny sedge and flea sedge. The site is managed by Natural Resources Wales, which has been restoring the site to encourage more life in the alkaline-dominated soil. There's a very small layby nearby for parking.

Coed y Cerrig National Nature Reserve (SO 293 211) is a quiet little spot near Abergavenny. In the valley bottom is an alder woodland that can be explored by the accessible boardwalk, taking just 30 minutes or so, while there are other trails around the reserve.

Not sure there's a more romantic ruin than that of **Carreg Cennen Castle** ④ (SA19 6UA). It's set 90m (300ft) above the River Cennen and was likely built by Edward I's baron, John Giffard, at the end of the 13th century. Open all year round, apart from Christmas Day. www.cadw.gov.wales/visit/places-to-visit/castell-carreg-cennen

Brecon is a hive of activity, and so the **Cathedral Church of St John the Evangelist** (LD3 9DP) is a peaceful hideaway. It was established in the 11th century as a medieval Benedictine priory, but it's possible there was a church on the site before then. Following the Dissolution of the Monasteries, it became a parish church for the people of Brecon.

The **Fforest Fawr Geopark** was established in 2005 and extends to 763 sq km (300 sq miles). Fforest Fawr itself, meaning 'great forest' in English, has plenty of places to explore, such as Garwnant and Taf Fechan Forests, Llandovery and the Black Mountain Quarries. www.fforestfawrgeopark.org.uk

Clydach Gorge is a complete gem between Abergavenny and Brynmawr. It was formed by the River Clydach, and its speed was utilised to power blast furnaces and mills. It's now a spectacular wooded gorge with plenty of places to explore. There are three walks from **Clydach Ironworks** (NP7 0LR), which used to employ more than 1,300 people in the 18th century. Part of the gorge is in the Cwm Clydach National Nature Reserve.

Must Dos

Form a quartet

Bannau Brycheiniog has four distinct regions, each with its own special landscape. **Y Mynydd Du** (the Black Mountain) is the most westerly and remote and, therefore, the least visited. **Fforest Fawr** has several isolated hills, while the **Central Beacons** are in the centre. Lastly, the **Black Mountains** (just to confuse you) are in the east.

A series of long-distance walks cross these areas, including, albeit very briefly, the 285km (177 mile) **Offa's Dyke Path**, which loosely follows the Welsh border. You can walk **The Beacons Way**, a 159km (99 mile) walk from Abergavenny to Llangadog, which climbs peaks such as Fan y Big, Pen y Fan and Twyn Swnd. The **Taff Trail** is 88.5km (55 miles) in length and runs between Cardiff and Brecon along a mixture of riverside paths, railway paths and forest roads. You could also do the 77km (48 mile) **Usk Valley Walk** from the Roman town of Caerleon to Brecon. www.ldwa.org.uk

Then there are the big and not-so-big hills of **Fan Foel** (481m/1,578ft), **Fan Brycheiniog** (802m/2,631ft), **Cribyn** (795m/2,608ft) and **Rhos Dirion** (713m/2,339ft). Let's face it, you're spoilt for choice!

The Park has also established **Cycle across the Beacons** – a 90km (56 mile) touring route from Llandeilo to Abergavenny. www.bannaubrycheiniog.org/activities

⬇ The Nant Cwm-du drops down into the Senni valley.

← Book shops and hiding places ... the Hay Festival is second to none.

↓ Penderyn Distillery – great tours, even better whisky.

can't visit when it is on, each bookshop offers a map that charts a book tour around the town – it's magnificent, and should be on the bucket list for all bibliophiles! www.hayfestival.com

Get in the woods

The **Garwnant Visitor Centre** (CF48 2HU) is set within 162ha (400 acres) of woodland on the shores of Llwyn-on Reservoir. It's a fantastic place for all the family and just £5 to park for the day. There are loads of things to do including biking (with hire facilities), walking, archery and disc golf, and there's also a large play area and café. www.garwnantvisitorcentre.co.uk

Enjoy great music

The annual **Green Man Festival** (NP8 1LP) is a huge event held every August near Crickhowell. This music, science and arts festival is sometimes called a mini (but much more relaxed!) Glastonbury. Tickets sell out quickly, so get on the waiting list.
www.greenman.net

For a more sedate, under-your-own-steam event, the **Hay-on-Wye Book Festival** is world-renowned, bringing authors and book lovers together in the beautiful town. If you don't fancy the festival, or

Feed the birds...

Tuppence a bag? You can get up close to red kites at the **Llanddeusant Red Kite Feeding Station** (SA19 9YG). www.redkiteswales.co.uk

More caves!

The deepest cave in Bannau Brycheiniog, and Wales, is **Ogof Ffynnon Ddu** at 274.5m (901ft) and containing more than 50km (31 miles) of passage. Discovered in 1946, its name translates to 'Cave of the Black Spring'. Access is restricted to experienced cavers only and is managed by the South Wales Caving Club.
www.swcc.org.uk

Bannau Brycheiniog | 245

Nearby is **Dan-yr-Ogof, The National Showcaves Centre for Wales** (SA9 1GJ). A ticket, which needs to be booked online in advance, gains you access to ten attractions, including Dan-yr-Ogof, Cathedral and Bone Cave, as well as a museum, Iron Age village and Mr Morgan's Farm Yard. Dan-yr-Ogof was discovered in 1912 after Tommy and Jeff Morgan entered through the River Llynfell. They set the way to find more than 16km (10 miles) of passage. Cathedral Cave and its acoustics take your breath away and are worth the admission alone. www.showcaves.co.uk

You can also discover the **Big Pit Coal Museum** (NP4 9XP), just outside the Park's southern boundary, where you can go underground to get a taste of what life was like for miners. www.museum.wales/bigpit/

← Formations in Dan-yr-Ogof.

CAR-FREE TRAVEL

→ For details on how to get around Bannau Brycheiniog, visit www.traveline-cymru.info.

→ There are hourly direct trains to Abergavenny on the Cardiff to Manchester line and to Merthyr Tydfil from Cardiff and Pontypridd. Llandovery is on the Heart of Wales Line, with trains from Llanelli, Swansea and Shrewsbury. www.heart-of-wales.co.uk and www.nationalrail.co.uk

→ The Brecon Mountain Railway runs from Pant to Torpantau and Pontsticill, following part of the original Brecon & Merthyr Railway, which closed in 1964. The heritage return route is 15.29km (9.5 miles). www.bmr.wales

→ Regular bus services operate through the Park. The T4 runs from Cardiff to Newtown via Brecon – and to the base of Pen y Fan – while the T6 runs from Swansea to Brecon. The X55 Cymru Clipper service from Swansea and Neath runs to Pontneddfechan. www.bannaubrycheiniog.org/getting-here/

→ The Explore Wales Pass offers unlimited travel on all rail services and most local bus services in Wales. It can be used on all local bus services in and around the Park, including Beacons Buses, except #1, #2, #442, T2 and X75. Passholders can also get discounted rates at other sites, such as Cadw Welsh Historic Monuments and National Trust properties and gardens. www.tfw.wales

↑ Cathedral Cave is worth the admission alone.

Down the road from Dan-yr-Ogof is **Craig y nos Country Park** (SA9 1GL), which forms part of the historic grounds of the Victorian Craig-y-nos Castle. www.bannaubrycheiniog.org/craig-y-nos-country-park

And, if you've still got energy after all that, on the shores of Llangorse Lake is the **Llangorse Multi Activity Centre** (LD3 7UH), where you can enjoy horse riding, climbing and archery. www.llangorse.com

Feet up time!

The magnificent **International Welsh Rarebit Centre** (LD3 8SL) is an utter joy, if somewhat understated for its lofty title. It celebrates the hot cheese with either ale or mustard delicacy through an array of tremendous recipes. Bliss!

The **Penderyn Distillery** (CF44 0SX) was the first distillery in more than 100 years in Wales. It produces a delicious range of whiskies using a unique copper single-pot still designed by Dr David Faraday, a relative of the great 19th-century scientist Michael Faraday. Combined with the fresh, natural spring water in the village, the whiskies are light and flavourful. Tours are available, and there's a horsebox coffee trailer in the car park. www.penderyn.wales

And finally, Bannau Brycheiniog has plenty of great pubs, but we were drawn to the **Bear Hotel in Crickhowell** (NP8 1BW). It's been a pub since 1432 and has a tasty menu alongside great beers. It feels ... well ... old, but the food and service are anything but. Enjoy! www.bearhotel.co.uk

CAIRNGORMS

DESIGNATED: 1 September 2003
SIZE: 4,528 sq km (1,748 sq miles), **HIGHEST PEAK:** Ben Macdui at 1,309m (4,295ft)
ANNUAL VISITOR NUMBERS: 2.15 million (2023), **POPULATION:** 18,000
OFFICIAL WEBSITE: www.cairngorms.co.uk

There was a point on the trail where I forgot where I was. Not in a 'I don't know where I am, let's pull out a map, grab a compass or use the sun to navigate' type of way, but in a sense of being held up by the Earth, progressing through something that was much bigger than me. The forest track had become a single-track path through remnant pine forest, undulating up and down to its destination. Trees that had been there for many years, were more than supportive as I avoided bare-root ankle snatchers and swung around difficult steps. In places, the bark was smooth through years of steadying hands; pines and birches providing wooded support for hikers, adventure seekers and the curious. Ahead was nothing but the white-grey path, gnarly branches and a long descent.

Eventually, I came back to the now, and rejoined the north of Scotland. The fact that this path was in the UK stunned me. When I stopped to ponder and take a

↓ The dramatic snow-capped peaks of Glenshee.

breath, I could have easily been walking through the forests of British Columbia, or on the Pacific Crest Trail, not rising through Glenmore to Ryvoan and Meall a' Bhuachaille. My sense of belonging had disappeared from a place to a feeling.

In *The Living Mountain* (1977), Nan Shepherd wrote: 'To aim for the highest point is not the only way to climb a mountain,' and those words spoke loudly on this walk. The Cairngorms are one of our most priceless landscapes, every sinew lit step after step. The Cairn Gorm is our 'arctic plateau', while a quarter of the UK's rare and endangered species call this National Park home. Mountain hares frolic in the winter; they are joined by ptarmigan, snow bunting and much more. The unique climate of those mountaintops sustains life for a multitude of species and supports local people.

Climate is central to the economy of the Cairngorms National Park. There are three key ski resorts, which employ people from all around the area, while its communities, from Grantown-on-Spey to Ballater and Blair Atholl, are vital bases for snow and ice seekers. Yet, research from the James Hutton Institute in 2020 found there had been a decrease in the observed maximum and average snow depth since the beginning of records in 1983/84. Maximum snow depth had declined by around 10cm (3.9in), and the average by approximately 3cm (1.2in). It also said that current trends demonstrated there would likely be a decline in snow cover days per year from the 2030s for Aviemore, the Cairngorm Chairlift meteorological station and the Ptarmigan Restaurant located at the top station of Cairngorm Mountain railway.

Clearly, should these findings be realised in the future, then the impact on the economy would be profound. The Cairngorm Mountain resort operates throughout the year, with mountain bike and other

← The World Porridge Making Championships are held in Carrbridge. Bobby Fisher won the top Speciality Dish in 2023.

← Crathie Kirk peeks out of the trees.

↓ River Luineag near Aviemore.

activities, while Glenshee runs its chairlift and café to ensure visitors can reach higher ground through the off-season to keep its business ticking over. At present, the Lecht ski resort is only open during the winter.

Yet, until we get a grip on the climate crisis, while there will still be snow, it'll be much less frequent, and we'll probably see a lot more rain. Tackling these issues takes a global effort, and it can often feel too big. The Cairngorms is aiming to be the first National Park to reach net zero by 2030, but we all must do our bit.

Visiting the Cairngorms and supporting those local communities is important, as is treasuring this special landscape all year round. The National Park is home to one-quarter of Scotland's native pine forest, and it has 7,028km (4,367 miles) of paths and rights of way that take you right into its heart. Its communities, from the tourist hotspot of Aviemore to the salt-of-the-earth regulars in the Claymore in Grantown-on-Spey, are some of the most welcoming around.

This is their National Park, our most cherished wilderness, and we all must look after it.

THE CHAMPION

Pete Crane
○○○

Pete Crane is the former Head of Visitor Services at the National Park and now Director, Access and the Environment, at Mountaineering Scotland. He also sits on the evaluation panel that manages asset transfer requests at Forestry and Land Scotland.

The restorative power of nature and outdoor spaces is being increasingly understood. Green prescribing is becoming popular, and we know that access to space and fresh air is vital for well-being. Access to National Parks has never been more important.

↑ Pete with his daughter Jo on Meall a' Bhuachaille winter 2025.

'Getting back into the outdoors, back on my bike and out walking, was an important part of my recovery. People said I recovered well because I was fit, determined and wanted to get back outside.'

When Pete was at the National Park, he managed the government-funded Snow Roads Scenic Route. It was a multi-faceted project that included two different main roads and the construction of three viewpoints, all of which were in three different local authority areas. It was a difficult, long, drawn-out project, but understandably a huge cause for celebration when it was completed.

'It was a nightmare at times, but something I really enjoyed,' he said. 'On the last day, when the final installation was going in, I had to be up on site at 8am with the landscape architect. I was standing chatting to him and felt really ill. I managed to get through the day, but after a couple of days wasn't getting any better, so my wife Lorna insisted I go to my GP. They couldn't find what was wrong, but I continued to get worse, and eventually I ended up in hospital being treated for half a dozen potential illnesses, including viral encephalitis. I'm really lucky they spotted it.'

Pete would stay in hospital for three weeks before being allowed home to continue his recovery. Encephalitis inflames the brain, often causing long-term damage, and is a slow illness to recover from.

'Effectively, I've had to deal with brain damage,' Pete adds, 'and while I made a relatively quick recovery, I suppose I'm still recovering. I sat at home for a week to make sure I didn't have epilepsy, which I was very fortunate not to have, and then I had a really good chat with Kate Christie, our head of HR, because I wanted to go back to work. I didn't want to sit at home and have what was left in my brain not functioning, and the Park Authority were fantastic in allowing me to do that. It was little and often at first – it took minutes to read a three-sentence email and more to reply – but it was one of the key things that drove me on to a good recovery ... alongside my physical fitness and stubbornness.'

Pete grew up in Worcestershire, did a degree in forestry at Bangor University and that brought him into Scotland, initially to Edinburgh and then Inverness. He worked in private sector forest investment management and, 'to the annoyance of my late mother', left the role to train in outdoor learning at what is now Edinburgh University.

'I went from working with the richest 5 per cent to the poorest 5 per cent, enabling young people to get outside, and then moved up to Fife to manage Lochore Meadows Country Park in Fife, in the ex-coal mining area. I was there for ten years, and then when the National Park was being established, I applied for a job there. I stayed for 18 years! One of my early projects was to mark the boundary of the National Park. We used 29 granite stones from the Balmoral Estate, and that was a huge project. We were working with four local authorities at first, and then, when the Park expanded, five.

The Land Reform Act also meant we needed to survey and designate core paths, and I worked very closely with my colleagues in tourism, so we would be doing what the visitor wanted, rather than what we thought was best. Although it's a mountainous National Park, the biggest activities that people do here are sightseeing, visiting attractions and going for short walks. Mountain walks are really important, but they're not the most important, and getting that data gave us the confidence to make sure what we were putting in place was right.

One of the initial challenges we had was that many of the communities had leaflets promoting the local paths, but only a few recognised the National Park. We did a year of consultation with those communities to ensure those leaflets were consistent. It was unbelievably hard work, because we were working with more than 20 communities, and all were volunteers. I think the National Park has been incredibly good at working with people and taking them along the journey.'

Pete says that areas like the Cairngorms are dependent on support, subsidy and private investment if they are to deliver on their promises. Like many National Parks, affordable housing is an issue, and this has already seen young people leaving the area. He says there is real concern that in the next decade or so, there won't be the workforce to sustain those communities.

'We know people want to come here; they want to work here and bring up their families. But where can they live?' he adds. 'The Cairngorms draw people because, in a UK context, it's a wilderness. It has a quarter of the country's rare and endangered species. It is a special place.'

> **Pete's favourite thing to do in the Cairngorms National Park:** 'There's no one sentence that can answer that because I love going into different parts of the National Park I haven't visited before. Even after retirement, I've been going up hills I've not been to. I also like going back to places I've been before and seeing the change. I've seen some remarkable changes on Meall a' Bhuachaille, with the montane woodland growing where, as a student 40 years ago, I was told it wouldn't grow that high. It's an amazing place. I just like being out there, on a bike, walking, skiing and being out in the space.'

FACTS AND QUIRKS

Golden Spurtle

The World Porridge Making Championships are held annually in Carrbridge. The first **Golden Spurtle event** was held in Carrbridge in 1994, the brainchild of Roger Reed. He was the owner of the Fairwinds Hotel, and wanted to raise the profile of the village and promote the warming food. www.goldenspurtle.com

Mysteries and myths

Is **Am Fear Liath Mòr** – the big grey man – stalking climbers up Ben Macdui? At a meeting of the Cairngorm Club in 1925, walker Norman Collie said: 'Every few steps I took I heard a crunch, then another crunch as if someone was walking after me but taking steps three or four times the length of my own. As I walked on and the eerie crunch, crunch sounded behind me, I was seized by terror and took to my heels.' The figure has been seen and heard several times on the mountain.

Castle Roy, once protected by Murdo the Highland Coo and his pal Buster the sheep, is said to have hidden treasure within its walls and a secret passageway to the nearby Old Kirk. However, should anyone try to find it, they would be exposed to the plague, which could be hidden within the site.

Glenmore is said to be the home of the King of the Fairies, Big Donald, while there is also a water kelpie at **Loch Pityoulish** near Aviemore. It is rumoured to have lured children into the water who were attracted by the 'pretty pony'. The freshwater lake of **An Lochan Uaine** is known as the green loch, not because of algae, but from fairies washing their clothes at night. Nearby, at **Loch Morlich**, there's the ghost of a Highland warrior who marches up and down the beach.

WALK 1

Ryvoan and Meall a' Bhuachaille

◇◇◇

Remote native woodland and glorious views.

This wonderful route from Glenmore Visitor Centre climbs quickly before crossing into forest, native woodland and descending to An Lochan Uaine, the green loch. You then have the option of following the lower route back to the Reindeer Centre and the visitor centre, while hardier walkers can continue along the Ryvoan Pass to Abernethy National Nature Reserve and Ryvoan Bothy before turning left and climbing Meall a' Bhuachaille. Whatever the option, this is a fantastic walk!

For the longer route, keep the visitor centre on your left and then climb up the road after it, turning right after a few metres. This forest track gives great views of the Cairngorms and their snowy peaks. The track climbs and undulates slightly before becoming a single path through native woodland. It does feel wild here, skirting through pine-remnant woodland and trickling forest streams. The path begins to descend – a little sketchy in places – before reaching An Lochan Uaine. Pause for a bit and then take the path to Ryvoan Bothy (pop in and remove any rubbish if you can) before turning left and climbing up to Meall a' Bhuachaille.

START/END: Glenmore Visitor Centre, PH22 1QU
DISTANCE: 5.8km (3.5 miles) to 8.7km (5.4 miles)
GRADE: Easy to Moderate/Strenuous in places

⬇ The walk begins with long views across the Cairngorms.

← Ryvoan bothy – a place of sanctuary, whatever the weather.

the Allt Coire Chondliach, and a welcome brew at the visitor centre.

In terms of classic days out in the Cairngorms, this walk might not pack the punch of bagging several Munros, but it's a cracking introduction to the National Park. It feels much longer a walk than it is, and you can stay in the bothy to break it up.

You'll feel all of its 810m (2,657ft), but the views are spectacular, as is the opportunity to see golden eagles and an emerging montane woodland. Onwards is the track down to Coire Chondliach and

The route is also accessible for wheelchair users, who can follow the lower route there and back.

WALK 2

The Beaver Trail
○○○

Beavers and woodland ... what's not to like!

This is a lovely, low-level and straight-forward wander along the Beaver Trail from Rothiemurchus to Loch an Eilein with the opportunity to see beavers at Lochan Mor and its tributaries.

Start at Rothiemurchus and follow the signs to the start of the trail. The walk travels through varied woodlands before emerging at Lochan Mor. There are information posts about beavers all along the walk, and you could even see one if

START/END: Rothiemurchus, PH22 1QH
DISTANCE: 6.9km (4.3 miles)
GRADE: Easy

↓ Beautiful woodlands en route!

256 | The Complete Guide to the UK National Parks

Why not try these great walks...

UATH LOCHANS AND FARLEITTER CRAG: A 5.3km (3.3 mile) wander around the four lochs in Glen Feshie.

LAIRIG GHRU: An epic and wild 30.5km (19 mile) linear walk from Coylumbridge to the River Dee near Muir. It climbs the Lairig Ghru, the best-known pass in Scotland, to a height of 835m (2,740ft).

ANAGACH WOODS: Enjoy a 9km (5.5 mile) walk around the ancient pinewoods in Grantown-on-Spey.

you go close to dawn or dusk. Eventually, you will emerge from the woodlands on to a road; turn left and walk a few hundred metres. Instead of rejoining the trail, walk down to the picturesque Loch an Eilein and see the remains of the castle in the water. A castle was built on the loch between 1222 and 1298 by the Bishop of Moray, while the remains are from the 1380s.

Return to the trail – much more open than before – and to Rothiemurchus.

↑ Lochan Mor on the Beaver Trail.

Key places

The rider...
The Cairngorms National Park has a variety of accommodation, including B&Bs, hotels, self-catering options, campsites and hostels. Wild camping is allowed in the National Park as long as people leave no trace – the Scottish Outdoor Access Code (SOAC) (www.outdooraccess-scotland.scot) has more information. www.visitcairngorms.com/plan-your-visit/places-to-stay/

Places to visit

Aviemore On the north-western side of the National Park, just off the A9. Busy hub all year round with cafés, restaurants, outdoor shops and the Macdonald Resort. Comes alive in winter, as skiers come together before travelling up to the Cairn Gorm.

Braemar In the centre of the National Park, along the A93 from Ballater. Has two popular pubs – the decadently decorated Fife Arms boutique hotel and Farquharson's Bar and Kitchen. You'll find a bakehouse, butchers and cafés, as well as outdoor shops, and the village is famous for its annual gathering at the Highland Games Centre, held on the first Saturday in September. Nearby is the community-owned and wonderfully preserved Braemar Castle. Braemar recorded the coldest temperature in the UK at −27.2°C (−16.6°F) on 10 January 1982.

Tomintoul The epicentre of the UK's largest Dark Sky Park on the A939 from Grantown-on-Spey. The village was commissioned by the Duke of Gordon, who was hoping to discourage cattle theft and illegal distilling in the area. The distillery is around 6.5km (4 miles) away, as well as the Lecht Mine and Corgarff Castle. Just outside the village is the

⬇ Braemar in the snow.

Tomintoul Dark Sky Discovery Site and Bird Hide.

Kingussie Near the spectacular Uath Lochans, just off the A9 in the north-west of the National Park. It's the capital of the historic Highland region of Badenoch, and its name means 'head of the pine forest' in Gaelic. It has pony trekking opportunities and a busy high street.

Grantown-on-Spey Near to the National Park's northern boundary, this is a thriving town with ancient pinewoods. Has a museum, town history trail, seasonal discovery centre and a couple of pubs. The Craig Bar, just off the main strip, serves amazing gourmet pies.

Why not try...

Ballater A pretty village where the A939 and A93 meet. Sits in the heart of Royal Deeside and was originally developed as a resort to welcome people who visited the Pannanich Mineral Well. It's also on the doorstep of the Balmoral Estate.

Newtonmore Busy village with the Clan Macpherson Museum, Wildcat Experience and open-air Highland Folk Museum. A quieter base for exploring most of the National Park.

Blair Atholl This village has a different feel to the others further north. Based in Perthshire, it has a working mill and Blair Castle, built in 1269 by John Comyn of Badenoch.

↑ The Anagach pinewoods in Grantown-on-Spey.

→ The River Dee runs through the centre of Braemar.

Must Sees

Loch Garten (NH 974 180) is one of the best place to see ospreys. Part of the Abernethy National Nature Reserve, its Caledonian pine forest is the perfect habitat for crested tits, red squirrels, siskins and common lizards. There are ant nests nearly 1m (3.3ft) tall, too. The Nature Centre, open daily from 1 April until 31 October, brings you up close and personal with ospreys, with a camera trained upon their nest and friendly staff to talk you through what can be seen. There are activities for the kids, too. www.rspb.org.uk/days-out/reserves/loch-garten-abernethy

Loch Morlich ❶ (NH 964 093) is a freshwater loch with the highest beach in Britain; the only one in Scotland to have a Rural Beach Award. The sandy beach emerges from woodland at Glenmore and is a hive of watersports activity. While busy, the peaceful water has great views of Castle Hill and Creag a' Chalamain as well as Lurcher's Crag and Cairn Gorm.

Insh Marshes ❷ (NN 774 998) is Britain's largest naturally functioning floodplain, at 8km (5 miles) long and 3km (2 miles) wide in places, as well as being a globally recognised Ramsar site. It has a lookout hide with vast views of the marsh as well as the more secluded Invertromie hide. Birds can be seen here all year round, but particularly in spring when greylag goose, tree pipit, curlew and willow warbler visit.

The **Falls of Bruar** (NN 818 664) are a beautiful series of waterfalls on Bruar Water. Robert Burns wrote a poem about them, and they can be visited from the popular House of Bruar.

The **Falls of Trium** (NN 680 923), a series of rapids on the River Trium around 6.5km (4 miles) south of Newtonmore, are worth seeing.

Loch Muick (NO 292 831) is a serene freshwater loch around 8km (5 miles) south of Braemar. It's surrounded by mountains and has the impressive Glas-allt-Shiel lodge, which was built in 1868 by Queen Victoria. She called it her widow's house, a place of retreat following the death of her husband, Albert. From there, you can follow Glas Allt to Cac Carn Beag at 1,155m (3,789ft).

The **Balmoral Cairns** (NO 263 949) are historic obelisks and cairns, built by the royal family on their Balmoral Estate to commemorate key events. They are an eclectic mix, 11 in total, with the most famous being the must-see **Prince Albert Cairn** (NO 259 934).

Mar Lodge ❸ (AB35 5YJ) is Britain's largest National Nature Reserve and one of its most stunning. It is 29,000ha (71,661 acres) of varied landscape from moorland and Caledonian pine forest to the Quoich wetlands. The site is being restored ❹: the native pinewood forests and 5,500ha (13,591 acres) of peatland are regenerating thanks to conservation efforts. www.nts.org.uk/visit/places/mar-lodge-estate

The **Uath Lochans** (PH21 1NX) are four small lochs nestled within the ancient pines of Glen Feshie. The water sparkles, whatever the weather, and the lochs are festooned in dragonflies and other insects throughout the spring and summer. The site has two trails – the Uath Lochans Trail (2.4km/1.5 miles), and the more challenging Farleitter Crag Trail (4km/2.5 miles), which has great views of the Spey Valley.

↑ Ski touring at Drumochter.

Must Dos

Enjoy the snow

The Cairngorms have three 'official' ski centres and resorts, but when the snow falls, the entire National Park can become a magnet for winter sports enthusiasts. Good snow can be found as low as **Creag Choinnich** (NO 160 918) in Braemar, with powder-like conditions occurring now and again, according to the locals.

The main resorts are:

◆ **Cairngorm Mountain** (PH22 1RB) has more than 30km (19 miles) of pisted runs and 13 surface tows and lifts. During the off-season, it offers tubing slides, mountain carting and mountain biking. There's also a funicular railway, the Ptarmigan Restaurant, a café, Cas Bar and a shop. Lower down the road, at the base of Coire Cas, is a large free parking area, ideal for hillwalkers and climbers accessing the Northern Corries. www.cairngormmountain.co.uk

◆ **The Lecht 2090** (AB36 8YP) is located between Tomintoul and Strathdon. It has 11 lifts and 20 ski runs, divided into three main areas: Osprey, Buzzard and Falcon. The centre does not open during the off-season. www.lecht.co.uk

◆ **Glenshee Snowsports** (AB35 5XU) has 22 lifts spread across three valleys. It opens in the off-season with a chairlift operating from June to September to take people up to The Cairnwell. The Tea@TheShee Cafe is also open. www.ski-glenshee.co.uk

Of course, winter sports are dependent on the weather, and it is best to check the forecast before you go.

Go curling ...

Strathspey Curling Club in Grantown-on-Spey has an outdoor rink just on the boundary of the Anagach pinewoods. Anyone can pop down and try their hand at the sport in the winter, when it has been filled with water by the club and frozen over. www.facebook.com/people/Strathspey-Curling-Club

... and snow touring

You can also strap on some skis and travel Nordic style around the National Park.

The **Cairn Gorm** (NJ 005 040) is an obvious place to start, as are the **Hills of Drumochter** (NN 657 761), which are on either side of the pass of Drumochter, on the A9.

In warmer times

Watersports are popular. **Loch Morlich** (NH 964 093) is an ideal base to learn how to paddleboard, canoe and kayak, with several operators offering training packages to take you on the water. **Loch Insh Outdoor Centre in Kincraig** (PH21 1NU) offers everything from pedalos and rowing to sailing and windsurfing. The centre even has a Jungle Float, a floating waterpark with slide, high dive platform and trampolines. The centre also offers winter sports training. www.lochinsh.com

The Spey is a great place for canoeists to hone their craft, with several activity providers willing to help you get the best out of a trip. Spirit of the Spey is based in Newtonmore. www.spiritofthespey.co.uk

The National Park is a magnet for mountain bikers. The Cairngorm and Glenshee resorts are good bases, as is **Laggan Wolftrax** (PH20 1BU), which is west of Laggan. This purpose-built single-track mountain bike centre has more than 32km (20 miles) of trails. It has two green, four blue and four red routes, alongside a severe black trail called the Wolf of Badenoch Black. Eesh! www.forestryandland.gov.scot/visit/laggan-wolftrax

↑ Glenshee has a chairlift that will take you up the 933m (3,061ft) summit of The Cairnwell.

↓ Watersports at Loch Morlich.

Munro bagging!

There are 55 Munros (mountains above 914m/3,000ft) in the National Park, four of which rank in the top five highest peaks in the UK. **Ben Macdui** (NN 989 989) at 1,309m (4,295ft), **Braeriach** (NN 953 999) at 1,296m (4,252ft), **Cairn Toul** (NN 963 972) at 1,291m (4,236ft) and **Sgòr an Lochain Uaine** (NN 954 976) at 1,258m (4,127ft) are a peak bagger's dream – as well as being serious undertakings. Cairn Gorm comes in sixth at 1,244m (4,081ft). The brilliant Walk Highlands is the site to visit for routes, hints and tips. www.walkhighlands.co.uk

Sgòr Gaoith (NN 902 989) and **Sgòran Dubh Mòr** (NH 904 002) are classics too, at 1,118m (3,668ft) and 1,108m (3,635ft) respectively – truly iconic in winter for those who can handle crampons and an ice axe.

The **Lairig Ghru** drovers' route connects Speyside and Deeside and is a 30.5km (19 mile) linear walk from Coylumbridge to the River Dee near Muir. There are two bothies on the way – **Corrour** (NN 981 958) and **Bob Scott's** (NO 042 932).

Both are incredibly busy, so if planning to stay, pack a tent just in case. It is also important to follow the Bothy Code. www.mountainbothies.org.uk/bothies/bothy-code/

If you do get caught out near Loch Avon, there's the **Shelter Stone** (NJ 001 015). It's not the most luxurious facility, but useful if in trouble.

The **Speyside Way** follows the Spey Valley from Buckie to Newtonmore. It's a 137km (85 mile) route, but you can also head over to Tomintoul, adding an extra 25km (15.5 miles) to your trip.

See amazing wildlife

Golden eagles can be spotted, if you're lucky, at **Glen Doll** (NO 251 764), **Glenmore** (NH 979 095) and **Glenlivet** (NJ 195 287) … but there's so much more to discover! The National Park is a haven for mountain plants and other rare wildlife such as pine martens, Scottish crossbill, snow bunting and black grouse. Rare insects include the small scabious mining bee, shining guest ant, Kentish glory and dark bordered beauty moths, and the pine hoverfly. In winter, mountain hares and ptarmigan patrol the arctic plateau of the Cairn Gorm.

At the Reindeer Centre in Glenmore you can take a guided tour to see (and feed!) Britain's only herd of free-ranging reindeer. www.cairngormreindeer.co.uk

To see animals such as the Amur tiger

⬇ Glenlivet – a stunning landscape packed with heritage features …

⬆ … and the world-famous distillery.

and the yak up close, visit the **Highland Wildlife Park in Kingussie** (PH21 1NL). www.highlandwildlifepark.org.uk

Wildcat conservation

Saving Wildcats has been releasing wildcats into the National Park to restore the population of what was once a widespread animal. You can find out more at Highland Wildlife Park in **Kincraig** (PH21 1NL). www.savingwildcats.org.uk

Enjoy more sedate pleasures

The Cairngorms have more than 60 Scheduled Ancient Monuments and a deep heritage. **The Clan Grant Centre**

← Looking towards Creag an Leth-choin.

(www.clangrant.org/clan-centre-trust) tells the story of the aforementioned Clan at Duthil, near Grantown-on-Spey, while Newtonmore has the **Clan Macpherson Museum** (PH20 1DE) (www.clanmacphersonmuseum.org.uk) and open-air **Highland Folk Museum** (PH20 1AY) (www.highlifehighland.com/highlandfolkmuseum/).

Balmoral (AB35 5TB) is the highland home of the royal family. www.balmoralcastle.com

The **Glenlivet Estate** is packed with heritage sites too, including the Scanlan Seminary, a place of exclusion for persecuted 18th-century Catholics; Lecht Mine; Knock Earth House, a stone-lined underground chamber that could have housed an illicit whisky still; and Blairfindy Castle. The whole area, while popular with whisky enthusiasts, is perfect for crowd-free wandering. www.glenlivetestate.co.uk

A wee dram

And what more perfect way to enjoy the Cairngorms than enjoying a wee dram? **Glenlivet** (AB37 9DB) is more than 200 years old and has a fascinating history. It is on the Malt Whisky Trail, which visits nine distilleries along the River Spey from sea to source. www.maltwhiskytrail.com

Glenlivet is the only site in the National Park on the trail, but there are several distilleries within its boundary, including **Tomintoul** (AB37 9AQ), **Dalwhinnie** (PH19 1AA) and **Cairn** (PH26 3NT).

The **Cairngorms Brewery** (PH22 1ST) offers tastings and has a shop. www.cairngormbrewery.com

---

CAR-FREE TRAVEL

→ Although the Cairngorms National Park is remote, there are train stations at Blair Atholl, Dalwhinnie, Newtonmore, Kingussie, Aviemore and Carrbridge. www.nationalrail.co.uk

→ Aviemore, Kingussie, Newtonmore and Dalwhinnie are on the Highland Main Line, with regular direct trains to Edinburgh, Glasgow and London.

→ The heritage Strathspey Steam Railway runs between Aviemore, Boat of Garten and Broomhill at Nethy Bridge. www.strathspeyrailway.co.uk

→ There are regular bus services into the National Park from London, Edinburgh, Glasgow, Aberdeen and Inverness, as well as local bus services between its communities, operated by Stagecoach and Ember. www.stagecoachbus.com/plan-a-journey and www.ember.to

→ The Aviemore Adventurer runs between Aviemore town centre and Cairngorm Mountain seven days a week, with space for bikes and skis. www.stagecoachbus.com/promos-and-offers/north-scotland/aviemoreadventurer

LOCH LOMOND & THE TROSSACHS

- Killin
- Tyndrum
- A85
- Ben More
- Falls of Falloch
- A84
- Glen Finglas Visitor Gateway
- A93
- Rest and be Thankful
- Arrochar
- Loch Katrine
- Callander
- The Cobbler
- Loch Arklet
- Loch Venachar
- Loch Lomond
- Aberfoyle
- Cashel Forest
- Lake of Menteith
- A82
- Glenbranter
- Balmaha
- A811
- Inchcailloch Island
- Puck's Glen
- Kilmun

LOCH LOMOND

LOCH LOMOND & THE TROSSACHS

DESIGNATED: 19 July 2002
SIZE: 1,865 sq km (720 sq miles), **HIGHEST PEAK:** Ben More at 1,174m (3,852ft)
ANNUAL VISITOR NUMBERS: Over 4.5 million (2024), **POPULATION:** 14,500
OFFICIAL WEBSITE: www.lochlomond-trossachs.org

'Twas there that we parted, in yon shady glen,
On the steep, steep side o' Ben Lomond,
Where in soft purple hue, the highland hills we view,
And the moon coming out in the gloaming.'

This verse is from the popular lament or folk round 'The Bonnie Banks o' Loch Lomond', which dates from the mid-18th century. There seem to be many interpretations of what it means, but for me, it's the strong sense of belonging, loss and a tinge of sadness that evokes a reaction.

The song was a real earworm for most of my travels around Loch Lomond & The Trossachs. It travelled some distance, gently over the breeze, from a cruise boat on Loch Lomond when I was not far from Beinn Bhreac, (pronounced *been-vraeachk* meaning speckled hill), near Luss. I heard it being whistled outside a pub in Arrochar, and then, while wandering through the woodlands above Ardentinny, it was being hummed by a man walking his dog. The song, such a simple, catchy and effective tune, is probably most people's first contact with Scotland; they'll know Edinburgh, because it's the capital, Hogmanay and all that, and, somehow, this ditty. They feel a sense of belonging to Loch Lomond, a misty-eyed sentimentality, and when they

➜ Puck's Glen and the surrounding woodland are an absolute marvel.

⬇ The Holy Loch, Cowal Peninsula – an often overlooked but rugged part of the National Park.

➡ The iconic Loch Lomond.

arrive the first time, it's like they've been here before.

It's therefore no surprise that when people head to Scotland, Loch Lomond is often one of the first places they come to. Half of Scotland's population live within an hour's drive of the National Park, which welcomes more than 4 million visitors a year. The majority of those people will visit the loch and feel satisfied they've answered that song, that call. You can't blame them either; Loch Lomond, the largest area of freshwater on mainland Britain, is stunningly beautiful. Luss, Balmaha, cruising on the Loch itself and climbing Ben Lomond are all must-dos here. But like most National Parks, this is a place of utter contrasts.

⬇ The bonnie, bonnie banks of Loch Lomond.

Alongside Loch Lomond, the National Park has three other distinct areas. Cowal to the south-west is more rugged, open and coastal. The Trossachs are huge, wide open forest ranges, while Breadalbane in the north-east is more mountainous, with long-distance views and a unique feel to the rest.

Despite the differences in landscape, this is a united population that wants the best for their region. Language is vitally important; Gaelic is embraced by many, and it connects with the landscape. Then, when you head to the Park's website, the first thing you read is:

'Nature is in real trouble here and the impacts of climate change are being felt more than ever. We can secure a positive future for people, nature and climate. But we must act now. Here. Now. All of us.'

Of all catchlines, those final five words struck a real chord. They empower and encourage people to stop and think what a special place Loch Lomond & The Trossachs National Park is, what all our designated landscapes stand for. They are humbling.

I wasn't prepared for what this National Park threw at me, and I cannot wait to return to the bonnie, bonnie banks o' Loch Lomond.

➜ Loin Water passes through Glen Loin before arriving at Loch Long.

| THE CHAMPIONS

Lucy Allen & Cordelia Murray-Brown

Lucy Allen and Cordelia Murray-Brown are members of the Youth Committee at Loch Lomond & The Trossachs National Park.

Loch Lomond & The Trossachs is one of the few National Parks that has a committee of young people to help it make decisions on key issues such as climate change, how land is used, public transport for rural communities and green career opportunities. It was formed in 2018 and has played an important role in guiding the Park Authority's interaction with young people and giving them a voice.

❝ 'I graduated from university in 2024 after studying social and public policy,' Lucy says. 'Although I live outside the Park, most of my free time has been spent in it, either climbing hills or going for cold swims, especially in the summer. I had a real interest in the environment and climate change, and how to engage with young people. When the opportunity came up, it made sense for me to give it a go, and so far it has been great. The Youth Committee helps me have an influence and engage with young people.'

'I grew up in this National Park and I think everything in my life revolves around it,' Cordelia adds. 'I go to the only secondary school in the National Park here in Callander, and I work part-time in Stronachlachar. I'm heading to university to study geography; the physical appreciation I have for this land is a big part of what I've got from the National Park. I joined the Committee because I wanted to be able to have some kind of influence over the Park and play a part in the protection of an area I love so much.'

⬇ Lucy Allen.

⬇ Cordelia Murray-Brown.

The Youth Committee meets regularly to discuss various issues affecting Loch Lomond & The Trossachs National Park. They set their agenda and programme for the year and then feed back to the National Park Authority Board.

'It's important for us that it's not tokenistic,' Lucy says. 'We take back what we have been working on to the main Board, and I have represented the Committee at that meeting. I told them what discussions we had planned for the year, and also fed back on what we are working on. In return, they help shape our discussions by asking our opinion on things, but we set our own agenda. It's good to feel we are listened to.'

One of the key reasons for the establishment of National Parks was to help local economies thrive. Sadly, in rural areas, it's difficult to provide opportunities for all, particularly for young people who often have to leave to find work elsewhere. Then, there is the perennial issue of public transport.

'It is hard, but there are working opportunities out there; it just depends on what you want to do,' Cordelia says. 'I've got a part-time job at a café in Stronachlachar, but it can be very difficult to get around without a car. In summer, there aren't many buses, and that's awkward because you have to rely on lifts. There have been services like the Trossachs' Explorer, which most of the Committee have used, but they need to be used, or there isn't a business case for them to stay. I know the Park hopes to have it running again soon.'

'The Park is set up to be enjoyed, that's the reason for it, but it's hard when it is inaccessible for some people,' Lucy adds. 'That said, to be able to just go out and enjoy it, for recreation or work, is very special. We're lucky that we don't have to pay to use it! We can climb the hills, swim in the lochs, go camping, and then there's the right to roam we have here too. There will always be issues at the hotspots when it's the first hot day of the year – parking, litter, or even finding random stuff on the beach – but I guess it's about education. One of the roles of the Youth Committee is to help people understand how to enjoy this special space responsibly, and we can connect with people.'

Cordelia adds: 'Lucy is right; this is a special place and I'm lucky to call it home. We are aiming to become a net-zero National Park, and I think you can see evidence of how important this place is in terms of climate and good air, even though we are so close to a big city. Then, there are other aspects too; I've got a camera full of pictures of different lichens, and then, as soon as you get a clear night, the stars are just amazing. It's great to think that Lucy and I can influence how people enjoy this place through the Youth Committee.'

> **Lucy's favourite thing to do in Loch Lomond & The Trossachs:**
> 'I'd climb up Conic Hill, look at the views, and then go for a dip in the loch at Balmaha. Ideally, I'm picturing a nice summer's night, with a lovely sunset. I'd then go for dinner at the Oak Tree and hear some live music. I'd be tempted to camp as well!'
>
> **Cordelia's:** 'There is a lot of choice in what you can do here, but I'd go up to some of my favourite spots around Kinlochard, which is where I grew up. I'd climb Ben Venue and then go to Loch Arklet, which is my favourite view of all time in Scotland. When you look down and see the dramatic peaks of the Arrochar Alps, it feels like you're properly in the highlands.'

Lots of water!

Loch Lomond is the largest body of freshwater in mainland Britain: nearly 39km (24 miles) long and 8km (5 miles) at its widest point – a surface area of 71 sq km (27.5 sq miles). The *Bathymetrical Survey of the Fresh-Water Lochs of Scotland* (1897–1909) worked out that there are 92,805 million cubic feet of water within the loch. That's a lot of Olympic-sized swimming pools! Scotland's only lake is in the National Park too – the Lake of Menteith. In its centre lies the peaceful, ruined island medieval priory of Inchmahome.

The Gaelic language

For hundreds of years, up until the 19th century, Gaelic was the dominant language of most of the inhabitants of the Park area. As late as the 1950s, native Gaelic speakers were still to be found in places like **Balquhidder**, **Brig O' Turk** and **Killin**.

Most of the present-day place names in the region have Gaelic roots, especially many geographical features, such as mountains, glens and rivers.

For example, **Ben Lomond** comes from Beinn Laomainn (pronounced LOEUmin), meaning 'beacon mountain', and Loch Venachar comes from Loch Bheannchair (pronounced VYANuchur), meaning 'horn-shaped, ie tapering, loch'.

Legends and most haunted

Rob Roy MacGregor, the Scottish hero immortalised by Sir Walter Scott, lived and died in the village of Balquhidder. After the Duke of Montrose seized his lands, Rob Roy launched a personal feud against the duke, which lasted until 1722, when he was eventually forced to surrender. Though later imprisoned, he was pardoned in 1727. He died at his home in Inverlochlarig Beg, Balquhidder, on 28 December 1734. Today, the village attracts many visitors who come to see Rob Roy's grave in Balquhidder Kirkyard.

The Drovers Inn may well be the most haunted pub in the Park. This 18th-century inn welcomed Rob Roy in 1716 and has several ghosts. The Little House of Horrors website says that Room 2 is haunted by a family, and in Room 6, the lights flicker. There's also a ghost girl that appeared in a photograph taken in the pub, while Angus, a young drover, stalks the inn to avenge those who killed him.

← The Drovers Inn.

WALK 1

Cashel Forest
◇◇◇

Disappear from the crowds with this varied route around Cashel's peaceful forest.

While most people are making their way up the nearby Conic Hill, you can enjoy similar scenery in relative peace just a few kilometres away. Cashel Forest is home to pine martens, adders, red squirrels, water voles, deer, and a variety of birdlife, including cuckoos. It's managed by the Cashel Forest Trust, which, since 1997, has established around 300ha (741 acres) of new native woodland here, overlooking Loch Lomond. The site also has 24ha (59 acres) of remnant oakwood, a traditionally managed coppice from the 18th century.

This walk takes you through varying stages of these superbly managed woodlands and climbs to around 300m (984ft). It's also relatively easy to follow – walking along the 'red' marked route until the 'black' posts appear on your right. This also gives you a handy get-out clause! The red route is bleakly steep in places, and should you not fancy the extra climb, you can follow it to a track and back to the Forest's visitor centre, for a shorter walk.

From the visitor centre, follow the red route and turn right before a metal gate. The path undulates, and you walk past a huge

START/END:
Cashel Forest, G63 0AW
DISTANCE: 6.5km
(4 miles)
GRADE: Moderate

↑ The woodland progresses through various age structures.

Loch Lomond & The Trossachs | 273

wild crab apple tree, a 300-year-old beauty and the largest in the UK and Ireland. The route then begins to gain some height through aspen and mixed woodland before turning right and climbing another 100 or so metres (328ft) to a stunning viewpoint. Another one follows a few minutes later, and it's breathtaking – Conic Hill on your left and Loch Lomond right ahead.

The woodland on your left becomes more sparse, while on the other side is an expansive peat habitat. Follow this route until it comes out onto an obvious forest track, but instead of heading down the hill, take a deep breath, head right, and climb up to another viewpoint and a very scenic picnic bench.

The way back down is on that forest track. It switches back and forth down the hill, eventually landing back at the visitor centre.

← Lichens in the older part of the forest.

WALK 2

Glen Finglas and The Great Trossachs Path

○○○

A hillside meander through Glen Finglas.

At 48km (30 miles), The Great Trossachs Path runs between Callander and Inversnaid through dramatic loch shorelines and mature woodland, including Brig o' Turk, Loch Katrine and Stronachlachar. It can be split into several sections, with the Park suggesting six that are suitable for walkers of all abilities.

This linear walk takes you from Glen Finglas Visitor Gateway to Kilmahog. It

START: Glen Finglas Visitor Gateway, FK17 8HR
END: Bochastle, FK17 8HD
DISTANCE: 8.5km (5.28 miles)
GRADE: Moderate

↑ The walk passes through ancient woodland.

→ Amazing views of Loch Venachar.

274 | The Complete Guide to the UK National Parks

Why not try these great walks...

CONIC HILL: From the centre of Balmaha, this is a 4km (2.5 mile) walk along the West Highland Way up the iconic 361m (1,184ft) hill.

THE COBBLER: A challenging 11km (6.75 mile) route from Arrochar to the 884m (2,900ft) hill also known as Ben Arthur – one of the Arrochar Alps, and probably its most stunning. From here, it's possible to link up with Beinn Nanain (926m/3,038ft) and Beinn Ime (1,011m/3,317ft).

AUCHMORE CIRCUIT: In the Breadalbane area of the National Park, a 4.5km (2.75 mile) circular walk from Killin. Enjoy woodlands, Loch Tay and the towering Tarmachan Ridge.

---

begins by climbing from the Gateway – a brilliant information and activity centre that will keep the kids entertained – into ancient woodland. Keep following the route up the hill and pause a while at the Drippan farmstead, which was in use until as late as the mid-19th century. Further on, turn right and follow the path up the hillside, which has amazing views of Loch Venachar and the invitingly secluded Loch Drunkie.

Around halfway, you emerge into the open hillside – Ben Ledi is on your left at 879m (2,884ft). Eventually, the path descends slightly, and you cross just below Dunmore, an Iron Age hillfort. Further on is Samson's Putting Stone, a huge glacial erratic. Both are more than worth the minor deviations!

The route ends at the Bochastle Car Park, with the inviting Lade Inn just over the road.

↑ The meadows at Callander.

Key Places

The rider...
All types of budgets and needs are catered for in Loch Lomond. There's a huge range of B&Bs, pubs, guesthouses, cottages and hotels, alongside a multitude of camping, caravan and hostel sites. The Park has implemented Camping Management Byelaws that cover the popular lochshore areas of the National Park from 1 March to 30 September every year. Camping is by permit only, which can be bought from the National Park Authority website. You can wild camp outside the byelaws management zones. www.lochlomond-trossachs.org/plan-your-visit

Places to visit

Tarbet On the west of Loch Lomond, where the A82 and A83 meet. A quiet but important hub with prominent hotel, tea room and visitors' site,

➜ Looking down the main street in Callander, towards Ben Ledi.

which received a £2.1 million upgrade in 2025. Overnight motorhome parking is available, while the pier is ideal for Loch Lomond cruises. Tarbet sits on a small neck of land that separates Loch Lomond from the sea and Loch Long.

Kilmun A small settlement on Holy Loch near the Firth of Clyde. It has an arboretum and an interesting historic tour that tells this quiet village's story. People settled in the area around 3500 BC, and the village was founded as a monastic community in the 7th century by Celtic monk St Fintan Munnu. There's the remains of a 12th-century church as well as a mausoleum, which was built by the Campbell Clan.

Balloch The first village you encounter in the Park if coming from the south on the A82. You'll find a castle, country park, the huge Loch Lomond Shores complex, and the National Park headquarters. Boat tours operate from 'the village on the loch', and there are plenty of places to eat and stay.

Callander In the east of the Park, on the A84, and the location for the original *Doctor Finlay's Casebook* television series. Has a thriving main street with boutique shops and restaurants, along a peaceful 'meadows' area, a stone's throw away from the centre, with ponds and places to relax. The town has a strong Roman heritage as the Roman Army was stationed beneath Callander's Pass, and there are visible fort remains. An interesting graveyard features an eight-sided watch-house that was occupied by night watchmen to ensure the graves weren't robbed to supply bodies for medical science.

Aberfoyle A good base for exploration into the Queen Elizabeth Forest Park (the Achray Forest) and the Trossachs Trail. You'll find cafés, bike hire facilities and the Scottish Wool Centre. It's on the intersection of the A873 and A81 towards the south-east of the Park, but is much quieter than the towns and villages further south.

↑ Beautiful pink bluebells in Luss.

Why not try...

Luss Historically known as the Clachan Dhu, the dark village, because it lay in the shadow of surrounding hills. The current village, self-titled as Scotland's loveliest village, was built in the 19th century by Sir James Colquhoun to house the workers of his nearby slate quarries.

Arrochar A small village around 3.2km (2 miles) from Tarbet on Loch Long. Has two pubs – the Village Inn and Ben Arthur's Bothy – and good access to the Arrochar Alps, with the distinctive Cobbler at 884m (2,900ft), a breathtaking walk from the lochside.

Tyndrum Another small village 8km (5 miles) north of Crianlarich. A good starting point for the Breadalbane area of the Park with Ben Lui, Ben Oss and Beinn Dubhchraig all nearby.

↓ Arrochar.

Must Sees

Inchcailloch Island ① (NS 409 903) is part of the Loch Lomond National Nature Reserve. Not only is the waterbus across Loch Lomond from Balmaha, Balloch or Luss a real delight, but the island is a rich habitat for birds. It's remote and quiet, and there's also a campsite in Port Bawn. The remains of a 13th-century church, dedicated to Irish missionary St Kentigerna, are a Scheduled Ancient Monument.

Glenbranter ② (PA27 8DJ) has three varied trails and two cycling routes, with the Waterfall Trail in the frankly jungle-esque Allt Robuic gorge the ultimate highlight. This trail climbs through native oakwoods festooned with lichens and mosses, and hides flowing and cascading waterfalls. In 2025, the route was affected by storm damage so, again, check before choosing a trail. www.forestryandland.gov.scot/visit/forest-parks/argyll-forest-park/glenbranter

The viewpoint at **Rest and be Thankful** ③ (NN 230 073) is second to none, giving gorgeous views of Glen Croe in the heart of the Arrochar Alps. Its name is taken from the words inscribed on a stone by soldiers who built the military road in the 1740s.

The magical **Puck's Glen** (NS 146 839), named after Puck, the spirit that appears in Shakespeare's *A Midsummer Night's Dream*, is part of the Argyll Forest Park. Beautiful waterfalls are visible along a Victorian walkway that follows a deep woodland gorge, while red squirrels ④ as well as, woodpeckers and other birds provide the backdrop. The site was closed in 2025 due to storm damage, which left some of the large trees blocking the trail. Check before visiting. www.forestryandland.gov.scot/visit/forest-parks/argyll-forest-park/pucks-glen

Above Callander are the **Callander Crags** (NN 626 085). Not only are they visited through lush woodland on a superb walk, but they also afford a panorama of the highlands and their mountains and lakes, and the countryside of the lowlands. They are part of the Highland Boundary Fault, formed when two ancient continents collided 390 million years ago.

The National Park has 22 large lochs and, much like in the Lake District, it is hard to choose a favourite. **Loch Lomond** (NS 376 888) is obviously the focal point, with islands, high mountains, valleys, secluded bays and native woodland all around. **Long Loch** (NS 477 525) is also beautiful and bold: amazing when shrouded in mist with the Cobbler and other Arrochar Alps rising high. **Loch Katrine** ⑤ (NN 453 101) feels more secluded, more so when on the water, while The Great Trossachs Path runs along its northern shore, through epic shorelines and mature woodland. **Loch Arklet** ⑥ (NN 377 091) is a real gem, best viewed from near Stronachlachar. Overlooking it, some way in the distance, are the jagged and dominating Beinn Ìme, Ben Vane and Beinn Narnain. In winter, it's an experience not to be missed. Sheer bliss!

The River Falloch drops 10m (33ft) at the **Falls of Falloch** (NN 338 208), a popular but beautiful spot around 5km (3 miles) from Crianlarich. Near the waterfall, Woven Sound is a trellis-like structure designed by John Kennedy. It wraps its way around trees and makes a fine viewpoint, but also amplifies the sound of the water.

Must Dos

Take a boat trip

There are plenty of ways to enjoy Loch Lomond and its associated lochs, but one of the best is the steamship on Loch Katrine. The **Steamship Sir Walter Scott** runs from next to the Pier Cafe in **Stronachlachar** (FK8 3TY) and **Trossachs Pier** (FK17 8HZ), and has been sailing since 1900! It's accessible for all and takes in the stunning scenery around the loch, including Ellen's Isle and Queen Victoria's Royal Cottage, which ironically she didn't stay in as the noise from a 21-gun salute shattered its windows. It's an informative heritage cruise, thanks to the Steamship Sir Walter Scott Trust charity. www.lochkatrine.com

Cruise Loch Lomond runs boat trips from Luss, Tarbet and Balmaha to various places around Loch Lomond and the islands. www.cruiselochlomond.co.uk

Sweeney's Cruise Co. also run tours from Balmaha, Luss and Balloch. www.sweeneyscruiseco.com

For more self-powered travel, **Milarrochy Bay** (NS 411 921) is ideal for paddleboarders and kayakers, as is the beautiful **Loch Venachar** (NN 570 057). There's a canoe launch point at **Jubilee Point** (NS 141 930) on Loch Eck.

Go island hopping

With 22 islands and 27 islets, there are plenty of places to get away from the busier shores of Loch Lomond. You can get to **Inchmurrin Island**, the largest inland island in Britain, from the burnfoot jetty at Arden (G83 8RD). You need to book the boat by contacting the Inchmurrin Hotel and paying them for the service. www.inchmurrin-lochlomond.com

Inchloanaig is apparently where Robert the Bruce grew yew trees in the 14th century. The wood was used to make bows for the Battle of Bannockburn.

Inchcailloch can be visited from **Balmaha Boat Yard** (G63 0JQ). www.balmahaboatyard.co.uk and by waterbus from Balloch or Luss.

Spot wildlife

From sealife to birdlife, Loch Lomond & The Trossachs is stacked with opportunities to get close to some of our most breathtaking wildlife. **Golden eagles** have been spotted across the Park, more so at Arrochar Alps, the Great Trossachs Forest and Argyll Forest Park, while you might also see white-tailed eagles too.

← Milarrochy Bay – a great place to paddle from.

↑ The *Steamship Sir Walter Scott* runs from next to the Pier Cafe in Stronachlachar and has been sailing since 1900!

Ospreys are now increasing thanks to conservation efforts across Scotland, and from mid-March to September they can be spotted from Balmaha to Inversnaid, and at the **Lake of Menteith** (NN 577 003).

As the Park has 62.8km (39 miles) of coastline, you can spot redshanks along the mudflats on **Holy Loch** (NS 168 810), and lots of oystercatchers at **Loch Long** (NS 477 525). **Ardentinny** (NS 186 880) has a sandy beach at Finart Bay and is a great place to explore rock pools, and you can also get into the woods and climb the 548m (1,798ft) Stronchullin Hill. There's a SEA LIFE Aquarium Centre in **Balloch** (G83 8QL). www.visitsealife.com/loch-lomond/

Walk among tall trees

Nearly 30 per cent of the National Park is covered in trees, with a quarter – some 13,300ha (32,865 acres) or so – established since 1860 or earlier. Twenty-five per cent is native woodland.

The Park has two main forest parks: **Argyll Forest Park** in Cowal (www.forestryandland.gov.scot/visit/forest-parks/argyll-forest-park) and **Queen Elizabeth Forest Park**, which is in the Trossachs (www.forestryandland.gov.scot/visit/forest-parks/queen-elizabeth-forest-park). Both are wild and untamed, with several trails for walkers and cyclists. The **Lodge Visitor Centre** (FK8 3SX) has four trails – one of which is accessible – and a Go Ape centre.

The **Great Trossachs Forest** – covering 16,500ha (40,772 acres) (www.thegreattrossachsforest.co.uk) is one of the UK's largest National Nature Reserves. At the **Glen Finglas Visitor Gateway** (FK17 8HR) there are nine waymarked walking routes from the challenging 24km (15 mile) Meall Route to the family-friendly Natural Play and Sculpture Trail through **Little Druim Wood** (NN 549 063).

Cashel Forest (G63 0AW) is another great place to explore regenerating woodland, **Honeymoon Bridge** (G83 7AS) is a peaceful spot just outside Arrochar, while the **Kilmun Arboretum** (PA23 8SJ) has hundreds of trees that were originally planted to see if they would produce good timber. www.forestryandland.gov.scot/visit/forest-parks/argyll-forest-park/kilmun-arboretum.

Boating on Loch Long.

Just 4.8km (3 miles) away is **Benmore Botanic Garden** (PA23 8QU), a beautiful mountainside treasure trove of botanical species. www.rbge.org.uk/visit/benmore-botanic-garden

Take a long hike

Being such a big National Park, there are loads of ways to link up several big walks. The 92km (57 mile) **Loch Lomond and Cowal Way** (www.lochlomondandcowalway.org) begins at Portavadie in Cowal and ends at Inveruglas at Loch Lomond. It connects with the **West Highland Way**, Scotland's first official long-distance route (www.westhighlandway.org). At 154km (96 miles), it's no mean feat, linking Milngavie on the outskirts of Glasgow to Fort William in the west, and passing through Drymen, Balmaha, Inversnaid, Inverarnan, Crianlarich and Tyndrum.

At Inversnaid, you can join the 18.6km (30 mile) **Great Trossachs Path**, which has 165km (103 miles) of routes coming off it. www.lochlomond-trossachs.org/things-to-do/walking/long-distance-routes/great-trossachs-path/

Still got energy? The **Three Lochs Way** goes from Balloch to Inveruglas – a 55.5km (34.5 mile) route, which also links to the John Muir Way, itself a 216km (134 mile) trail from Helensburgh to Dunbar. www.threelochsway.co.uk

And finally, the **Rob Roy Way** runs for 127km (79 miles) from Drymen to Pitlochry. www.robroyway.com

Pedal it...

Most of these long-distance routes are accessible, in some part, by bike. The Lodge Visitor Centre has some great trails, and nearby is **Aberfoyle**, which notes itself as 'Gravelfoyle' because of its fantastic gravel riding surfaces. There are three routes from the village – from a 10km (6.2 mile) Faerie Loop through the south of the Queen Elizabeth Forest Park, to the challenging 30km (18.6 mile)

→ There's a pebble beach at Ardentinny on Finart Bay and a great place to explore rock pools.

Lomond View, which is an extension of the 20km (12.4 mile) Aqueduct Loop. You can hire bikes at Aberfoyle and Loch Katrine.

Climb big hills

There are 21 Munros, mountains above 914m (3,000ft), in the Park, with the highest being **Ben More** (NN 432 244), near Crianlarich at 1,174m (3,852ft). There are also 19 Corbetts – mountains between 762 and 914m (2,500 and 3,000ft).

Easier climbs include:
Ben Lui (1,130m/3,707ft),
Ben Vorlich (985m/3,232ft),
Beinn Ime (1,011m/3,317ft),
Beinn Narnain (926m/3,038ft) and
Ben Lomond (974m/3,196ft).

Adventurous climbers can also enjoy bouldering, multi-pitch routes, bolted sport climbing and winter classics. www.lochlomond-trossachs.org/things-to-do/climbing/

CAR-FREE TRAVEL

→ The Park is trialling a National Park Journey Planner that shows all the potential travel options for a journey within Loch Lomond & The Trossachs. You can plan a trip, check the carbon impacts and pay for your journey. **www.lochlomond-trossachs.org/plan-your-visit/national-park-journey-planner/**

→ Two key train lines provide access to the National Park. ScotRail operate a direct line from Glasgow to Balloch, while its West Highland Line has stations in Arrochar, Tarbet, Ardlui and Crianlarich. **www.scotrail.co.uk/inspiration-hub/great-places-to-visit/loch-lomond**

→ A waterbus from Tarbet or Ardlui can take you to Loch Lomond's eastern shores and the West Highland Way, Ben Lomond and Balmaha. **www.lochlomond-trossachs.org/things-to-do/water-activities/waterbus/**

→ There are several bus services to get you around the Park **www.travelinescotland.com** and **www.traveline.info**:

→ West Coast Motors runs the #484 and #486 between Dunoon and Cowal Peninsula.

→ McColl's run the #305, which takes you from Balloch to Luss, the #306 from Balloch to Helensburgh and the #309 from Balloch to Balmaha.

→ Garelochhead Coaches run the #302 from Luss, Inverbeg, Tarbet, Arrochar, Rest and be Thankful, Lochgoilhead and Carrick Castle.

ACKNOWLEDGEMENTS

During the course of writing this book, I was asked several times what my favourite National Park is. Cards on the table… my heart will always be in the Yorkshire Dales. That's where I grew up, caved, walked, penned books and now work. However, I was stunned by the sheer variety and warmth from our other 14 National Parks. I have never met a more welcoming group of people than in each of these breathing spaces. From chats in pubs with locals, business owners, farmers, and walkers sharing paths, to Park protectors, rangers, visitors and volunteers, this book has been special to be a part of and is something I will look back on forever with fondness and with humility.

Writing a book about the UK's 15 National Parks, their nuances and uniqueness is not a task that can be accomplished single-handedly. I've been lucky to work with the best editorial team ever at Bloomsbury – Elizabeth Multon, Kate Savage and then Clara Jump, who, even when I most doubted myself, stood firm in her belief in me and this project. She is an absolute gem, and this book wouldn't have happened without her.

To the Comms leads at each of the National Parks: Charlotte Easton & Emma Pearcy; Caro Cook; Hilary Makin & Maria Court; Catriona McLees; Caroline O'Doherty; Ruth James & Jeff Travis; Sarah Calderbank; Rob Leigh; Tom Marshall; Mark Sadler; Bronwyn Lally; Marie Parkin; Ioan Gwilym; Olly Davies; Sarah Ormerod, Kate Bouchier-Hayes & Cathy Owen; and those at National Parks UK, thank you from the bottom of my heart.

Then there are the Champions: Alan Bowring; Pete Crane; Richard Gray, Alun Gethin Jones; Dr Lucy Shipley; Will Clark; Cordelia Murray-Brown; Lucy Allan; Andrew Parry-Norton; John Packman; Nick Sanderson; Jackie and Ian Berry; Rebecca Wilson; Robin Dower; James Parkin; Paul Gorringe; and Neil Heseltine - your passion for your life, your Park and your world shone through, and I'm indebted to have spent just a few minutes with you. Likewise, Laura Clapham from the South Downs, Gary Pickles, the anecdote extraordinaire at Northumberland, and Ian Johnstone in Dartmoor.

Thank you also to my family and friends for giving me the strength and support to carry on, even when various vicious wet and windy storms curtailed my best efforts to get some great pictures and left me locked me in bunkbarns for hours. My family was more than supportive during the many weeks spent on the road researching. I'm not sure I can ever repay that faith.

And finally, a huge thank you to the people I either met, stayed with, or helped me along the way: Tara Maxamed; Derek Robbins at Fix Tor Café in Princetown; Graham Boswell at Base Lodge in Minehead; Lorraine Binfield at The Shimmerings in Ringwood; Helen Ashby at Wayside in Little Plumstead; Esmeralda Guds; Marian Stanley; Amy Norton; Claire Onslow; Kate Lock at the South Downs Bunkhouse; Sarah Hubbard at the Cranford Guesthouse in Braemar; Fiona Busfield; Pete Mayles; Reuban Elliot; and Rhian Hughes. I am truly sorry if I have omitted anyone.

I wrote, while in the Broads National Park, that it was a privilege to cross timelines with that part of the country for just a few brief hours. In essence, I feel that way about each and every person I met along the way.

Thank you.

Mike Appleton

PICTURE CREDITS

Top/Middle/Bottom = T/M/B, Left/Right = L/R. All photos belong to the author, with the exception of:

Adobe Stock: 8, 18, 23(T), 24, 35, 38(B), 40, 41(#2–5), 56, 57(T), 75, 93(T), 95(#3+4), 96, 106, 114(#3R), 121, 122(T), 127, 128, 129, 130, 131(T), 133(#4), 139, 144, 145, 146, 148, 151(#3), 154(B), 155, 158(T), 164(B), 169(#3), 173, 180, 183, 185(B), 190(T), 193, 200(B), 203(T), 205(#7), 207, 221, 223(#4+6), 226(T), 241(T), 249, 250(T), 256(B), 257, 281; **Alan Bowring:** 234; **Alasdair Mackenzie/NNP:** 19(T); **Alastair Hubbard:** 258; **Alastair Humphreys:** 7; **Alun Gethin Jones**: 196; **Andrew Parry-Norton:** 160; **Bill Nix:** 63(T); **Bill Smith:** 104(R), 110; **Cordelia Murray-Brown:** 270(R); **Dartmoor National Park Authority:** 151(#2); **David Taylor/NNP:** 20; **Dr Lucy Shipley:** 124; **Ebor Images:** 66(B), 67(T); **Exmoor National Park Authority:** 133(#5), 137(B); **Fiona Busfield:** 61, 137(T) 194(B); **Geograph:** 77(#2), 131(B), 272; **Geopictures.net:** 246, 247; **Getty:** 151(#4), 154(T), 167(T), 225, 227, 231, 233(B), 239, 243(#1,3+4), 244; **Jackie & Ian Berry:** 68; **James Bass:** 118–19(B); **James Hines:** 9, 79; **James Parkin:** 214; **James Ross:** 250(B); **John Packman:** 104(L); **Judy Rogers:** 50; **Julian Claxton:** 114(#1); **Loch Lomond & The Trossachs National Park Authority:** 267, 268(TL), 269, 276, 277(B), 278(T), 279(#1,5+6), 283; **Lucy Allen:** 270(L); **Marian Stanley:** 81; **Neville Stanikk:** 133(#1); **New Forest National Park Authority**: 159(B), 165, 166(T); **Paul Gorringe:** 178; **Pete Crane:** 252; **Peter Mayles:** 199; **Richard Gray:** 142; **Rueban Elliot:** 262; **Sally Ann Norman/Ad Gefrin Anglo-Saxon Museum & Distillery:** 26(T) **Sarah Hodgson:** 48; **Shaila Rao:** 261(#3); **Steve Bell/NYMNP:** 78 ; **Tara Maxamed:** 123(M), 133(#3); **Tom Barrett:** 102(T+M), 103(T), 116(T), 117; **Twice Brewed Inn:** 25(T); **Will Clark:** 32; **Yorkshire Dales National Park Authority:** 86

INDEX

A
Aberfoyle 277
Abergavenny 240–1
Acle 111
Allen, Lucy 270–1
Alnwick 21
Amberley 185
Ambleside 39
Appleton le Moors 68–9, 74–5
Arrochar 277
Arundel 184
Ashburton 148–9
Ashford-in-the-Water 93
Aviemore 258
Aysgarth Falls & Freeholders' Wood walk 54–5

B
Back Tor, Mam Tor, Hollins Cross, Back Tor & Lose Hill walk 89–90
Bakewell 92
Ballater 259
Balloch 276–7
Bannau Brycheiniog National Park 230–47
 Govilon Line walk 238–9
 Pen y Fan walk 237–8
Barmouth 202
Beaulieu 167
The Beaver Trail 256–7
Beccles 110–11
Beddgelert 202
Bellever Tor walk 145–6
Bellingham 21
Berry, Jackie & Ian 68–9
Betws-y-Coed 202
Blair Atholl 259
Blencathra 35–6
Bovey Tracey 149

Bowring, Alan 234–5
Braemar 258
Bransgore 167
Breamish Valley Hillfort Trail 18–19
Brecon 240
Brecon Beacons *see* Bannau Brycheiniog National Park
Broad Haven 220
The Broads National Park 100–19
 Irstead Staithe & Barton Broad Boardwalk walk 107–8
 Upton Marshes walk 108–9
Brockenhurst 166–7
Buckfast 149
Buckfastleigh 149
Bungay 110
Burley 167

C
Cairngorms National Park 248–65
 The Beaver Trail 256–7
 Ryvoan and Meall a' Bhuachaille walk 255–6
Callander 277
Cashel Forest walk 273–4
Castleton 92
Chagford 149
Clark, Will 32–3
Combe Martin 131
Coniston Water 39
Crane, Pete 252–3
Crickhowell 241

D
Danby 75
Dartmoor National Park 138–55
 Bellever Tor walk 145–6

Haytor Quarry and Rocks walk 146–7
Dolgellau 203
Dower, John 86–7
Dulverton 130–1
Dunster 130

E
Eryri National Park 192–209
 Mawddach Trail 200
 Yr Wyddfa walk 199
Exmoor 120–37
 Simonsbath to Wheal Eliza walk 127
 Tarr Steps walk 128–9
Eyam 92

F
Fishguard 221
Fordingbridge 167
Freeholders' Wood, Aysgarth Falls & Freeholders' Wood walk 54–5

G
Garbutt Wood, Sutton Bank & Garbutt Wood walk 72
Gilwern 241
Glen Finlas and The Great Trossachs Path walk 274–5
Glenridding 39
Gorringe, Paul 178–9
Govilon Line walk 238–9
Grantown-on-Spey 259
Grasmere 38–9
Grassington 56
Gray, Richard 142–3
The Great Trossachs Path, Glen Finlas and The Great Trossachs Path walk 274–5
Grosmont 75

H

Hadrian's Wall 16, 24, 27
  Hadrian's Wall meander 17–18
Haltwhistle 21
Harbottle 21
Harlech 203
Hassocks 185
Hathersage 92
Hawes 56
Hawkshead 39
Hay-on-Wye 240
Haytor Quarry and Rocks walk 146–7
Heights of Abraham 93
Helmsley 75
Heseltine, Neil 50–1
Hexham 21
Hole of Horcum, Levisham Moor, Hole of Horcum & Skelton Tower walk 71
Hollins Cross, Mam Tor, Hollins Cross, Back Tor & Lose Hill walk 89–90
Holne 149
Holystone 21
Horner Woods 131
Horning 111

I

Ingleborough epic walk 53–4
Ingleton 57
Ingram 21
Ingram Valley Farm 14–15
Irstead Staithe & Barton Broad Boardwalk walk 107–8

J

Jones, Alun Gethin 196–7

K

Keswick 38
  Keswick to Threlkeld walk 37
Keyhaven walk 164–5
Kilmun 276

Kinder Scout walk 90–1
Kingley Vale circular walk 181–2
Kingussie 259
Kirkby Stephen 56–7
Kirkbymoorside 75

L

Lake District National Park 28–45
  Blencathra walk 35–6
  Keswick to Threlkeld walk 37
Lawrenny walk 218–19
Levisham Moor, Hole of Horcum & Skelton Tower walk 71
Lewes 184–5
Leyburn 57
Llanberis 202
Llandeilo 241
Llandovery 241
Loch Lomond & the Trossachs National Park 266–83
  Cashel Forest walk 273–4
  Glen Finglas and The Great Trossachs Path walk 274–5
Loddon 111
Lose Hill, Mam Tor, Hollins Cross, Back Tor & Lose Hill walk 89–90
Luss 277
Lymington 167
Lyndhurst 166
Lynmouth 130
Lynton 130

M

Machynlleth 202–3
Malham 57
Mam Tor, Hollins Cross, Back Tor & Lose Hill walk 89–90
Matlock Bath 93
Mawddach Trail 200

Merthyr Tydfil 241
Midhurst 185
Miles Without Stiles 32, 33, 39, 61
  Aysgarth Falls & Freeholders' Wood walk 54
  Bellever Tor walk 145
  Chattri Memorial walk 183
  Farndale Wild Daffodil Walk 73
  Keswick to Threlkeld walk 37
Minehead 131
Moretonhampstead 149
Murray-Brown, Cordelia 270–1

N

New Forest Commoners Defence Association 160
The New Forest National Park 156–73
  Keyhaven walk 164–5
  Tall trees and mighty oaks walk 163–4
Newgale 221
Newtonmore 259
Norfolk Broads National Park 100–19
  Irstead Staithe & Barton Broad Boardwalk walk 107–8
  Upton Marshes walk 108–9
North York Moors National Park 64–81
  Levisham Moor, Hole of Horcum & Skelton Tower walk 72
  Sutton Bank & Garbutt Wood walk 72
Northumberland National Park 10–27
  Breamish Valley Hillfort Trail 18–19

Hadrian's Wall meander 17–18

O
Okehampton 149
Oulton Broad 111

P
Packman, John 104–5
Parkin, James 214–15
Parry-Norton, Andrew 160–1
Peak District National Park 82–99
   Kinder Scout walk 90–1
   Mam Tor, Hollins Cross, Back Tor & Lose Hill walk 89–90
Pembroke 221
Pembrokeshire Coast National Park 210–29
   Lawrenny walk 218–19
   Strumble Head walk 217
Pen y Fan walk 237–8
Petersfield 185
Pickering 75
Porlock 130
Portmeirion 203
Priddons Farm 142–3
Princetown 148
Pulborough 185

R
Ringwood 167
Rosedale Abbey 74
Rothbury 21

Ryvoan and Meall a' Bhuachaille walk 255–6

S
St Davids 221
Sanderson, Nick 104–5
Sandsend 75
Saundersfoot 221
Settle 57
Seven Sisters to Beachy Head walk 182–3
Shipley, Dr Lucy 124–5
Simonsbath 131
Simonsbath to Wheal Eliza walk 127
Skelton Tower, Levisham Moor, Hole of Horcum & Skelton Tower walk 71
Skipton 57
Snowdon *see* Yr Wyddfa
Snowdonia National Park *see* Eryri National Park
Solva 221
South Downs National Park 174–91
   Kingley Vale circular walk 181–2
   Seven Sisters to Beachy Head walk 182–3
Stalham 110
Staveley 39
Steyning 184
Strumble Head walk 217
Sutton Bank & Garbutt Wood walk 72

T
Tall trees and mighty oaks walk 163–4
Tarbet 276
Tarr Steps walk 128–9
Tenby 221
Threlkeld, Keswick to Threlkeld walk 37
Tideswell 93
Tissington 93
Tomintoul 258–9
Town End Farm 68–9
Tyndrum 277

U
Upton Marshes walk 108–9

W
Wheal Eliza, Simonsbath to Wheal Eliza walk 127
Wilson, Rebecca & Ross 14–15
Windermere 38, 40
Wooler 21
Wroxham 110

Y
Yorkshire Dales National Park 46–63
   Aysgarth Falls & Freeholders' Wood walk 54–5
   an Ingleborough epic 53–4
Yr Wyddfa walk 199